*"If today were the last day of my life, would I want to do what I am about to do today? Whenever the answer has been "No" for too many days in a row, I know I need to change something."*

— STEVE JOBS

# PEOPLE ARE TALKING

*"Brilliant!"*

—SARAH CHAUNCEY

*"What am I thinking after reading this?! I am thinking of a way to paper my office with it. To distribute it to the people I work with, the management, my friends, elementary school play dates from 25 years ago, and every person I meet on the street. This is an incredibly relevant idea."*

—TALIA HAYKIN

*"Brilliant! Just brilliant. Thanks for what is the best read (for me) this year so far."*

—WILL TELANT

*"Awesome! Love it! I'm looking for a few "adults" right now!"*

—TERRY TREXLER

*"You have a terrific mission and organizational culture and some solid wisdom to share!"*

—TODD KEMP

*"I. love. this. The title may scare you but read it anyway."*

—CONNIE WINCH

# WHY EMPLOYEES ARE ALWAYS A BAD IDEA

# WHY EMPLOYEES ARE
# ALWAYS
## A BAD IDEA

(and Other Business Diseases of the Industrial Age)

CHUCK BLAKEMAN

Crankset Group
PUBLISHING

Crankset Publishing, 1324 Shadow Mountain Drive, Highlands Ranch, CO 80126

10 9 8 7 6 5 4 3 2 1

ISBN- 978-0-9843343-4-6

Crankset Publishing books are available at special quantity discounts to use as premiums and sales promotions, or for use in educational or corporate training programs. For more information, please email us at Grow@CranksetGroup.com, or write to the Chief Relationship Officer, Crankset Publishing 1324 Shadow Mountain Drive, Highlands Ranch, CO 80126, or contact your local bookstore.

This book is printed on acid-free paper.

Chief Editing by Madalyn Stone  Cover design by Josh Mishell
Layout by Lauren Kelley

Library of Congress Cataloging-in-Publication Data

Why Employees Are Always a Bad Idea (And Other Business Diseases of the Industrial Age) / by Chuck Blakeman.


1. Leadership. 2. Management. 3. Entrepreneurship.
I. Title. II. Why Employees Are Always a Bad Idea (And Other Business Diseases of the Industrial Age) III. Blakeman, Chuck


LCCN: 2013915879

www.cranksetgroup.com

*To my dear and patient wife, Diane,*
*my stable influence,*

*and our great kids,*
*Grant, Laura and Brie,*
*who all grew up in the Participation Age.*

# CONTENTS

Preface                                                                      xiiii
Introduction: The Participation Age Company                                    xvi

## Part I: The Seven Core Business Diseases of the Industrial Age

Chapter 1: The Human Carnage of the Industrial Age                              2
Chapter 2: Disease One - The Problem with "Big"                                17
Chapter 3: Disease Two - The Twenty-First-Century Industrialist                34
Chapter 4: Disease Three - Why Employees Are Always a Bad Idea                 50
Chapter 5: Disease Four - Why Managers Are a Bad Idea Too                      66
Chapter 6: Disease Five – 9 to 5 Disease                                       84
Chapter 7: Disease Six - Separation of Work and Play                          96
Chapter 8: Disease Seven - Retirement—A Bankrupt Industrial Age Idea          106

## Part II: Embracing the Participation Age

Chapter 9: Stakeholders—A New Model for the Participation Age                 119
Chapter 10: Why What You Believe Matters so Much                             129
Chapter 11: The Results-Based Business: Our Story                            144
Chapter 12: Companies Thriving in the Participation Age                      159
Chapter 13: From Manager to Leader – Moving Into the Participation Age       177
Chapter 14: How to Hire People You'll Never Have to Manage                   190

## Part III: Reframing Our Business Practices

Chapter 15: Other Business Diseases: Preplanning, Scarcity,                  202
            Education, Competition, Rugged Individualist, Balance
Chapter 16: The Solution: The Fourth "S"—Significance                        226


Afterword: How Capitalism Will Solve Poverty                                 231
Appendix                                                                     236
Acknowledgements                                                             240
Resources                                                                    242

# Preface

The Industrial Revolution, wasn't.

Only someone looking back over three hundred years in one afternoon could have called this a revolution. Revolutions take a few months to a few years, but not three hundred years. Next to the Stone Age, Bronze Age, and other ages, it looks like a quick revolution. But compared to what's going on today, it's a snoozer. From 1700 to 1970, very little of the change was rapid enough that people born in one decade would be wondering what happened in the next one. In contrast, the shelf life of many technologies today is less predictable than that of a can of soup.

So we're going to call 1700 to 1970 what it actually was—the Industrial Age, and focus specifically on the Factory System period of 1850 to 1970.

## THE SEVEN CORE BUSINESS DISEASES
## OF THE INDUSTRIAL AGE

In *Why Employees Are Always a Bad Idea* (*WEAAABI*), I describe the seven core business diseases of the Industrial Age. These archaic business practices are still central to the way most companies are run today. *WEAAABI* shows how we can move away from these Industrial Age practices to embrace a new way of doing business in the Participation Age. There are companies in every industry that are already there, or moving quickly in that direction.

In the Participation Age, managers are replaced with leaders (and a lot fewer of them), and employees are replaced with self-managed, self-motivated Stakeholders. Promotions, titles, departmental fiefdoms, work hours, vacation time, benefits, written policies, and even HR departments are also going away, even for companies with 10,000 Stakeholders.

## INDUSTRIALISTS ARE NOT CAPITALISTS

In *WEAAABI*, I also describe why the Industrialists of the 1800s, who gave us the business practices we still use, were not Capitalists, how Industrialists are markedly different than Capitalists, and why many present-day companies are simply twenty-first century Industrialists masquerading as Capitalists. People don't hate Capitalists; they just think they do. Their disdain is actually for twenty-first century Industrialists pretending they are Capitalists. In *WEAAABI* we clarify the difference and restore the good name of Capitalism; we return it to its rightful spot as the engine of growth, progress, and economic prosperity, where it has been for thousands of years.

## A TIDAL WAVE OF PARTICIPATION AGE COMPANIES

We built Crankset Group in the Participation Age, rejecting the traditional business practices still in use by most organizations. After a few years of helping other companies do the same, I wanted to know who else was thinking this way. In the process of researching this book, I "discovered" greats like Marvin Weisbord, Douglas McGregor, W. L. Gore, and Ricardo Semler (and his Brazilian company, Semco), and even a book titled *The Age of Participation* by Patricia McLagan and Christo Nel. I also found hundreds of companies in every industry, both old and new, small and large, who were approaching business the same way we were. It turns out the Participation Age is already widely populated by those pioneers. It's the privilege and responsibility of these early adapters to work together to move the rest of the business world out of the Industrial Age.

## HOW TO READ THIS BOOK

The Introduction describes a Participation Age company. Don't skip it – it's not a throw-away Introduction, but a vital cornerstone to this book.

Part I first describes the human carnage of the Industrial Age. Too much of our focus is on the incredible technological advances of the Industrial Age, without addressing the human toll we are still paying for having built the Factory System the way we did. Those technological advances of the Industrial Age are unassailable, but we believe they came at a very dear cost to our humanity. Participation Age companies have found a way to be even more successful while embracing what Douglas McGregor calls *The Human Side of Enterprise*. Part I also describes the seven core business diseases of the Industrial Age, which were put in place to help the Industrialists build the Factory System, at the expense of just about everyone else.

Part II tells the stories of many companies who have left these archaic business practices behind and embraced the Participation Age. Many of the examples I use are from manufacturing and other traditional industries, because those are the companies most likely to claim that the Participation Age is only possible for newer service and technology companies. Nothing could be farther from the truth. In fact, the very best examples of companies that have left every aspect of the Industrial Age behind make washing machines, meat slicers, airplane parts, textiles, and groceries.

Part III gets practical and in-the-trenches, and describes how to move from being a manager to a leader, and how to hire Stakeholders you'll never have to manage. It concludes with a quick overview of other business diseases of the Industrial Age that continue to plague too many businesses today. Part III will encourage and challenge you to build your career or company, on Participation Age practices that go beyond the "Three S's" of the Industrial Age.

## WHY THE STORIES ON AFRICA?

One of the core business diseases of the Industrial Age is *Separation of Work and Play*. The Industrial Age taught us that work was for making money, and then you went home to Make Meaning. We reject that premise and so does human history. With the advent of the Participation Age, we can now go back to a more normal relationship between work and life.

At the Crankset Group, we do business and life without separation. Some of it happens to occur in the U.S. and some of it, for me in particular, happens in Africa, but it is all purposefully braided together throughout my life, our company, and this book. As a result, in *Why Employees Are Always a Bad Idea*, you will see that our intention to help solve poverty in Africa is fully intertwined with what we do every day in our Crankset Group business headquartered here in the U.S., even though the two are thousands of miles apart and don't have a thing to do with each other in traditional business terms.

I trust you'll find meaning and direction for your own work, life, and business as I share my integrated, unbalanced, abundance-minded life with you through my experiences in Africa.

## THE PARTICIPATION AGE IS NOW

The Participation Age is not something that will happen in the future. It is all around us and it is the present. The only remaining question is whether we will leave the archaic business practices of the Industrial Age behind us and become Stakeholders and true Capitalists in a Participation Age world. Those who do will thrive, and those who don't will be left behind in a world that no longer needs or wants the business practices of the Industrial Age.

# Introduction

**W**hy *Employees Are Always a Bad Idea* (*WEAAABI*) describes the **seven core business diseases of the Industrial Age**, and what a Participation Age company looks like when they reject these business practices. Let me ask you to imagine that company with me.

**Imagine** a company that discarded everything it learned from the Industrial Age about how to run a company. Imagine a company, **of any size**, without employees or managers, with people simply known as Stakeholders.

What if this imaginary company didn't have a single written policy and no HR department, because they believe **rules destroy creativity?** What if it also had no titles, no departments, no corporate ladder, no office hours, unlimited vacation time, profit sharing for everyone, and with all that, was still highly profitable?

Would you want to work for that company, or maybe even build one like it yourself? *Why Employees Are Always a Bad Idea* is about **these** companies.

The companies I just described are already all around you, ***RIGHT NOW,* in every industry, even in manufacturing**, with as few as a couple of Stakeholders or more than 10,000. Some are new and others have been around for decades.

*WEAAABI* shares the stories of companies like Semco, W. L. Gore, Whole Foods, TD Industries, Container Store, and many others, and describes how each of them confronted the seven core business diseases of the Industrial Age so they could move into a new era we call the Participation Age, where people want to Make Meaning, not just money.

The Industrial Age is over. The *Dilbert* comic strip should no longer be funny. Becoming a Participation Age company is not optional.

## EMPLOYEES – A BUSINESS DISEASE
## OF THE INDUSTRIAL AGE

The Industrial Age gave us cool toys and a cushy life, but it also came with some business diseases. One of the most rabid of the seven core business diseases of the Industrial Age is the concept of an employee. It is a very new idea in the history of man, and one that needs to go away.

When machines took over most production, they couldn't run themselves, so the Industrial Age recreated people in the image of machines because it needed people to run the machines.

## EMPLOYEES ARE "SILENT"

Over time, companies made it clear they only wanted the productive part of the person to show up. They required people to leave the human being (the messy part) at home. As a result, the generation that entered the work force at the very peak of the Industrial Age (1945-1960ish) was given the worst generational label in history – The Silent Generation. If you had a *Silent* as a parent, you learned to live life the way your parent had been taught: "Be loyal to the company. Do what you're told. Show up early, leave late. Shut up, sit down, don't make waves, live invisibly, and go out quietly. The company will take care of you, from cradle to grave."

## EMPLOYEES ARE CHILDREN

This view of work (and life) turned adults back into children. You were taught that the most mature person was one who obediently took orders, did what they were told, didn't question authority, was blindly loyal to those in charge, and lived passively as others directed their life. Pretty much what we want a four-year-old to do.

In order to keep the children from ruining the house, and to make them extensions of machines, the Industrial Age herded people into company day care centers, boxed them in with extremely clear and narrow limitations on what they could do, the hours in which they could do them, and endless limitations on being human and *adult* at work. It stripped them of their need to ask, *Why?*, to create, and to solve problems, because machines didn't need them to ask, *Why?*, or to create, or to solve problems. Machines just needed them to *do*.

## EMPLOYEES ARE A DISEASE, NOT A CURE

We reject the business culture of the Industrial Age as a bad idea that needs to be corrected. Employees are one of those business diseases that should be eradicated. Because of the Industrial Age, the word *employee* has become synonymous with *child*. Many of the companies we profile can't even use the word anymore. They don't want to hire children who need to be told what to do and managed closely so that they don't run into the street.

## EMPLOYEES ARE REPLACED BY "STAKEHOLDERS"

Hundreds of Participation Age companies like ours don't hire employees, but have replaced them with *Stakeholders*. Our Stakeholders are sold on the idea of living well by doing good, and are not employees who punch clocks. Stakeholders are first and foremost adults who can think, take initiative, make decisions, carry responsibility, take ownership, be creative, and solve problems. And we love it when they ask the most human of questions, "Why?"

## STAKEHOLDERS ARE ADULTS

Our Stakeholders are all adults. *Employee* is a four-letter word for Participation Age companies. Adults don't need someone to keep them from running into the streets or ruining the carpets. Adults ask questions. They don't live passively, but are self-directed, creative, and solve problems. They don't expect the company or other adults to take care of them. And the whole messy person comes to work, not just the extension of the machine.

## STAKEHOLDERS ARE OWNERS

Ownership is the most powerful motivator in business. Adults own stuff. Even if they aren't a stockholder and don't physically own a piece of the company, Stakeholders own their work as a natural part of being an adult. And as Stakeholders, they receive profit sharing, just like an owner should. They may not own the company, but Stakeholders in all the Participation Age companies profiled own some of the fruit of their labor.

## STAKEHOLDERS REQUIRE LEADERSHIP, NOT ADULT SUPERVISION

If you hire Stakeholders (adults) instead of employees (children), it changes the way you direct people. Crankset Group, as with others described in chapter 12, don't have office hours, vacation time, or personal days. We're not interested in whose car was in the parking lot first or who left last. We believe office politics is a waste of time, so no one will ever be promoted. Participation Age companies provide leadership, not management, which is nothing more than adult supervision.

## STAKEHOLDERS FOCUS ON WORK, NOT PROMOTION TO THE NEXT TITLE

Every adult who works at Crankset Group has a title that includes the word *Chief*: Chief Results Officer, Chief Connecting Officer, Chief Transformation Officer, Chief Operations Officer, Chief Relationship Officer, Chief Development Officer, Chief of MIH (Making It Happen).

We don't have supervisors or managers or directors or VPs – just Chiefs. None of us will ever need to be promoted; we're all already at the top. We'll just grow into more responsibilities as we become better at things. As we do them, we will be recognized, and somebody might change our title (there is no centralized title-giver). Each of us makes more money by making a broader impact and contribution to the business.

## STAKEHOLDERS ARE BETTER TEAM PLAYERS

Participation Age companies believe in working together as adults in *Committed Community* to get results for each other and for our customers. We don't have loners, rugged individualists or people clawing their way to the top by trampling others. Participation Age Stakeholders don't believe in zero-sum games. They live in a world of abundance and believe what Zig Ziglar said: "You will get all you want in life if you help enough other people get what they want."

## STAKEHOLDERS ARE SELF-MOTIVATED

Although our company leases office space for training and also rents other spaces around the city, none of us have an actual office there. Like many Participation Age companies, we all work from our homes and from places like breakfast joints and coffee shops. If it helps somebody to get things done better, we'll get them an office.

## STAKEHOLDERS MAKE YOU AND THEMSELVES MORE MONEY

In *Why Employees Are Always a Bad Idea*, you'll read why Participation Age companies in every industry make so much more money than the average company. Our own business grew 61 percent in 2010, 41 percent in 2011, 66 percent in 2012, and is projected to finish 2013 at 45 percent growth. Why? Because we reject the widely used business practices of the Industrial Age and embrace a Participation Age approach to business. Every Stakeholder is an adult, taking responsibility, creating, problem solving, making it happen, and taking ownership of whatever needs to be done to bring our clients the best experience and the most tangible results possible. And everyone is a lot happier because they all work with adults who contribute and pull their own weight.

In the Participation Age, employees are always a bad idea. Stakeholders will replace them.

Come join us in the Participation Age.

# PART I

---

# THE SEVEN CORE
Business Diseases of The Industrial Age

# The Human Carnage of the Industrial Age

*"There's something about the Industrial Age that's epic and tragic."*
— CARLOS RUIZ ZAFON, best selling author of *The Shadow of the Wind*

The call came at 8:30 p.m.

I was already deeper into central Africa than when H. M. Stanley supposedly uttered that famous line in 1871, "Livingstone, I presume," to the man he had tracked for two years. Livingston had been presumed dead until Stanley presumed otherwise. I had friends who wondered the same about me that day.

I had been invited to come build businesses to help solve poverty. I lay on a small rickety cot in my tiny mud-brick room in the middle of the Democratic Republic of the Congo, staring up at a ceiling I couldn't see in the darkness. The whole village was in bed, but I was wide awake on my first night there. My unscheduled meeting with the two local village chiefs had gone well that afternoon, but that wasn't why I was there.

It was sultry and raining softly outside. I could hear the dripping on the tin roof right above me, and I could feel the slightest breeze through the open hole in the wall that passed for a window. The mosquito net would be my friend for the night.

And it was deathly black without electricity. The village generator had been on from 6:30 p.m., when it got dark, to 8:00 p.m. The overcast darkness near the equator is so deep that even flashlights seemed ineffective, their narrow column of light swallowed by the darkness they attempted to describe. It made more sense just to go to bed like everyone else.

I picked up my cell phone as it buzzed at me and tapped "Answer." Cell phones work everywhere in Africa, except where I was about to go.

I said hello, and the voice of my Congolese friend on the other end said, "It's time to go." He is a widely respected chief in the Congo and is the only reason I could make the connection I was about to make.

"What do you mean, 'it's time to go'? Do you realize it's 8:30 p.m. and everyone is down for the night, including me?" He was in the United States at the time, so I assumed he had momentarily forgotten the nine-hour time difference.

"Yes, I know. The Big Chief's contact just called and said the Big Chief wants you to come now. You go when the Big Chief says to go. A motorcycle will pick you up in a few minutes."

"Chief, it's raining and it's pitch black. There are no roads here, just mud. How far is it to the Big Chief?"

"Not too far, probably two hours."

"Sitting on the back of a motorcycle, driving in mud, at night, in the rain?" I was tightening up fast.

"You must go when the Big Chief says to go. This is very important. He would not ask you to come now if it wasn't the right time. Gather your things; the motorcycle will be there right away." Earlier that day I was told by Pauli, the only local who spoke broken English, that only one other man of European descent had been in this village in the last two years, and the Chief had refused to let him come any closer or to meet him. I felt honored, but very distracted by the unknown journey ahead.

As I quickly threw my things together, Pauli knocked on my door. He had somehow heard I was leaving early, probably from one of the motorcycle drivers via cell phone. I asked him how far it was to the Big Chief's village. He assured me it was no more than five hours. The timeline was going in the wrong direction.

A few minutes later, we were churning, grinding, and bumping along deep into the bush at 5 to 30 mph, depending on the condition of the path. There were four dirt bikes and eight people. A guy on the back of one of them was wearing a suit and tie. I later learned he was called "The Secretary" and was a trusted confidant of the Big Chief, along with an elderly woman, Bernice, who was on the back of another bike. She was also dressed to the nines in a long flowery dress. The Big Chief governs six million people and owns land the size of all of Colorado and half of Wyoming. You don't go see him without putting on your best clothes. All I had was dirty hiking pants and a polo shirt. It would have to do.

There was no road. We switched repeatedly from muddy paths to muddy gullies cut by prolonged downpours, to mud-filled ditches, back to gullies, then back to walking paths. Amazingly, I only fell off twice the whole night, the driver just once.

We stopped in the middle of the trail about three hours in. Bernice spoke some English and I was using a little battery-operated translator to talk to the others. She said one of the other bikes had a flat tire. Forty-five minutes later, we were back on the trail. Two hours later, we stopped again to patch the very same tire in the very same place. It wouldn't be the last time.

At 4:30 a.m., eight hours after we left (not two, and not five), we pulled into the Chief's village of about eight hundred people. This village was off the grid. There was no electricity, no running water, no generator—no modern conveniences of any sort. Just thatched huts, beautifully crafted and laid out, in a grid along wide dirt paths. I learned later it was a "three-day walk" from the next village. We were put right to bed, then were awakened abruptly at 7:30 a.m. for a ceremonial breakfast.

The journey here from Colorado had taken four days, three continents, five countries, four airplanes, a jeep, and a dirt bike, with almost no sleep. I met with the Chief for a few hours with Bernice translating in broken phrases, then walked around the small village with Bernice for a few hours to meet people. We came back to the Chief's compound, signed some papers, took endless cell phone pictures, and were done for the day. I was looking forward to finally getting a full night of sleep. But Bernice walked up to me and casually said we would be leaving in a half hour at 4:00 p.m., and that for security reasons we would go out a different way that night than we came in. Oh, and it would take ten hours this time, not eight.

I finally slept that next night, then the next day I did the reverse trek out of Africa back to Colorado. In seven days, I had barely slept a night and a half, to visit someone I had never met, for just a few hours.

Why? Because as much as the Industrial Age had tried to remanufacture me in the image of its machines, I had escaped and made it into the Participation Age, where people make both money and meaning, and where there isn't a separation between the two. We are able to do things like this because we built a company that encouraged us to change the rules of what it means to do business, a company built on business practices of the Participation Age, to Make Meaning, not just money.

## MAKE YOUR OWN BUSINESS RULES

He who makes the rules, wins, and I had learned, much later in life than I should have, that I didn't need to play by the rules of the Industrial Age. I didn't have to be loyal to the company. I didn't have to blindly do what I was told. I was a product of the Industrial Age, but had escaped to Make Meaning in both my business and in Africa. Millions more are doing the same, in a tidal wave of change leading us into the Participation Age.

## THE HALLMARK OF THE PARTICIPATION AGE IS SHARING

In 2006, a couple of us were flown out to Silicon Valley to accept an award given by Sun Microsystems for branding, messaging, and design work. At this internal conference of a few hundred Sun employees, Sun leaders and outside consultants were talking about the new "Age," called *The Participation Age*. Quite a few leaders and publications have used it since as well, and I found it to be a compelling description for the age in which we find ourselves. And as the leaders at that conference said, "The hallmark of the Participation Age is *SHARING*."

> Make Meaning, not just money.

Since that conference in 2006, and before that for over a decade, we have seen the organic and viral growth of a dizzying array of sharing systems, from weekend software projects tackled by people all over the world who don't know each other, to bike sharing, car sharing, house sharing, virtual assistants, coworking spaces, incubators, and the cocreation of products and services by companies interacting directly with their customers. Linux, an open-source, *shared* software operating system, owned by no one, runs the fastest computers in the world and tens of millions of cell phones.

Airbnb.com lets people share their homes with people around the world. ZipCar.com, Car2go.com, Getaround.com, RelayRides.com and others allow you to share your car with people around your city. And other sharing platforms encourage crowd funding, cocreating, innovating, swapping, selling, and renting of everything imaginable to people just about anywhere. None of this was conceivable forty years ago as the Industrial Age was closing.

The development of Web 2.0 internet technologies was a big step forward because Web 2.0 is based on sharing—the sharing of information, services, products, knowledge, and opinions to the point that companies don't even own their brand anymore; those who participate in sharing what they think about a company on the Internet are the real owners. Sharing is the new and uncontrolled economy that is baffling the twenty-first-century Industrialist.

But the sharing economy is here to stay. As Emily Badger said in *City 2.0: The Habitat of the Future and How to Get There*, "The open-source culture of the web has taught us how to share, and made sharing a default of social interaction."[1] Sharing is becoming so pervasive that *Shareable Magazine* was created to do nothing but track and report on the sharing economy.[2]

> The hallmark of the Participation Age is SHARING.

Sharing in the Participation Age shows up in many ways. United Airlines' stock value plunged US $180 million in a few days because Dave Carroll wrote a song about how they broke his guitar and stuck it out on YouTube. Before the Participation Age, United, and others similar to them, regularly blew off one badly treated customer after another, knowing they had a limited reach among their friends. But now, in the Participation Age, one person's shared view of the world has a power that it never had before in history.

On the positive side, we've also seen sharing create massive responses from all over the world to a single person's plight, and the proliferation of crowd-sourcing and crowd-funding companies that help people in ways they could have never imagined before such participation was possible. Now we also regularly find vendors, suppliers, and people to fix our sinks and buy our books based on websites that aggregate the shared reviews of others.

## THE PARTICIPATION AGE HAS CHANGED THE WAY WE WORK

The Participation Age has changed the way people relate to each other. But most importantly, it is changing the way we relate to work, allowing us to go back to a more natural relationship with work that was dominant for thousands of years before the extremely short, unique, and interruptive blip in history we call the Industrial Age.

Past generations who grew up in the intimidating presence of the Industrial Age were taught to react, respond, and at times even to contribute, but never to participate and share. Today, the Participation Age demands that we be proactive and creative, which is our basic human nature. The Industrial Age did not want us being proactive and creative; it wanted us to be extensions of machines, and loyal, almost indentured servants to the company (via the golden handcuffs of in-house retirement plans).

## THE FAR-REACHING EFFECTS OF THE INDUSTRIAL AGE

The Industrial Age had far-reaching effects because it was the most unique economic period in human history. Before it, economic expansion was largely nonexistent, and since then, economic expansion has slowed to a crawl, with many proclaiming we will never see expansion like it again. People who are addicted to *Big* (see the next chapter) love to wax eloquent about "the great Industrialists" and the incredible advances of society and nations as a result of the Industrial Age.

But on a microscale, where all of us normal people live, the biggest impact of the Industrial Age was a Jekyll-and-Hyde experience – raising our standard of living, while methodically stripping us of many of the things that make us human; most importantly, our ability to create and to participate in the world around us in real and meaningful ways. At our core, we are not made to be extensions of machines, or to find our personal validity in four decades of gutting it out just so we can sit on a beach for a few years before we die. In short, we are made to Make Meaning, not just money. The Industrial Age ignored this. The Participation Age celebrates it.

## MAKE MEANING, NOT JUST MONEY

In the Participation Age, the trip I shared at the beginning of the chapter is a natural extension of our business. Our company is not in the business of solving poverty anywhere in any direct way. But we have recognized that the best, most capitalistic way we can build and grow a company with expanding revenue and a great bottom line is to build a company where people can Make Meaning, not just money.

## A DIFFERENT VIEW OF "WORK"

This requires that we treat everyone like creative adults who want to Make Meaning with their whole lives, not just by holding down a job. This means a different view of *work*. Each one of us has the privilege and responsibility of making something more of our lives than is convenient for the present, most common corporate structure, which is still dominated by archaic, Industrial Age practices.

## MAKE ROOM TO MAKE MEANING

In most companies today, it would be inconvenient for me to run off to Africa because some Chief called, or for someone to leave at 10:00 a.m. to watch a school play, or take two days to accompany their young basketball star to a tournament. Giant Corporation, Inc. has labels for that, with special names like "personal time" and "vacation time," so that you know you're getting a gift of time, and that you shouldn't get used to it. These are archaic Industrial Age constructs that were invented to keep me on the assembly line as much as possible, and make me feel indebted because I was getting "time off."

Where did these kinds of business practices originate? Are they normal and an inescapable part of modern life, or are they throwbacks to a short period in history that needs to be left behind?

## THE INDUSTRIAL AGE – GREAT TOYS. BAD KARMA.

The toys that came from the Industrial Age have improved our standard of living exponentially, even if sometimes they haven't actually improved our lives. But the human carnage of the Industrial Age is the unaddressed collateral damage of how we decided we would produce those toys. The business practices we invented during that time had a lot of built-in problems I call business diseases. They were put in place as cures for problems faced by the Industrialists as they created the Factory System in the 1800s, but they were actually the diseases, not the cures. And they are still with us, infecting our business world and holding us back from fully entering the Participation Age.

> The human carnage of the Industrial Age is the unaddressed collateral damage of how we decided we would produce those toys.

## DILBERT STILL REIGNS IN THE FRONT OFFICE

It's fascinating to see the phenomenal change on the production side of business in the last fifty years. The furnace, smokestack, and assembly line have been replaced with clean suits, clean rooms, and nanotechnology. The production side of the business has been revolutionized. But in the front office, the Industrial Age Dilbert Society still reigns.

Humor is most often the intersection of two ideas that don't belong together. If the out-of-place idea is really old and was at some point tragic (but not now), it's even funnier. That is why Industrial Age management practices used in today's office situation are so funny.

Scott Adams, the creator of the *Dilbert* comic strip, has a made a living off of identifying the foibles of the ongoing presence of the Industrial Age front office. It is still with us, long after we've dumped the Factory System production floor. Through all the changes from 1970 forward that have regularly reshaped the way companies produce, the front office is the Factory System gift that just keeps on giving. The old saying "Much truth is said in jest" couldn't apply more to *Dilbert*. It's been so funny and so timeless because it plays on such a deep and wide-scale tragedy – the continuing human carnage of the Industrial Age. The popularity of *Dilbert* is a sad indictment of our failure to bring the front office forward into the Participation Age.

Despite an unrelenting parade of management fads, the structural and cultural landscape in the front office looks largely like it did in 1960. And despite the righteous jumping up and down of people like Douglas McGregor in *The Human Side of Enterprise*, Marvin Weisbord in *Productive Workplaces Revisited*, and Michael Hammer and James Champy in *Reengineering the Corporation*, along with many others like them, the overwhelming majority of companies are still running their front offices on Factory System values and constructs dragged forward out of the Industrial Age.

## PRODUCTION FLOOR VS. OFFICE FLOOR

In some ways it's easy and simplistic to see why the production floor has progressed so well while the Dilbert Society is still in full control of the front office. The production floor is much more directly tied to revenue, and when revenue is affected, companies respond quickly.

Front-office folks like me see a direct correlation between the product being made and the effect it has on revenue. So, if the production changes and the revenue flows again, we stop looking for problems that aren't so directly tied to the production. But the front office is more like government – there is usually no clear and direct line of profitability or loss from the business models we employ in the front office. The path from the front office to its impact on revenue gets murky. Lousy practices in the front office don't get exposed because we don't trace our profitability directly back to them. But the indirect cost will be enormous and life threatening to businesses that don't adapt to the new economy of the Participation Age.

In short, Giant Corporation, Inc., the most visible product of the Industrial Age, has always been focused on the production floor itself – its processes, its management, and its bottom line. It has resisted changing leadership practices that don't have a direct impact on revenue. As a result, companies have done a bad job of seeing the human carnage of focusing on production and ignoring the long-term impact of archaic front-office practices that have changed very little in decades. As long as those business practices allowed us to be successful, there was little motivation to change them. But while they allowed us to make great toys, what impact did they have on the people running the factories? And how will they work going forward in the Participation Age?

We trumpet the successes of the Industrial Age, the quality and efficiency processes we've built since, and all the mind-boggling advances it has brought to our lives, but we never ask the producers, the people who do the work, "How'd that work out for *YOU*?"

So let's ask them, "How'd that work out for you?" The answer coming out of the peak of the Industrial Age is devastating.

## THE FACTORY SYSTEM STARTED IT ALL

The Industrial Age began in the early 1700s, with its roots back as far as the 1600s. For the purposes of this book, we'll focus on the establishment and dominance of the Factory System, the source of today's business culture, circa 1784-1970, and really only from 1850 on, since the system was not dominant until then.

The 120-year dominance of the Factory System (1850-1970) replaced hand manufacturing in homes and workshops with machine-based production. For the first time in history, this required people to regularly leave their homes and *go to work* at a centralized factory location to *perform work*. The Factory System changed every aspect of business and aspects of home life that had been in place for thousands of years.

By the 1880s, industrial production exceeded what the economy could absorb. For the first time in history, this degraded the value of an individual's work. Prior to the Factory System and for thousands of years, the home and workshop system had always assured that productive work was a virtue that was always rewarded, and excess goods were not a problem. But now that the factories could produce more than the nation needed, hard work and productivity no longer led to an assurance of prosperity, which devalued work in ways we had never seen.[3]

The peak of the 120-year dominance of the Factory System came after World War II, from 1945 to 1965, when a few hundred years of Industrial Age momentum converged with the end of the war and the beginning of an era of optimism. In less than a century of building an economy based on the Factory System, the United States was basking in the glory days of the Industrial Age. The system encouraged everyone to GO to work from 8:00 a.m.-5:00 p.m., with the promise that the system would take care of them and their families from the cradle through retirement to the grave.

The generation born between 1925 and 1945 were the beneficiaries of this Industrial Age peak. They entered the work force from 1945 to 1965. The boys came home from World War II to a booming economy built on the backs of a Factory System engine built one hundred years before and fine-tuned during the war.

As a result, the suburbs exploded with cute little Cape Cod houses and white picket fences, occupied by two parents, 3.8 kids, and a dog. All the dads left in unison for their offices at 7:30 a.m. in their shiny, new, and very large Fords, while the moms stayed home and got the kids off to school and made curtains. Then all the dads got home at 6:00 p.m. to wives with not a hair out of place, dinner on the table, and 3.8 perfect and heavily scrubbed children.

The TV shows *Ozzie and Harriet, My Three Sons*, and *Leave It to Beaver* were idyllic pictures of what the Industrial Age held for all who fell in line. The peak of the Industrial Age was an amazing time in many ways. The economy was expanding at record rates, and the future looked bright for everyone.

As a result, everybody wanted to work for "Giant Corporation, Inc.," because that's where you were most likely to find the American dream. The giant industrialists of the 1800s like Vanderbilt, Rockefeller, Carnegie, Mellon, and J.P. Morgan had designed a system that would take care of you from cradle to grave, as long as you didn't question the system and did what you were told.

Nobody argues with the incredible advances in products, services, and lifestyle that converged to make 1945-1965 an amazing period. The Factory System was an amazing advancement. But what effect did it have on the generation that entered the workforce during that twenty-year span that was the peak of that system? How did the very heights of the Industrial Age, from 1945 to 1965, work out for them? The label given them by generational scholars paints a haunting picture.

## THE LUCKY FEW, OR...?

If you look first at it from the Industrialist's side of the equation, the plight of this generation doesn't look so bad. Elwood Carlson wrote that those born between 1929 and 1945 who entered the workforce after World War II from 1945-1965 should be called "The Lucky Few." They came on the scene at the peak of the industrial age and were showered with its benefits. He says the Lucky Few had the *Ozzie and Harriet* life. They were:

> *The luckiest generation of Americans ever. As children, they experienced the most stable intact parental families in the nation's history. Lucky Few women married earlier than any other generation of the century and helped give birth to the Baby Boom, yet also gained in education compared to earlier generations. Lucky Few men made the greatest gains of the century in schooling, earned veterans benefits like the Greatest Generation, but served mostly in peacetime with only a fraction of the casualties, came closest to full employment, and spearheaded the trend toward earlier retirement. More than any other generation, Lucky Few men advanced into professional and white-collar jobs while Lucky Few women concentrated in the clerical 'pink-collar' ghetto.*
>
> *In their young adulthood, they went to work and got promoted like crazy. The Lucky Few had a much smoother and more prosperous transition to adulthood. . . . The transition to adulthood was early, fast, and easy.*[4]

Carlson also writes that the Lucky Few were also the only generation to benefit fully from the security of corporate retirement plans. Many of those who followed have been bitterly disappointed by retirement plans that evaporated in bankruptcies and acquisitions.

## "WHY ARE YOU?"

The Lucky Few received all the benefits promised by the Factory System. But the Factory System was careful not to promise them a few things, like the ability to express their creativity, to think, to be fully human, and to ask the most human of questions, "Why?" It did not promise them that they could Make Meaning, only that they could make money.

Living a personal life of meaning was not part of the Factory System plan. You were to get your significance through the company. In the 1950s, it was the company's job to become significant, and your job to make it happen. The legacy of finding our significance through our job is so engrained that today, when we meet someone, the first question is always, "What's your name?" and the second is always, "What do you do?" or, in the negative, "What machine are you tied to?" That was not the normal greeting 150 years ago. People were more focused on their own personal identity, not on an identity based on work. We never ask "Why are you?" only "What do you do?"

The Industrial Age beat the "why" out of us, and today we are still much more comfortable avoiding and finding our meaning through our vocational identity, as if that defines who we are. We don't see our business as a tool for building something greater, but as an end in itself. That mindset is a legacy of the short-lived, but incredibly influential Factory System of the Industrial Age.

Elwood Carlson was very much alone in labeling the generation entering the workforce after World War II *The Lucky Few*. He isn't wrong. He was just seeing it from the Industrial Age vantage point. They got all the stuff and the easy road through life because they played the Industrialist's game the way the Industrialists needed them to play it. They played by other people's rules, and it seemed to work out for them. Or did it?

## THE SILENT GENERATION

The mainstream demographers labeled this generation in radically different terms than Elwood Carlson. On November 5, 1951, *Time Magazine* ran a cover story describing the young people entering the workforce. It characterized them as "grave and fatalistic, conventional, possessing confused morals, and expecting disappointment." This 1951 article stated:

> *Youth today is waiting for the hand of fate to fall on its shoulders, meanwhile working fairly hard and saying almost nothing. The most startling fact about the younger generation is its silence. With some rare exceptions, youth is nowhere near the podium. By comparison with the Flaming Youth of their fathers and mothers, today's younger generation is a still, small flame. It does not issue manifestos, make speeches, or carry posters. It has been called the 'Silent Generation.'* [5]

The American historian William Manchester carried the label forward, calling those entering the work force in the late '40s to late '50s, "withdrawn, cautious, unimaginative, indifferent, unadventurous, and silent." The Silent Generation has lived with this damning label ever since. In 1970, *Time Magazine* did a follow-up issue on *The Silents*, and in 1991, Strauss and Howe used it in their book *Generations*,[6] which describes American history from 1584 forward in generational cycles.

*The Silent Generation.* I can't think of a more condemning label for an entire generation than this one. And they have lived down to their label. Not a single president or Supreme Court justice has come from this generation, the only twenty-year generation in two hundred years with that forgettable record.

Human beings are first and foremost creative problem solvers. Creativity in art, music, science, technology, innovation, problem solving, and human relationships sets us apart from other animals. The Silent Generation was stripped of their creativity. In order to serve the Factory System, they had to be.

## THE ROOTS OF THE "SILENTS"

The Industrialists of the 1800s had to build silence into the system. In so doing, they laid the foundation for the generation at the peak of the Industrial Age to be silent and forgotten. While designing a system that would provide the basic securities of life in the suburbs, the Industrialists needed to reengineer humans in the image of machines. Being creative was the most detrimental attribute you could have as an Industrial Age extension of a machine.

No human who was wondering, thinking creatively, or trying to innovate would ever do well tied to a machine. As a result, one specific question became about more than any other during the Industrial Age. The question that promotes some of the greatest creativity in people, and makes us more human than any other question we can ask, became forbidden: "Why?"

You were more likely to get fired for asking why than for asking any other question. Asking why became a symbol of insubordination, rebellion, and the inability to work well with others in the Factory System. Above all, the Silents were taught to not question *any* authority by asking why. It was authority that was giving them their suburban security. You don't question the hand that feeds you and gives you a stable, predictable, *Ozzie and Harriet* life.

## THE TALE OF TWO RESULTS

The quantity and variety of products rolling off the assembly line in the 1950s were unprecedented. That was one result of the Industrial Age. But the human product at the peak of the Industrial Age was the most *undesirable* result we could have feared: blind loyalty to the corporation, conditioned to do exactly what we were told. The responsibility doctrine of the Silent Generation was, "Show up early and leave late, shut up, sit down, don't make waves, live invisibly," and worst of all, "Go out quietly," maybe even with a gold watch. If anything demonstrates the chasm between the tremendous production of the Industrial Age and the result for Industrial Age people, it is the effect it had on this generation: Great toys. Really bad human results.

The Silents would never have felt they had permission to go to Africa and meet chiefs. They were taught to find their meaning through making the company successful, not by building a life of significance.

## THE '60S BABY BOOMERS—WHAT CHANGED?

So it's no wonder that the generation that followed the Silents, the Baby Boomers who started coming of age in the '60s, gave rise to a time of rebellion, questioning authority, asking "Why?" as a standard way of life, exhibiting dislike for The Man (Corporate America), and a responsibility doctrine that read, "Never trust anyone over thirty." The Silents were all over thirty by then. Those not-so *Lucky Few* got the short end of the stick again.

But the '60s came and went and the only thing that really changed in Giant Corporation, Inc. was the production side of the house. The smokestacks were either outsourced offshore or more often replaced with technological marvels and a mixed service/information-based economy. The Industrial Age was gone, but the front-office system that was built to run it is still in place.

## THE PARTICIPATION AGE FRONT OFFICE:
## NO TURNING BACK

In the Participation Age, there is another way – a way that makes the company even more money by creating systems and processes that focus on both the health of the production line and the joy of the staff. The Participation Age demands that we allow people to share in the creative process of building the corporation and in the rewards that come from doing so.

> The Participation Age demands that we allow people to share in the creative process of building the corporation and in the rewards that come from doing so.

Many companies are already living fully in the Participation Age and have been for years. In a few rare cases we'll look at later in the book, pioneering corporations have already been there for a few decades. And it is encouraging to see companies of all sizes leaving Industrial Age practices behind and embracing the Participation Age.

There is no turning back. The Industrial Age is behind us and the Participation Age is fully upon us. Going forward, the companies that are committed to encouraging their workforce to participate and to Make Meaning will also make more money as a company – in most cases, a lot more.

## IT'S NOT YOUR FATHER'S CORPORATION ANYMORE

Multiple corporate movements, led by dozens of CEOs of large corporations, have sprung up around the need to move into the Participation Age and Make Meaning. One of them, Conscious Capitalism, led by John Mackey (Whole Foods) says, "Unlike some businesses that believe they only exist to maximize return on investment for their shareholders, 'Conscious Businesses' focus on their whole business ecosystem, creating and optimizing value for all of their Stakeholders, understanding that strong and engaged Stakeholders lead to a healthy, sustainable, resilient business." This isn't your father's corporation anymore.

The producers who are the backbone of every company don't necessarily want to confront the challenges of Africa. But everyone living in the Participation Age wants to Make Meaning, not just money. They all shudder at the thought of thought of ending up like the Silent Generation. There is an earnest search by people now looking for companies that will encourage them to participate and to share in both the creative process of building a company and the rewards of doing so. We call them Stakeholders. The good news is that a fast-growing number of companies are looking for those Stakeholders. And as they find each other, together they are creating companies that are flourishing and setting themselves up for a long run at success.

Conversely, the employees and companies who find the Participation Age unsettling, annoying, or disruptive to their present world will find themselves on the outside looking in. The only choice for both people and companies in the Participation Age is to jump in with both feet, share, create, and participate together in putting the Industrial Age behind us.

To get there, we have to recognize and confront the seven business diseases of the Industrial Age described in Part I – those practices that were developed to serve as cures for issues in the Factory System that morphed into diseases for the people who staffed the factories. The Industrial Age and its Factory System are behind us; the leadership practices that served them both will not serve us in the Participation Age. The cure has become the disease. It must be eradicated.

## NOTES

1. *Share Everything: Why the Way We Consume Has Changed Forever, City 2.0: The Habitat of the Future and How to Get There,* co-produced in partnership by The Atlantic Cities and TED Books, eBook format only (TED Conferences, February 20, 2013)

2. *Shareable Magazine,* Neal Gorenflo, http://www.shareable.net/

3. Roger B. Hill, PhD. *The History of Work Ethic: Historical Context of the Work Ethic,* Program of Workforce Education; College of Education (Athens, GA: University of Georgia Press, 1992)  http://rhill.coe.uga.edu/workethic/hist.htm

4. Elwood Carlson, *The Lucky Few, Between the Greatest Generation and the Baby Boom,* Florida State University (Tallahassee, FL: Springer Science+Business Media B.V., 2008)

5. *The Younger Generation, Time Magazine,* November, 5, 1951, Volume LVIII, No. 19 http://ti.me/185MFtZ

6. Strauss and Howe, Generations: *The History of America's Future, 1584 to 2069* (New York, NY: Morrow and Co., 1991)

# The Problem with "Big"

*"Too much of anything is just enough."*
— JERRY GARCIA

### THE MOSQUITO WOMEN

It is 3:00 a.m. in The Democratic Republic of the Congo (DR Congo). It's one of my first trips to Africa. I'm staying at the home of a former government Minister of a large national bureaucracy. He passed away a few years ago and is survived by his elderly wife and their grown children, who live elsewhere in the world. I've been awakened by the sound of angels singing softly. At first I thought I was dreaming. I'm in the poorest country on earth, in a city of eleven million people, and in my fog I assumed I was dreaming about what it should really be like in this incredibly beautiful country. It was a strange feeling to suddenly realize I was awake and that the angels were real.

As I got my wits about me, it sounded like eight or more women singing African harmonies: beautiful, soft voices. This close to the equator, night is deep. The blackness of the night made the voices seem like they were just yards away. My bedroom faced the front courtyard of the compound. I groped my way to the window. Although I could not see anything beyond the open window, it became clear to me that the women were just a few yards to my left, singing on the veranda to our house. I stood and listened for a while. They would sing, pray softly, then sing again.

They had momentum; it was clear they were not going to stop for some time. I stumbled back to my bed. I could have closed

> Anyone who thinks they are too small to make a difference has never been to bed with a mosquito."
> - Gandhi

my window, but it seemed appropriate to leave it open and join them, at least in spirit. I learned later that they come every Saturday night to pray and sing for the whole night at the house of the widow whose late husband and grandfather are so revered in DR Congo.

Will Africa be different because of these women who sing and pray with such dedication? This is a massive city without a single working traffic light, no waste disposal, and no running water inside the houses. This huge country with incredible natural resources has been run into the ground by decades of kleptocracy and unfocused leadership. How can these few women make a difference? Gandhi had the answer. He once said, "Anyone who thinks they are too small to make a difference has never been to bed with a mosquito." Just maybe these *mosquito women* will change the world.

Back to sleep, if I can, if I dare. Africa…

## "BIG" — A CORE BUSINESS DISEASE

*Big* is one of the core business diseases of the Industrial Age; it is a solution devised by famous Industrialists in the late 1800s to serve themselves and the Factory System. The people hired to run the factories were not considered in its formation, except as extensions of machines. Big serves Big, almost always at the expense of Small.

Everybody seems to love Big. It's impressive and showy. We love big marching bands, big stadiums, big buildings, big stars, big houses, big trucks, big universities, big cities, big budgets, big jewelry, big dinosaurs, big TVs, and a thousand other Bigs. Mega size, king size, double gulp, triple burger; anything that smacks of Big – we're in. "Big is better."

It took a long time for us to fall in love with Big, almost at the very end of the Industrial Age. Even in 1960, an average bagel, cup of coffee, burger, or beer was half the size it is today.[1] With our new and recent addiction to Big, those traditional products wouldn't stand a chance.

Today, there is a restaurant in the upper Midwest that has a 10 lb burger on its daily menu. A candy store in the Southeast makes and sells a 5 lb Gummy Bear. It's the same shape as the regular one, but it's Big. It's very popular.

Big sells better than small in a lot of other ways, not just in food. We love big software applications, too. We use less than 2 percent of the features of common word-processing and software office applications. We just assume that bigger is better. *Big* has become a qualitative statement.

The bottom line: we're addicted to Big. We can't help ourselves. Big is just too cool for school.

## WHY IS BIG SO BIG NOW?

Big isn't a new thing; it's been around for thousands of years – big pyramids, big empires, and even big business. The Hudson Bay Company, with thousands of employees, was incorporated in 1670 and is still going strong. And, of course, Big Governments have been a way of life for thousands of years, with an insatiable desire to conquer their neighbors and get even bigger. But Big Business as a dominant economic force is a very new thing.

There are just 167 companies in the world older than five hundred years. Only one of them, StoraEnso, has more than one hundred employees. The rest are Smalls. The phrase *big business* did not even enter the common lexicon until the 1950s. Big Government has been around a long time, but Big Business as a dominant force is brand, spanking new.[2]

> Big Business as a dominant economic force is a very new thing.

Even today, only about 17,500 companies out of the 28 million in America have more than five hundred employees. That's a tiny percentage – just 6/100ths of 1 percent. It's an even smaller fraction of the tens of millions of additional Schedule C businesses. About 98 percent of businesses have one to nineteen employees, and those with fewer than ten employees constitute 96 percent of all businesses in America. The ratio is even smaller in the rest of the world. Big is actually freakishly rare. But because of its size, we trot it out front all the time. As with many rare things, we're in awe of Big.

Even though there are still very few Bigs, there are a lot more than there used to be, which allows them to dominate parts of our economy. Our fascination with Big, and their very recent economic dominance, make them the assumed and shining example of what all businesses should aspire to become. Today, venture capitalists make it sound like there is almost something wrong with you if you don't want to be one. After thousands of years of running economies on the backs of the Smalls, we assume Big is now the best and only way to go.


## BIG FOR THE SAKE OF BIG

How did Big come to dominate? The rise of Industrialism within democracies in the 1800s, for the first time in history, allowed men to become immensely powerful without being in government. The modern Capitalist haters are wrong (as we'll show later in this chapter). Greed was not the driving force of the Industrialists any more than it has been throughout history for kings and politicians. It was all about power.


## BIG HAS HAD ITS DAY

We don't realize how unusual and unique it is to have so many Bigs around. We've grown up with them and assume it's always been this way. But macroeconomic trends show a slowing dominance of Big. The bell curve has topped out, and many believe that Big has a shelf life and will fade in the coming century, like the railroads faded from their glory days in the early 1900s. In 1960, the nation's largest employers were all manufacturers.

Today, only three of the top fifteen employers are manufacturers, and they make almost everything overseas.[3] And in general, the Bigs, as a cohort group, aren't expanding as they did for a hundred years. They are still the dominant economic group, but from 1999 to 2009, US multinational corporations lost a net half million jobs.[4] This is not surprising, because the Participation Age is allowing us to go back to living and working locally, and is creating less and less dependence on Big.

Big is one of the core business diseases of the Industrial Age. And like all of the business diseases we will tie to the Industrialists, it was a solution built to create power for the Industrialists, which became a disease for the rest of us. But as the Participation Age continues to spread, Big is going to become less and less important to our future. In a February 2010 cover story article for *Wired Magazine*, Chris Anderson described a new Industrial Revolution. The headline on the cover summed it up – "The factory, the investors, the workers—obsolete. In the age of DIY manufacturing all you need is a garage and a great idea." Technology like 3D printing, electronics assembly, the Internet, and our inborn need to live locally will return us to our roots as a world full of Smalls, with fewer and less dominant Bigs. In this 2010 article, Anderson said, "The collective potential of a million garage tinkerers is about to be unleashed on the global markets, as ideas go straight into production, no financing or tooling required." We are already well on our way there.

## THE PROBLEM WITH BIG

Big has special problems that it doesn't share with Small. Whether it is business, government, dinosaurs, hurricanes, or snowstorms, the really big ones have two intrinsic problems that Small doesn't have:

1. The bigger they are, the more problems their complexity creates, for themselves and the world around them.

2. The bigger they are, the greater impact their mistakes and problems have on the world around them.

## HOW DOES "BIG" AFFECT US?

In 2008, one giant financial institution, Lehman Brothers, collapsed, which created a domino effect, threatening the entire banking system. As a result, in 2009, and for almost two years after, the US economy was stunningly rated by the National Security Agency (NSA) as the highest threat to US national security, higher than terrorism or any other outside threat. The United States' addiction to Big had become her own worst enemy.

But not all of us were our own worst enemy in 2009. Just the Bigs. While one side was bashing big government and the other side was blaming big business and big banks, virtually no one was angry with local business or local government. The only consensus during that time was that the Smalls weren't the problem.

## TWO TICKS, NO DOG

An illusion is that these Bigs are always at odds, but more often they recognize the advantage of propping each other up for the sake of keeping Big alive in all its forms. This symbiotic relationship was most publicly demonstrated in late 2008. Big government gifted hundreds of billions of dollars to a few giant banks without so much as an I.O.U. – free money with no strings attached. Big government had to do it. Big business was holding the government and the entire country hostage by sheer virtue of its size.

## WHAT DID BANKS DO WITH THE MONEY?

They put it in their pockets and didn't lend it. Then, with their pockets stuffed, and with the full knowledge of the government, they turned around and took credit lines away from millions of small businesses in the middle of the night without so much as an e-mail notice. You just woke up in the morning and your credit line was gone. This was perhaps one of the most spineless and shameful acts in banking history. Big government stood by and watched. That shouldn't be surprising. Big rarely attacks Big. They sometimes don't like each other, but like two ticks with no dog, the Bigs need each other desperately.

I was told by the branch manager at a local Wells Fargo bank that the bigwigs at Wells Fargo headquarters didn't bother to look at anyone's small business credit rating when they did this. It was a universal deletion of credit to small and local business owners by most giant banks nationwide, who all the while were sitting on hundreds of billions of dollars in free government handouts and the lowest Federal Bank interest rates in history.

## HOW DID THIS AFFECT YOU?

It got worse. After hundreds of thousands of very successful business owners turned to their personal lines of credit to stay afloat, the banks then jacked those interest rates through the roof. The inability of small and local businesses to obtain financing is perhaps the biggest, most influential factor in the slowest and longest economic recovery in history.

In 2009, one business owner described to me how her forty employees had been successfully cleaning skyscrapers for over twenty years. She had used her line of credit every month to buy supplies and then paid it off every time she got paid. When the banks ripped her credit line out from under her, she had US $80,000 in contracts in hand for the next month, but couldn't buy the $15,000-$20,000 in supplies she needed to clean the buildings. Losing her line of credit drove her under in just one month. She closed her doors, laid off her employees, and was done.

Hundreds of thousands of small and local business owners had similar experiences. Small business in America was crippled by this one act that went largely unreported by Big Media. It is the largest underlying cause of the slow recovery from the *great recession*. And it is again important to remember that the government had full knowledge and just stood by and watched. In fact, the banks were able to blame the government, which had put in place new lending restrictions. This, in turn, gave the banks an excuse for taking away everyone's credit without regard to their actual credit worthiness.

## THE PROBLEM OF "BIG"—REVISITED

This series of events – the failure of just one giant bank, the gift of hundreds of billions of dollars to a few dozen other giants, the subsequent universal destruction of small business credit, and the lack of any pushback from Big Government – is as good an example as you'll find of *The Problem of Big*. When a few giant businesses can become the greatest threat to their own nation's security, something is out of balance.

As this shows, bad decisions by the Bigs can have far-ranging and devastating consequences. When Big does something stupid like Lehman Brothers did, the impact is global. When Small does something stupid or intentionally detrimental, it's no less acceptable, but the scope of the damage is localized and controlled. It's like the difference between the mistaken detonation of a hand grenade or a nuclear bomb. Both are bad, but only one is global in scale.

## ALL THREATS, FOREIGN AND DOMESTIC

How does Big affect government and its relationship to business? Every Congressman, Senator, civil servant, and armed forces inductee takes an oath of office swearing to protect us "from all threats, foreign and domestic." As mentioned previously, the NSA said our biggest threat for almost two years was a domestic threat – companies that were too big. What did our government do? It passed legislation, Dodd-Frank, vowing to keep businesses from ever getting *too big to fail* again. But within twelve months of its passing, the eighteen largest banks in the nation that had been the target of Dodd-Frank had an even larger share of the market than they did before the passage of Dodd-Frank, and they have grown bigger ever since.

This kind of patronage between the Bigs is not isolated and is actually standard practice. In 2012, the US Justice Department found that HSBC, one of the world's three largest banks, had "spent years committing serious crimes," regularly laundering money for terrorists and drug cartels. These kinds of crimes should automatically have resulted in the loss of HSBC's banking license. But the Justice Department decided HSBC was "too important to subject them to disruptions" and shielded them from criminal prosecution.

In the last five years, the Justice Department has shut down hundreds of small and local banks for much smaller and less intentional infractions of banking rules. But Assistant Attorney General Lanny Breuer told a press conference in 2013, "Had the US authorities decided to press criminal charges, HSBC would almost certainly have lost its banking license in the United States, the future of the institution would have been under threat, and the entire banking system would have been destabilized."[5]

## IN THE END, THE SMALLS GET THE SHAFT

As with Dodd-Frank, Washington barks a lot about the Bigs, then regularly passes regulations that hurt only the Smalls, which by default helps the Bigs. Giant Corporation, Inc. is one domestic threat they aren't about to address, because if they did, it might just endanger their own power as a Big. Big doesn't attack Big if it can be avoided. It only pretends to, so the rest of us will rise up in indignation until the feeling passes.

## MACROSOLUTIONS FOR MICROPROBLEMS

Another problem with Big is that it creates macrosolutions for microproblems. Even with the best of intentions, it is simply too big a task to ask macroentities to solve local problems. The problem is not the systems, but the size of the systems: the size of business, the size of government, and the resulting accumulation of power and decision making into those few hands.

The old adage is that "all politics is local." That, of course, is an oversimplification, but it has a lot of truth to it. The same is true for problems: "All problems are local." Again, with exceptions. But certainly most problems and most politics are local. Microsolutions are more likely to solve microproblems.

Does Small always work better than Big? No. It is easy to find both local businesses and local governments that make self-preserving decisions that aren't in the best interest of their constituency, just like the Bigs. But because they are small and local, the negative effects are never as damaging.

Turning to local government and local business for answers to our local problems would push as many decisions down the food chain as possible. This is difficult, if not impossible, for both national politicians and big business leaders to accept,

> Big creates macrosolutions for microproblems

because they lose control over their own macropower. There is a place for both Big Business and Big Government, but experience says we would be better off – and certainly safer as a nation – with less of both.

## GREED—IT'S NOT WHAT IT USED TO BE

The motives of the giant Industrialists of the 1800s were not about building a better mousetrap or producing something the public needed, even though they did those things. And it wasn't about greed.

One of the great misunderstandings of the Industrialists' motivations is that they were greedy, when in fact greed played almost no role. In his 1835 book, *Democracy in America*, the French political thinker Alexis de Tocqueville wrote of the United States, "I know of no other country where love of money has such a grip on men's hearts." This was not something he observed uniquely in the wealthy, but as an obsession of virtually everyone in America. This all-inclusive obsession with greed was imputed onto the Industrialists by those who saw the world through that lens. But nothing could be further from reality. The Industrialists had motivations much less common and pedestrian than greed.

## IT'S REALLY ABOUT POWER – I WIN

As with all empire builders who passed before them, for the Industrialists it was about *power.* Money was just a new measure of power. The Industrial Age provided new opportunities for people to pursue power and control on a massive scale without being in government. In the newly democratized world and for the first time in history, you could build a fiefdom alongside a government that would not send armies to destroy you, but would actually protect your right to do so.

As de Tocqueville observed, greed is widespread and is actually the motive of the Small who doesn't already have a lot of money. Bit players on Wall Street are greedy. And owners of small shops who want to overprice their gas cans during a hurricane— they're greedy. When someone doesn't have much money and sees the opportunity to get more by any means, morality and ethics often take a back seat to accumulating more money. This very common and broadly practiced obsession is wrongly imputed by the masses onto the Industrialists.

There is little doubt that most of the Industrialists, when they were also Smalls, likely ignored some moral or ethical boundaries to begin to accumulate wealth. But once Industrialists experience real wealth, they ignore moral and ethical boundaries in order to be more powerful, not for more money.

Bernie Madoff may have been greedy when he was a bit player on Wall Street, but he perpetuated his Ponzi scheme long after he stole billions because it made him powerful, well known, and respected. Athletes may get stars in their eyes when they get their first US $1.5 million contract, but five years later they're holding out for an extra $500,000 on a $40 million contract because the extra $500,000 will make them the highest paid player – a seat of power. After someone has significantly more than they need, it becomes about power. And power requires winning, beating the other guy.

> As with all empire builders who passed before them, for the Industrialists it was about power. Money was just a new measure of power.

The desire for power is much rarer than greed. Most people are not motivated to pursue sweeping power. But the basic motivations of feudal lords, politicians, and Industrialists are identical. For all of them, the most intoxicating motivation is to be able to manage and direct the lives of other people, which gives them power, control, and prestige. The feudal lord accumulates armies, the politician accumulates votes, and the Industrialist accumulates money, all with the same motive: domination of their respective worlds and elimination of potential threats. Being the most powerful person is a rare motivation, and that is the motivation of Industrialists.

## LORDS BY BIRTH VS. LORDS BY AMBITION

In the preindustrial world, your ability to be powerful was controlled by birthright; you were either born into power or not. But by 1800, with a fledgling US democracy just getting on its feet, this was a new world where people could rise from nothing and be lords of their own feudal systems, regardless of their birth status. All they needed were the same feudal aspirations, drive, and blind ambition to be powerful, and then some ingenuity to find a path in the free enterprise system to make it happen. It was also necessary to possess the ruthlessness to economically destroy those in your path.

Industrialism was the same power-grabbing game rulers had played for thousands of years, but instead of attacking someone physically, you did it economically. As with feudalism, Industrialism was seen as a zero-sum game. There was only so much land (or in this case, market) to go around, and every little bit that someone else controlled was that much less over which the Industrialist could reign. The more an Industrialist controlled, the more powerful he became. Competitors were seen as challengers to the throne, and were therefore treated as treasonous rebels to be attacked and destroyed. The early Industrialists learned well from their royal and feudal predecessors. Attacking and destroying others became as much a part of business as it had been a part of governing for thirty centuries.

## THE RISE OF THE INDUSTRIAL AGE LORDS

Cornelius Vanderbilt was a feudal lord ruling over a fiefdom. He was so powerful, he was able to destroy the entire railroad industry by shutting down the Albany Bridge, the only rail bridge into New York City, which he owned. Some say the act was partially motivated by competitors who felt Vanderbilt was old and washed up – no longer influential. His became the biggest railroad as he bought up competitors for pennies on the dollar. That's power.

In 1895, J. P. Morgan was so wealthy that the American government, which was nearly out of gold following the Panic of 1893, begged him for a loan. The United States was bailed out by 3.5 million ounces of gold from Morgan, saving the US Treasury and the country from bankruptcy.[6] He bailed out the government a second time a few years later, and was reported to say that if they needed it a third time, he wouldn't have done it. That's power, and it was deeply satisfying to Morgan to know he alone controlled the future of our country.

And in 1907, J.P. Morgan single-handedly caused a national recession by making a few cheap-shot comments to the press about Westinghouse. That's power.[7] He did it to destroy George Westinghouse so Morgan could take control of Westinghouse's company. The objective, of course, was to take over 100 percent of the fledgling electricity industry. It didn't occur to Morgan to just be better; rather, the path to success was destroying Westinghouse. John D. Rockefeller, whose fiefdom was oil, returned the favor and spent untold sums of money trying to destroy the credibility of J.P. Morgan's electricity in hopes that he could ensure his kerosene empire would be the only source of light going forward.

"They don't think in terms of money, they think in terms of winning. Not sometimes. Every time."

Money and market dominance gave the Industrialists power, so they chased both. Not for greed, but for power and the sheer joy of beating the other guy, which became their favorite demonstration of power. Money was just a tool. Winning at all costs, and the power that came from being on top, was the intoxicating way of life for the Industrialist. And it still is for many business people, sports figures, and politicians who make up the twenty-first-century version of the Industrialist.

Sumner Redstone, the American media magnate (CBS, Viacom, Paramount), spoke clearly about Industrialist-minded business people, "They don't think in terms of money, they think in terms of winning. Not sometimes. Every time."

Vanderbilt, America's first giant Industrialist, set the pace. In 1867, before he closed the Albany Bridge, Vanderbilt invented the hostile takeover in an attempt to acquire the Erie Railroad. He wanted to own the whole industry to gain the power that would come with that monopoly. Vanderbilt would end up being the biggest railroad magnate ever and the richest man on earth, until Rockefeller toppled him. But greed wasn't the motivation; money was just one of many measures of his power.

John D. Rockefeller didn't have to dethrone and behead the last king in order to gain power. He simply dethroned and beheaded the competition.

Rockefeller controlled 90 percent of refineries and pipelines, and his objective was always to control 100 percent. He was considered one of the least ruthless of the Industrialists, but don't tell Tom Scott that.

Mr. Scott, head of the Pennsylvania Railroad, the largest corporation in the world at the time, tried to stick his toe into the oil business. So Rockefeller shut down his own Pittsburgh refineries, which were providing the biggest share of Scott's rail cargo. Shutting down those refineries cost Rockefeller a fortune (remember, it's not about greed), but crushing a potential threat to his throne was more important. It wasn't about building a great company that would contribute to the world around him. It was about being the sole feudal lord of the oil industry and squashing any insurrection that might arise in his fiefdom. Power is the motivation of the Industrialist. The true Capitalist has no such interest, as we'll see later.

The focused desire to be the biggest, to win and crush all others, to monopolize whatever they put their hands on, was the Industrialists' greatest motivation. They were not in business to deliver a great product, but to become the most powerful men on earth. J.P. Morgan had proof that he was the most powerful man on earth when he held in his hands the fate of an entire nation.

These weren't Capitalists in any way, any more than hard-hearted kings or power-hungry politicians are Capitalists. They were relentless power-mongers, who chose business as the means to build their economic dictatorships. They were building fiefdoms just like medieval lords. The only difference was their weapon; they used money instead of the sword.

## THE DISTORTION OF CAPITALISM

These guys, and thousands who aspired to be like them, distorted Capitalism to the point that it lost its original meaning. Capitalism for centuries had its roots in *the velocity of the dollar*. The baker bought some shoes, the shoemaker took that money and bought some candles, the candle maker bought some wheat, and with that same dollar, went back to the baker and bought a cake. Capitalism, before the Industrialists, almost always added value along the local community continuum, over and over, many times with the same dollar. Capitalism was what made the town a great place to live. It raised the standard of living of everyone in the town. Trading with the next town carried the same advantages.

The Industrialists usurped this basic exchange-of-money-for-goods concept, and pretty much ignored the rest of the Capitalist *value-adding* equation, which had always created benefit or *good* in the local community beyond just the exchange of money. Much like feudal lords, Industrialists were *USERS* of the local community, intent on stripping it of anything and anyone who could make them more powerful, by virtue of making them richer. The Industrialists took as much money out of the local economy as possible and brought it back to the Industrialists' banks.

## GOVERNMENTS ARE NOT IMMUNE

Too many people naively believe government is somehow immune to wrongful motivations. But not only is government not immune to wrongful motivations, such as power-grabbing, governments are more likely to have wrongful motivations than private business. The Ethics Resource Center says that, "Fraud is more common in government than in business," and that an Enron-sized scandal is "more likely to happen next in government than in business."[8] The Ethics Resource Center report goes on to say, "Nearly 60 percent of government employees indicated that they have witnessed a violation of government ethics standards or the law. Many of these incidents have gone unreported. Of greater concern still is the fact that signs point to further deterioration in the near future."[9]

As these reports show, people are the same whether they work in business or government. The Industrialists simply learned from the governments that preceded them. The feudal lord liked his wealth, but it was only a measure of his power, which was much more intoxicating than the accumulation of money. The Industrialist was nothing more than a feudal lord, with the very same drive to be powerful. The only difference was that Capitalism was usurped as the weapon of choice for building the economic kingdom.

## ECONOMIC POLLUTION OF THE INDUSTRIALISTS

There is no doubt that many giant corporations do very good things and provide a few products and services that Smalls would struggle to provide right now. But in general, the Bigs also leave behind economic pollution of epic and lasting proportions. The eighteenth-century Industrialists polluted more physically; the economic pollution of the twenty-first-century Industrialist is much less obvious, but every bit as caustic. Following are a few examples of the economic pollution of the Bigs:

1. *Recessions and depressions*—We rarely had one until Giant Corporations of the 1800s made them a regular and frequent occurrence. Before that, only giant governments could cause recessions. In the 1800s, that kind of power was transferred to Industrialists. Vanderbilt shut down one bridge and created havoc. J. P. Morgan bad-mouthed "risky" stocks one day in front of the press and drove the stock market down so he could buy Westinghouse and grab the Niagara Falls turbine project. At 1:45 a.m. on September 15, 2008, Lehman Brothers declared bankruptcy, with most economists pointing to that as the beginning of the Great Recession of 2008, from which we had not fully recovered as of 2013.

2. *National security threats*—As stated before, in 2009, the NSA rated our nation's economy as the number one threat to our national security,

above terrorism or any other outside threat. The aggregate ability of giant corporations to destroy us from within was seen as our biggest problem. Those giant companies are now all bigger.

3. *Net job destruction*—"Redundant" employees, as the Europeans like to call them. As smaller businesses are bought out, redundant employees are considered collateral damage necessary to the buyout. And research shows that the Bigs are *net job destroyers* as a whole. It is a myth that big businesses create jobs (more on that later). Big business creates recessions and depressions; small business brings us out of them with new job creation.[10]

4. *Government bailouts*—The cost to the taxpayer of shoring up businesses that are *too big to fail* has been in the trillions. The Smalls never get a dime when they do something stupid (nor should they), but Big Government throws hundreds of billions at the Bigs, regardless of how stupidly or irresponsibly they have acted.

5. *Bad policy*—Giant Corporations and Giant Government, working together to solve giant problems that are mostly local, create regulations that make it hard for the Smalls to compete against the Bigs. Countless books and articles have documented the negative effects of regulation on the Smalls. As one example, small business carries an extra US $10,500 per employee burden just to comply with government regulations and spends twice as much on tax compliance as the Bigs.[11]

But the Bigs are in control, so you're not about to see regulations that actually curb the Industrialist's appetite any time soon.

6. *Crony Industrialism*—The squeaky wheel gets the pork and the giant wheel squeaks loudest. The Bigs have always had virtual tunnels to each other's caves, but the Internet and other fast-moving means of communication are exposing them to the light of day. It's not crony Capitalism, it's simply the ongoing appetite of twenty-first-century Industrialists. Call it crony Industrialism if you like, but it has nothing to do with Capitalism.

7. *Lack of innovation*—Small businesses create sixteen times more patents per employee than large companies.[12] Most of the great advances of the last fifty years or more have come from new and small businesses, not from the Bigs. The reasons for this will become clear in the next chapter, as we separate Industrialists from Capitalists.

## A GREEN ECONOMY

The concept of being green revolves around conserving the resources of the earth for future generations. That concept should be applied more to business as well. We need to ensure our economy is around for the next generation, and leaving it up to the two Bigs to sort it out is a recipe for disaster. Neither Industrialists nor politicians give a rat's patootie about future generations.

A true Capitalist builds something that will last long after he's gone. Read Steve Jobs's Stanford commencement address, delivered June 15, 2005. He had a little bit of Industrialist in him, too, but viewing his mortality and asking questions about his legacy were formative things for him. A question he asked himself daily was, "If today were the last day of my life, would I want to do what I am about to do today? And whenever the answer has been 'No' for too many days in a row, I know I need to change something." He understood the need to think long-term and to build something sustainable for future generations.[13]

> A true Capitalist builds something that will last long after he's gone.

## WHICH BIG DO YOU LOVE?

The two Bigs may not love everything about each other, but they are codependent and *DO* love key things about the other Big that will help them both remain in power. They need each other and don't feel they need Small. Most people find themselves rooting for one Big or the other, without realizing that both Bigs have lost touch with the Small and the local some time ago.

Fans of either Big Business or Big Government are both fooled regularly. Those who love Big Business love it when their Bigs talk about how government is causing the problems. Those who love Big Government love it when the darts go the other way. We're so mesmerized that we listen to our favorite Bigs as if they are actually addressing the problem, or representing us, the Smalls.

What both audiences are missing is that these two Bigs are intrinsically attached at the hip, and are dedicated more to the preservation of Bigs of both persuasions than to fixing problems. HSBC is a perfect example, able to escape the hand of government completely simply because of its size.

## IN THE FINAL ANALYSIS. . .

In the final analysis, both Bigs have a cozy, symbiotic relationship in which donations, cronyism, favors, free trips, power, and money are flying in both directions regardless of party affiliation. It's almost never about what will work for you and me, but about preserving the power and position of the two Bigs. They may not love each other, but they understand how much they need each other.

## CAPITALISM IS NOT THE PROBLEM

The Industrial Age brought us big business and made it seem normal. In the process, it created confusion between historically good local Capitalism and what the Industrialists were practicing, which was nothing different than what feudal lords have been doing for centuries: trying to dominate the world.

As a result, on the business side, we have been led to believe for decades now that Capitalism is the problem, but no one ever means small and local business when they say that. Capitalism has unfortunately become synonymous with Big Business. But we don't actually hate Capitalism, and we never have. We have trouble with Big Business or Big Government when either one acts in the spirit of the giant Industrialists of the 1800s, which leads us to the need to redefine a lot of what we think of as Capitalism as what it really is, i.e., Industrialism. We don't hate Capitalism. The object of our fury is actually the twenty-first-century Industrialist, who is a very different species than the Capitalists of the last few thousand years.

> We don't hate Capitalism. The object of our fury is actually the twenty-first-century Industrialist.

## CAN BIG COMPANIES GET IT RIGHT?

Emphatically yes, and some have been getting it right for decades already. Many of the Bigs are rightly worried as they watch the world move into the Participation Age. The rapid changes in our culture, the leveling effect of the Internet, the rejection of the still-common, Industrial Age employment practices by the young, the pace of innovation, and even advancements in technology all favor the small, the nimble, the local solution provider. For over a century now, we have all assumed that being Big had a stranglehold on all the advantages and held all the power. The advantages and power are both melting away at breathtaking speed. Big is in big trouble going forward.

That doesn't mean Big can't make it in the Participation Age. As with most problems, the solution is simple, but hard to implement without full resolve and total commitment from the leaders in a company. But with that commitment, Bigs can thrive in the Participation Age. W. L. Gore & Associates, Inc., founded in 1958, now has around ten thousand Stakeholders in thirty countries and $3 billion in revenue. It is the shining beacon for the Bigs, showing that a company of any size can choose to be Capitalist instead of Industrialist. We'll showcase them later (and many others) as a truly Capitalist company that has resisted taking on any Industrialist attributes for over fifty years. They and dozens of other Bigs have led the way into the Participation Age for all the Bigs.

## CAPITALISM IS NOT INDUSTRIALISM

The problem is that many of the giant corporations of today don't understand that they are still just Industrialists with a digital smokestack. Too many of the Bigs are still using the outmoded business practices of the Industrial Age. It's the same old game in a shiny new digital box. If they are to change, they must see that they are actually just Industrialists and not Capitalists at all. And to that end, we have to take the definition of Capitalism back from those Industrialists who share very few things in common with good Capitalists.

Capitalism has been around for centuries and at times was questioned by narrow-minded religious leaders. But only recently, as it has taken the form of Industrialism, has it been the target of such widespread disdain. That recent rise in the negative view of Capitalism can be traced directly to the rise of Big Business starting in the 1800s. In the next chapter, we will draw the clear distinction between a twenty-first-century Industrialist who is an anachronism in our time, and a Capitalist, whom we should all love and embrace.

# EMBRACING THE PARTICIPATION AGE

1. What is your mindset – to be big, or to be great? What one thing do you need to do to ensure that your organization is focused on being great?

   _____

   _____

   By When? _____ /_____ / _____ : _____ a.m./p.m.

2. Is there anyone in your organization who needs help refocusing? What one action is required to help them refocus?

   _____

   _____

   By When? _____ /_____ / _____ : _____ a.m./p.m.

## NOTES

1. L.R. Young, *The Portion Teller Plan: The No-Diet Reality Guide to Eating, Cheating, and Losing Weight Permanently* (New York, NY: Morgan Road Books, 2005).

2. http://en.wikipedia.org/wiki/List_of_oldest_companies_in_the_United_States.

3. *Second Annual Conference on The Renaissance of American Manufacturing, Jobs, Trade and The Presidential Election*, Committee to Support US Trade Laws, Slide Presentation, http://bit.ly/1cxA3zN March 27, 2012

4. Ibid

5. *Gangster Bankers: Too Big to Jail; How HSBC Hooked Up with Drug Traffickers and Terrorists,—and Got Away with It*, Matt Taibbi, Rolling Stone Magazine, February 14, 2013 8:00 AM ET, http://rol.st/ZXokjE .

6. *In American History*, John Pierpont Morgan, Blogspot.com

7. http://www.historynet.com/the-men-who-built-america-a-preview.htm

8. Ethics Resource Center's National Government Ethics Survey on Public Trust, Arlington, VA, Ethics Resource Center, Sec 1:1.

9. Ibid, Sec1:4.

10. *Firm Formation and Economic Growth: The Importance of Startups in Job Creation and Job Destruction*, Kauffman Foundation Research Series, July 2010.

11. Nicole V. Crain and W. Mark Crain, *The Impact of Regulatory Costs on Small Firms*. White paper for the Small Business Administration (Easton, PA: Lafayette College, September 2010).

12. *Frequently Asked Questions*, United States Small Business Association, Office of Advocacy, September 2012

13. http://news.stanford.edu/news/2005/june15/jobs-061505.html.

# The Twenty-First-Century Industrialist

On one of our trips to Kinshasa, the Chief and I were standing and looking out over Kinshasa on a beautiful July day, and we talked about people. My Chief brought up how critical it is that a leader have a vision of where to lead the people. He is a true visionary and sees DR Congo as a country that is rich and gives back to its people: full of life, purpose, and vision.

On that day, we talked about integrity in the context of building a country that would encourage everyone to particpate. This Chief wants to see the whole country brought back to life, and understands clearly that everyone will benefit by giving, not taking. He is very adamant about setting an example for the rest of the Congo to follow. He believes the country is a diamond in the rough and from what little I've seen, I'd say he's right.

The twenty-first-century Industrialist is one of the core business diseases to come out of the Industrial Age. And, as with all the business diseases of the Industrial Age, the twenty-first-century version of the Industrialist needs to go away. The smokestacks of the Factory System that dominated the landscape from 1850 to 1970 may be gone, but the archaic, front-office business practices put in place by the likes of Carnegie, Morgan, Vanderbilt, and Rockefeller are still used to run most businesses today.

People who hate Wall Street think that Wall Street and all of its excesses actually represent Capitalism, and therefore hate Capitalists. But Wall Street and most of the Bigs of today are not Capitalists at all, just old-fashioned Industrialists running smokeless, digital factories. I'm a fire-breathing, rabid Capitalist, but I can't find much in common with either the Industrialists of the 1800s or companies of today that masquerade as Capitalistic. The Capitalists we love to hate today are simply twenty-first-century Industrialists without factories. They are not real Capitalists.

> The twenty-first-century Industrialist is one of the core business diseases to come out of the Industrial Age.

## CAPITALISTS VS. INDUSTRIALISTS

The most common definitions of Capitalism revolve around private ownership as the means of production, with the objective of making a profit. But there is much more to the picture.

There are seven distinct attributes (discussed later in this chapter) that make the Industrialists unique enough in history to disqualify them from being considered Capitalists. In short, the form of capitalism that grew up around the Industrial Age is commonly called *corporate capitalism*, a very new and vastly different type, which has wandered far away from traditional Capitalism. It's what most people refer to as *crony capitalism*, but what we described in chapter 2 as *crony Industrialism*; not Capitalism at all.

You will find crony Industrialists in just about every industry, not just manufacturing. They do not like us drawing these distinctions, because it is much more convenient for them to masquerade as Capitalists.

## WHAT TIME IS IT?

Many of today's Bigs are simply Industrialists who forgot which century it is. As we've shown in the two previous chapters, Industrialists of the 1800s were more motivated by kingdom building than anything else. The Industrialist is a user of people, assets, and resources and is more likely to be a threat to our stability and to our future as a nation than any Capitalist could ever be.

Industrialism is not something that just played out in the Factory System from 1850 to the 1970s. It is a *mindset* and a *value system* that was learned during that period, but still dominates a majority of business practices in many corporations today. Industrialists don't need a smokestack or an assembly line to be Industrialists. Industrialism is more about dubious values motivations, and practices, than a specific time period.

As we define the difference between a Capitalist and an Industrialist, it is important to say that no business leader, founder, or CEO is immune to modern-day Industrialism. Industrialist values and practices can be found in very small businesses, and great Capitalist values and practices can be found in giant corporations. But the bigger or older a company gets, the harder it is for it not to fall into the habits we all learned from the 1800s Industrialists, what might be called *creeping Industrialism*. We'll show later how some giant corporations started well, but unfortunately have headed back toward Industrialism, and how others have avoided becoming Industrialists, even as they grew to be giants in their industries.

**Industrialism is more about dubious values, motivations, and practices, than a specific time period.**

Small businesses shouldn't be complacent, thinking that these legacy habits only haunt the Bigs. You can be a company of two people that is three years old and be driven by Industrial Age business values that will keep you from succeeding in The Participation Age. We all need to be watchful that these values and practices don't become part of the way we do business, regardless of the size and age of our businesses.

## ARE INDUSTRIALISTS MORE LIKE SOCIALISTS?

The first Industrialists had very little in common with traditional Capitalists. In fact, Vanderbilt, Carnegie, Rockefeller, Morgan, and the like were in some scary ways much more Socialist than Capitalist.

1.  The Socialist Karl Marx believed economies were zero-sum games, in which there is only so much to go around, and if a lot of it were in one person's hands, others would not get any. The Industrialists believed the same things. They believed markets were zero-sum games where they should own 100 percent of a market. In doing so, they could keep everyone else from getting a piece of the pie. Monopolies actually function on this core Marxist principle of zero-sum accumulation of power into the hands of the few.

2.  Marx did not believe in free and open markets. Neither did the giant Industrialists. They conveniently believed in them *BEFORE* they dominated, but once they dominated, they were rabid about having a closed market. The Soviets also believed in free speech and freedom of assembly until they were in power.

3.  Marx believed that the relationship between employer and employee was naturally, and by necessity, exploitive and coercive, benefiting the employer at the expense of the employed. The Industrialists openly believed that

the employed existed to make them rich at the expense of the employed. Exploitation was, and still is, a core practice of the Industrialist.

4. Marx believed in the centralization of production, because those at the center would know best what was needed. The Industrialists believe in the centralization of production for each industry, as long as it is under their one company flag. AT&T truly believed the world was better off if telephones were all made by them, and rented to (not bought by) customers. Rockefeller in his heart truly felt he was on a mission from God to dominate the oil business for the good of the world around him. With his company's dominance, the world would be a better place. All of them preferred and could make a case for why each market should be in the hands of the very few, for the betterment of the many, just like Marx.

5. Marx preached world dominance of his one system, by force if necessary, to bring to pass a future utopia. The giant Industrialists all preached world dominance of their one company as the best answer, and many times used force, guns, and violence to keep it moving in that direction.

## THE RESULT

Under these conditions, in which the system was set up solely for the benefit of the few at the top, the predominate, cynical joke of employees in the Soviet Union applied to Industrial America quite well: "We pretend to work, and you pretend to pay us."

These Industrialists are not people with whom I identify. Their most well-known attributes have nothing to do with Capitalism. They used and abused some convenient aspects of Capitalism to get what they wanted, but what they built was fundamentally anti-Capitalist.

## THE SEVEN ATTRIBUTES OF THE TWENTY-FIRST-CENTURY INDUSTRIALIST

There are seven distinct attributes of Industrialism that separate it from traditional Capitalism. These attributes still dominate the business practices of the overwhelming majority of businesses today, including those with no historical ties to the Factory System. Too many of us are just mimicking the way the Industrialists viewed the world, as if it's the only way to run a business.

### ATTRIBUTE #1—BEING BIG VS. BEING GREAT

The number one value of Industrialists is that they are motivated more by being big than by making a contribution to the world around them. They might talk about adding value, or creating and innovating, but the motivation for doing so would be to get big.

Many of the new Bigs mimic the old Industrialists and are more focused on crushing their competition, winning, and holding the seat of power than on building something that contributes to the world around them.

## A FEW EXAMPLES

Some of the most common examples of companies that focus on size more than contribution are, of course, those tied historically to the Factory System, like oil companies and banks. Those industries are the easy targets. But plenty of companies that were started after the end of the Industrial Age share the same overriding motivation to be Big over everything else.

Microsoft had a largely Industrialist start, although in their defense they have been moving in the direction of Capitalism in recent years. In the first few decades, Microsoft seemed driven more by a desire to be big than to make a creative and innovative contribution to the world around them.

David Theilen, a former high-ranking manager at Microsoft, wrote *The Twelve Secret Rules of Microsoft Management*, in which he claims that the unspoken Management Rule #1 for Microsoft in those days was "Total World Domination."[1] Whether fully accurate or partially a figment of Theilen's imagination, this kind of objective – being big for the sake of being big – is a core motivation of the Industrialist. Theilen says the motivation was to "go for 100 percent of every market you enter. Every employee knew the rule implicitly, and that it was the goal for every product or service being developed." Owning 99 percent of the market was unacceptable for Microsoft in its early days; 100 percent was required. That's Industrialism at its core.

Industrialism is more about dubious values, motivations, and practices, than a specific time period.

Microsoft had this need to be big as part of its DNA from very early on. Some companies don't actually start out with the motivation to be big; they grow into it. At some point, being big can become more important than being great. Krispy Kreme existed for decades before it decided that being big was going to be a core driver. In its case, it led to a quick rise and a quick fall.

Capitalists have much different motivations. Capitalists are not motivated first and foremost by being big. They focus on the pursuit of creativity, innovation, and the desire to make a great impact on the world around them. If being big helps them be great, they will be big. If it doesn't, they won't.

Apple isn't immune from Industrialist tendencies, but Steve Jobs's quote to open this chapter is a classic Capitalist mindset: *"Being the richest man in the cemetery doesn't matter to me. Going to bed at night saying we've done something wonderful, that's what matters to me."* There isn't an Industrialist from 1800 through today who would embrace that statement. For them, doing something wonderful always takes a back seat to accumulating the most power.

Bill Hewlett and Dave Packard were two great Capitalists. The Hewlett Packard website gives "The Real Reason HP Exists." It says, "Our founders had big ideas about their company and its place in the world: 'I think many people assume, wrongly, that a company exists simply to make money,' said Dave Packard. 'While this is an important result of a company's existence, we have to go deeper and find the real reasons for our being.'"

Bill Hewlett also said he knew from the beginning that they wanted to make an impact in the world of technology. HP calls this "The First Rule of the Garage: Believe you can change the world." That's a Capitalist speaking – motivated by being great, not by being big. An Industrialist would have said, "I knew from the beginning that we were going to dominate the world of technology." That was the statement of all the giant Industrialists, wanting to own 100 percent of their market. A Capitalist like Bill Hewlett thinks about what technology he can create that will make an impact on the world around him. Neither Hewlett nor Packard were driven by being big, but by doing something great. That is pure, old-fashioned Capitalism – making money by first and foremost intending to add something of value to the world around you.

If you're motivated first by being big, you're an Industrialist, not a Capitalist, no matter how small you are.

> "I think many people assume, wrongly, that a company exists simply to make money," said Dave Packard. "While this is an important result of a company's existence, we have to go deeper and find the real reasons for our being."

## ATTRIBUTE #2—CLOSED MARKETS

The famous Industrialists of the 1800s – who the Bigs of today are still mimicking – did not believe in a Free Market. They believed in a market that would allow them, the elite, to control everything at the cost of every other business owner's economic freedom. The Industrialist's goal was not to be the best, but to destroy everyone else, to be the last man standing in a zero-sum game of dog-eat-dog. In their minds, there was a finite amount of business to be had, and they were going to have it all. The modern-day, twenty-first-century Industrialist works hard to keep the markets closed to others.

> "A zero-sum game is like poker. We all sit down at the table and I only win if somebody else loses. That's not the way a market works. That's not the way wealth is built."

Today, the war cry of "free enterprise" is one of the biggest ruses of the giant Industrialists who dominate Wall Street, the banking industry, and many other sectors of our economy. Like their 1800s counterparts, the Industrialists of today don't believe in a free market, free enterprise, or any other freedom that would jeopardize their position as Bigs. This is one of the reasons giant corporations engender so much hostility. As crony Industrialists, they suck at the teat of government, write regulations for their political cronies to vote on that will destroy the Smalls while helping the Bigs, and create any barrier they can to keep small business from flourishing.

All the giant Industrialists of the 1800s were deeply involved with politicians to an extent that would be difficult to understand today. The two Bigs worked in symbiotic synchronicity to ensure the ongoing survival of each other. Today's twenty-first-century Industrialists are as committed to today's politicians as their nineteenth-century brethren, it's just a lot harder to flaunt that commitment publicly.

## ATTRIBUTE #3—RESIST PROGRESS;
## MAINTAIN THE STATUS QUO

Industrialists are brilliant at creating efficiencies around their present products and their present positions in the market. They are fanatically obsessed with squeezing the last dollar of profit out of the present market, and are unparalleled at doing so. This is driven by the need to keep shareholders happy and to get more money faster, to create the cash cow that feeds the investors. But this massive investment in making existing systems highly efficient is expensive. More importantly, such deep commitment to the present creates legacy systems that make it very difficult to adapt and move forward in a fast-paced world.

That constantly changing world threatens the Industrialists' dominance, and puts them at an extreme disadvantage to newcomers. Southwest Airlines has made mincemeat of the legacy airlines because it entered the market without a commitment to decades of systems, airplanes, processes, and culture that were all outdated. Industrialists are so tied to milking the existing cash cow that it makes it very difficult for them to change, or even want to change. One of the problems with Big is that changing it is like turning the Queen Mary in a bathtub.

> Progress is the enemy of the Industrialist. The status quo is their friend.

Progress is the enemy of the Industrialist. The status quo is their friend. It is much easier to dominate and control a world that is static and unchanging, which is why dictators have always tried to keep people from becoming educated and learning about the outside world. Industrialists, like dictators, are very aware that the next great invention could likely destroy their power by simply refocusing the consumer on a newer, better product or service. We see this Industrialist commitment to the status quo even today. United responded to Southwest by repainting some airplanes, taking out the first-class seats, and declaring a new airline called TED. Seasoned flyers saw through the ruse and referred to TED as "the back half of UniTED," conjuring up images of the business end of a jackass.

Industrialists are at their best when creating efficiency of scale – getting things humming in the present world with the fastest throughput and the least amount of overhead. It's why companies like GM loved mergers and acquisitions as a way to get big – you can cut thousands of redundant jobs and skim off the creativity and innovation of the company being acquired, and make even bigger margins. It's a very savvy game they play to create efficiencies in the present. It's much easier, and much more profitable, to resist progress and maintain the status quo. New technologies, products, or services threaten all of that, making resisting progress an attribute of the Industrialist.

## ATTRIBUTE #4—DESTROYING JOBS

One of the great misperceptions regularly promoted by both politicians and giant corporations is that the Bigs are job creators. As a group, it is wholly untrue. According to government Business Dynamics Statistics and private research organizations using those statistics, Bigs, as a whole, are *net job destroyers*.[2]

If you look at big companies individually, you will find that over time some increase their staff and some reduce their staff. But as a cohort group, more jobs get destroyed in these older, bigger companies than are added to the economy. There are some big companies that are truly net job creators and should be applauded for their growth. However, there are a lot more big Industrial companies that, while giving the appearance of job creation, actually destroy jobs.

Capitalists, on the other hand, create jobs largely by organic growth, based on having introduced new products and adding value to their offering. That increases demand and results in expanded hiring: a great way to grow.

Very rarely is a company acquired without losing jobs. Sometimes, it's done by attrition over a few years; sometimes it's an immediate layoff. When Company A, which has ten thousand employees, buys Company B, which has one thousand employees, Company A will lay off two hundred people and declare that it has added eight hundred jobs. It's a lot like taking all the nutrients out of wheat by bleaching it, adding a few back in, and calling your product *enriched white bread*, which companies have done for decades.

*Inc. Magazine* ran two articles on December 4, 2012 that demonstrate the myth of job growth in larger companies. One was titled "Meet the Top Job Creator in America," referring to Steve Jones, co-CEO of Universal Services of America. The subheading read, "He's created 17,330 jobs," followed by a big picture of Steve Jones, and the caption, "Blue-collar hero."[3] The other one was about the same company, titled "We Hired 17,000 People in Three Years," and went on to tell the glorious details of how Universal Services of America created 17,000 jobs in just three years.[4] All this hoopla was enough to make you want to stand up and sing "God Bless America." But none of it was true.

Halfway through the first article, the reporter casually inserted, "Universal has grown in large part through acquisition." I then looked at the second article in the same issue of *Inc. Magazine*, which said, "Universal Services of America's strategy is to grow through acquisitions."[5] Then I visited their website and found that thirteen of their last nineteen press releases were about how they had grown by buying another, existing company. None of the press releases were about how they had added jobs by organic growth.

How, in anyone's definition of job creation, does that count as creating jobs? Job transfer, sure, but job creation? The definition of *creation* is to bring something to life from nothing. Da Vinci created the *Mona Lisa*. It didn't exist before that. All of these jobs existed at other companies before Universal Services bought them, and they admitted in these articles that there were redundancies and people had to be let go. So what's the real net job creation here? Not 17,330. Possibly zero, and taking into consideration the layoffs required due to redundancies in the acquired companies, possibly even a negative number.

This company was being celebrated as the single biggest job creator in America when it had created no jobs, and destroyed many. This kind of skewed reporting goes back to our addiction to Big. Once again, we celebrate Big just for the sake of celebrating Big, with no discernment as to what is actually going on: in this case, job destruction by multiple mergers.

GM, a classic twenty-first-century Industrialist, is another example of a company hailed for providing two hundred thousand jobs, when it has in fact destroyed untold numbers of jobs over the last one hundred years, with a net gain of zero or less.

GM was started in 1908 by a ruthless and swash-buckling Industrialist named William Durant. He started it as a pure holding company.[6] This holding company didn't create a single product, but made its first acquisition of Buick, from David Dunbar Buick, a number of years after Buick invented his car and had the company up and running. GM then went on to acquire over thirty other car companies and parts manufacturers in the early 1900s, including Oldsmobile, Chevrolet, Cadillac, and Pontiac, and in later years a bunch more, including Hummer, Saab, Daewoo, and Vuaxhall, along with companies in other industries.[7]

All they did for many decades was buy other highly successful automobile manufacturers, lay off redundant people, and then transfer jobs into GM. General Motors has about two hundred thousand employees, virtually all of whom would have existed in the acquired companies as they grew organically. And who knows how many tens of thousands of jobs they destroyed along the way to acquiring all those companies? Yet, we bailed them out because the political Bigs told us how important GM was to creating jobs in America.

## ATTRIBUTE #5—USERS, NOT CREATORS:
## THE CASH COW RULE

Because one of their main motivations is being big – or world domination – twenty-first-century Industrialists are usually not very creative or innovative. In contrast, Capitalists create, innovate, and add to the world around them as their primary motivation. They create new products, services, and even whole industries from scratch.

Industrialists, on the other hand, are users, like William Durant, not creators like Henry Ford. They are more focused on acquiring power for themselves, and as a result, they are users of existing products, services, sectors, and industries to obtain this goal. They have an uncanny knack for finding early-stage products or industries others have invented or started – like railroads, oil, steel, electricity, and cars – upon which to build their fiefdoms. They look around for a potential cash cow that can be controlled and spun up to great efficiencies, with bigger opportunities to dominate and be powerful.

Vanderbilt didn't invent the railroad, Rockefeller didn't invent kerosene or gasoline, Carnegie didn't invent steel, J. P. Morgan didn't invent electricity or banking, and William Durant of GM never invented, engineered, or designed an automobile. The Industrialists were simply users, focused on using these industries to create cash cows. As a result, they created little added value because they were consumed with controlling and using the industry as it existed, not inventing the next thing that might jeopardize their existing market.

If we look at the Industrialist DNA of GM versus the Capitalist DNA of Ford, we see why the two have had such radically different financial results in the last few decades. Durant's objective was to set up a holding company that would use the creativity of other companies and their innovations. There was no emphasis on creativity or innovation. Henry Ford started a car company that created and especially innovated as its core motivation.

Unlike Durant, Ford was a great innovator, insatiable about building a great car and about creating the future of the car industry by figuring out how to make the automobile inexpensive enough for more people to buy. Ford started as a Capitalist: creating, innovating, willing and very excited about regularly destroying his own present market for the future one that would be better. Durant started as an Industrialist who was most motivated by becoming big through acquisition, or in some cases by destruction of the competition, and who had no nose at all for how to create the future of the automotive industry. Is it any wonder these two companies have ended up in two very different places economically and financially?

Besides using existing inventions rather than creating new ones, Industrialists also use people, local economies, and resources. The Industrial Age is full of stories of people being used for the benefit of the corporation, local economies being dominated and then left as ghost towns, and resources being abused. We've cleaned it all up visually today, but corporations led by Industrialists still use people, local economies, and resources in ways that are beneficial first and foremost to the short-term gain of the corporation, without regard to the long-term consequences to either the company or its people. Remember Enron?

## ATTRIBUTE #6—FOCUS ON THE COMPETITOR: DESTROY, MIMIC, OR BUY

Chris Peters, when he was head of Excel Development for Microsoft wrote, "We didn't write Excel to make money, we wrote it for the sheer joy of putting the largest computer software company out of business." Sounds a lot like Vanderbilt closing the bridge. At the time, Lotus software was bigger than Microsoft. The people at Microsoft back then were more motivated by crushing them and becoming the biggest Big than by writing great software that would make people want to switch.

Sometimes, destroying the other guy is just easier than coming up with something better. It's what they learned from the old Industrialists – the quickest route to being big is to ensure nobody else is competing in the fiefdom.

I see signs of positive Capitalism at Microsoft now. But way too many other Bigs are still living out the same Industrialist mindset and are focused more on being big by destroying *the competition* than on building the next advancement for their consumers.

> Sometimes, destroying the other guy is just easier than coming up with something better. The quickest route to being big is to ensure nobody else is competing in the fiefdom.

Industrialists worry a lot about what the other guy is doing, because the other guy could end up creating something that will take market share away from their fiefdom. Capitalists are just the opposite. They are so busy creating the next great innovation that they have very little time to worry about what the next guy is doing. And they believe that if their innovation is game-changing, being big will be one of the evidences of their success. They don't try to be *big*; they try to be *great*. And big just follows, if big is what will help them be even better.

Competition is irrelevant for the creative and innovative company. Unlike Microsoft, Apple did not become big by focusing on how to destroy its competition. That's not to say Apple doesn't have some Industrial Age values and practices; it does. But Apple is known for creating new products that make their own existing product obsolete. For most of its corporate history, it has been a lot more focused on creating, innovating, and making a contribution to the world of technology than on getting big by destroying the other guy.

## DON'T DESTROY—JUST MIMIC

Some twenty-first-century Industrialists aren't focused on destroying the other guy, just mimicking them. They are always twelve months behind and are focused on finding out what part of someone else's great innovation they can exploit in order to make money and get bigger.

In the 1980s, a group of investors decided to mimic McDonald's, which was growing like gangbusters at the time. They studied McDonald's and concluded that the key thing that had to be replicated was *speed of service*. They built their entire concept around that notion, with the intent of beating McDonald's at their own game. They even built pneumatic tubes that shot food at people in their cars and called their franchise "Chutes."

They were successful at getting their food to the customer faster than McDonald's, but went belly-up anyway. Later, they discovered McDonald's was exploding because people loved two things – the taste of their french fries and the consistent "okayness" of everything else. People liked the taste and they liked the consistency, no matter which McDonald's they visited.

One of the dangers of trying to mimic others is that you will likely guess wrong about what makes them successful. In many cases, the successful company you are trying to mimic isn't even sure why they are successful.

The route to "big" can be achieved through destroying, mimicking, or buying the other guy, or it can be achieved through creativity and innovation.

> The route to "big" can be achieved through destroying, mimicking, or buying the other guy, or it can be achieved through creativity and innovation.

## ATTRIBUTE #7—SHORT-TERM DECISION MAKING

A heavy reliance on short-term decision making is a necessary attribute for the twenty-first-century Industrialist. It supports and enables all six of the attributes of an Industrialist described above. Being big, closing markets, resisting change, growth by acquisition that destroys jobs, and a focus on the competition; all these require a pattern of short-term decision making. Those first six attributes, along with the need to satisfy the incessant pressure from shareholders to be profitable every month, causes modern Industrialists to regularly mortgage their futures and focus on instant gratification.

The demise of US West in 2010 – one of the beneficiaries of the breakup of AT&T's phone monopoly – started with short-term decisions that began nearly thirty years earlier. In 1984, when AT&T's Bell System was broken up, US West decided not to aggressively buy wireless licenses because it was well known it would be years before wireless communications would be a big player in the phone industry. Buying those licenses would have hurt shareholder value in 1984, so US West passed.

Then in 1998, to once again increase present shareholder value, US West sold its small remaining interest in wireless communications to AirTouch. In a press release, US West touted the decision "as a way to strengthen our balance sheet."[8] A few months later, it sold its cable TV operation to MediaOne with the same rationale – it made the balance sheet look better at the time. US West was taken over by Qwest in 2000, which also lived by short-term decisions. The CEO went to jail and Qwest was sold off to CenturyLink.

Almost all of the decisions that led to the demise of both US West and Qwest focused on mortgaging their future to look better in the present. It's one of the things Industrialists do best. Twenty-first-century Industrialists are not focused on legacy, or sustainability, but are focused on milking the present situation for all its worth, regardless of the impact on the long-term future of the company.

## IT'S HARDER FOR BIG...

In light of the seven attributes of an Industrialist, it's true that smaller companies have an easier road to maintain Capitalist business practices. The bigger a company gets, the more likely it is to be motivated by Industrial values, but as we'll see in chapter 12, there are plenty of Bigs doing it right. It's not a matter of possibility, but of an intentional commitment to be a Capitalist and not an Industrialist.

The following chart is a comparison of the two to make it easier for us to see the separation between them.

# INDUSTRIALISTS VS. CAPITALISTS

Take the test: Are you a twenty-first-century Industrialist or a Capitalist?

| Industrialist | Capitalist |
|---|---|
| **Being Big**– Focused on size; commitment to being the biggest | **Being Great**–Making what people need to build a legacy. |
| **Closed-Market System**–Keep others from getting in on what we have, so the biggest of us can stay on top. | **Free-Market System**–Makes us all better and creates a level playing field in which the best get to the top. |
| **Destroy Jobs**–By a focus largely on acquisition or elimination of the competition. | **Create Jobs**–By a focus on creativity, innovation, and organic growth. |
| **Resist Change**–Change threatens the big, efficient cash-cow machine we've created. Present-oriented; short-term profit focused. | **Embrace Change**–Change creates opportunities to make more money. Future-oriented; long-term profit focused. |
| **Users**–Using people, local economies, resources, and existing products for the purpose of feeding the cash cow. | **Creators**–Creating the next invention, or innovation. Creating a better place to live and work. "Doing something wonderful" –Steve Jobs. |
| **Competition**–We win by destroying others. Don't build a taller building, just level everyone else's. | **Internal Excellence**–We rise to the top by focusing on our own internal excellence–we are our only competition. |
| **Cronies**–Closely aligned with government– helping write regulations that keep others out. | **Autonomous**–A strong need to be independent of government. Inviting others in. |
| **People as Machines**–Or extensions of them. Valuing productivity over creativity. | **People as Owners**–Valuing the innovative, creative ownership of the producer. |
| **Fear of Improving the Industry**–If my "competitors" get better, I could be left behind. | **Working to Improve the Industry**–If my industry is better, we're better off. A rising tide lifts all boats. |
| **Company Focused**–Use customers to make us more money so we can get bigger. | **Customer Focused**–Make what they want/ need; they will want to pay us. |
| **Centralized System**–Extracting power and control from the local economy, which might get a mind of its own and walk away. | **Disbursed System**–Creating local power and control, which will be more creative and will help us to know the problems better. |
| **Shareholders**–Cash cow decisions dominate–we must feed the shareholder beast. | **Stakeholders**–Decisions based on what is best for Stakeholders (customers, employees, vendors, and shareholders). |
| **Efficiency**–The need to be big–the bigger we get, the better our model works. | **Effectiveness**–The need to be effective. We'll be whatever size makes us most effective to our market (not our shareholders). |
| **Time-based**–The car in the parking lot the longest wins. Pay ranges for specific jobs. | **Results-based**–The person who contributes most is rewarded the most. |
| **The Three S's**–Safety, Security, & Stability. | **The Fourth S**–Significance, making meaning. |
| **Takes Big Risk**–To capture and sustain the existing market. | **Takes Big Risks**–To build something new that might destroy the existing market. |

Some of these attributes, e.g., Stakeholders and the three S's vs. the fourth S, Significance, we will be discussing in later chapters.

## CAPITALISM IS GOOD

Capitalism is good. For centuries, it thrived on the local velocity of the dollar, always with just a few Bigs hanging around who were in collusion with kings or lords, but who rarely affected local trade. Today, there are many Bigs that do not exhibit the seven attributes of a twenty-first-century Industrialist, and that can stand proudly as value-adding Capitalists.

Although the Bigs will have a great deal more trouble adjusting to the Participation Age, this isn't about big companies vs. small companies. It's about who rejects the seven attributes of Industrialism and who embraces them, and who decides that Capitalism is good or Industrialism is good.

Let's stop lumping Capitalism in with Industrialism. Instead, let's identify which companies are embracing twenty-first-century Industrialism for their own short-term gain, and which ones are focused on building sustainable companies that Make Meaning in the world around them, for the benefit of everyone in the process.

> Let's stop lumping Capitalism in with Industrialism.

---

# EMBRACING THE PARTICIPATION AGE

1. What is your mindset? Review the seven attributes of a twenty-first-century Industrialist, and/or the previous table. Are there any adjustments you need to make? Pick only one.

   _____

   _____

   By When? _____ / _____ / _____ : _____ a.m./p.m.

2. Is there anyone in your organization who needs encouragement to practice business more like a capitalist? What one action is required to help that individual?

   _____

   _____

   By When? _____ / _____ / _____ : _____ a.m./p.m.

## NOTES

1. David Theilen, *The Twelve Secret Rules of Microsoft Management* (New York: McGraw-Hill, October 30, 2000).

2. *Firm Formation and Economic Growth: Where Will The Jobs Come From?* (Kauffman Foundation Research Series, November 2009); and *Firm Formation and Economic Growth: The Importance of Startups in Job Creation and Job Destruction* (Kauffman Foundation Research Series, July 2010).

3. http://bit.ly/100DcNu.

4. http://bit.ly/SMLBTX.

5. http://bit.ly/TXhqvh.

6. Ed Cray, *Chrome Colossus: General Motors and Its Times* (New York, NY: McGraw Hill, 1980). And Maryann Keller, Rude Awakening: The Rise, Fall, and Struggle for Recovery of General Motors (New York, NY: Harper Collins, 1990).

7. http://en.wikipedia.org/wiki/History_of_General_Motors .

8. *US West divestitures boosted bottom line at expense of Qwest's future,* Andy Vuong, Denver: The Denver Post, 05/02/2010.

# Why Employees Are Always a Bad Idea

*"Of all the things that contribute to a happy workday, the one thing that stands out is making progress on meaningful work."*
— TERESA M. AMABILE, coauthor of *The Progress Principle*

The overwhelming majority of people in the Democratic Republic of the Congo are entrepreneurs, working hard every day to build their own businesses and carve out a path to success. With few exceptions, the choice is either to work for the government (including the military) or to start something yourself and see if you can make a living at it. Jobs in both the private economy and the government are few and coveted, which is odd, considering that a lot of government workers rarely get paid, perhaps one paycheck about every few months.

In fact, many government employees who go to work every day haven't been paid in years. I asked my Chief, "Why do they bother to show up?" He responded, "What else would they do? At least they can be together and talk about their plight with others just like them who have the same issue. And who knows, it might be payday." As a result, most of the people in the government also have a business on the side so they can survive.

DR Congo is the poorest country on earth. But among most Congolese, it is amazing how few of them see themselves as victims. Many of the higher-ups in government and in the state-run businesses complain and play the victim role, but few people on the street view life that way. They are optimistic, working hard, and always looking for a way to build something that will feed their families and create some stability in their lives.

The majority of Congolese are adult Stakeholders and do not have the childlike mindset of the Industrial Age employee. In the DR Congo, the mindset is, "It's my responsibility to make things happen." It's an entrepreneurial world where they aren't looking for someone else to care for them, because frankly there isn't anyone who would.

They know it's their responsibility, and the stakes are much higher than they are here. So they get out of bed every morning as Stakeholders and proactively greet the world looking for a way to make life happen. If only people in the Western world, with all its ready-made opportunities, could adopt the same positive *owners* outlook as those living in the poorest country on earth.

## THE SHORT AND SCURRILOUS HISTORY OF THE EMPLOYEE

The concept of an employee as we know it today did not exist before 1800, and really wasn't pervasive until the late 1800s. It is a core business disease of the Industrial Age. The familiar employee system of today was designed over a hundred years ago to support the Factory System, and is largely unchanged in most companies today.

So how is it working out? Very badly, it turns out. In 2013, 86 percent of people were in a job they didn't like, and 55 percent planned to look for a new job that year alone.[1] The cost to employers of shuffling those people around the economy is staggering. If only 10-15 percent of the workforce changes jobs (the annual estimate is 13 percent), it costs American businesses a mind-boggling US $2 trillion a year just to replace them.[2] The archaic employee model of the Factory System is not wearing well in the Participation Age.

## WHY ARE EMPLOYEES LOOKING TO LEAVE?

There are many other factors, but ownership of their tasks, processes, jobs, decisions, and results top the list. Ownership is the most powerful motivator in business. I pay much better attention to my own bicycle than to a bicycle I walk by parked at a cafe. Most employees are just *walking by* at work, because employees don't own anything there, least of all their lives and their ability to Make Meaning at work.

It doesn't have to be this way. In fact, it shouldn't be this way in any company. Successful companies of every size and age have already figured out how to live without the concept of an employee and have replaced them with Stakeholders who own everything, even if they don't own a piece of the company. Those

> Ownership is the most powerful motivator in business.

companies who are creating ownership throughout the workplace are the most successful financially, and are also voted the best places to work every year. In chapters 10 and 11, we will share the stories of some of them. But first, how did we get here? Where did this modern and very broken concept of *employee* originate? And why does it need to go away?

## PEOPLE—RECREATED IN THE IMAGE OF MACHINES

When the Factory System and its machines took over most production after 1850, the machines couldn't run themselves. So, the Factory System recreated people in the image of machines in order to run them. In the process of creating Factory System employees, the most desirable human traits were stripped away as undesirable in the factory: the desire to create, innovate, solve problems, reason, ask why, share, live in community, and be recognized for a unique contribution. All of these human attributes were in the way of the Industrial Age Factory System. The employee was not there to Make Meaning, but only to make money– for the factory first, and secondarily for themselves.

> The Factory System recreated people in the image of machines.

In the past, people had gathered in groups to work together, but the Industrial Age ushered in a whole new way of organizing work, moving away from the Domestic System, where artisans and craftspeople had made goods in or attached to their homes for centuries. This new system was distinctive in a number of ways:

1. It began to bring large numbers of people together in one place to work, increasingly segmenting work away from the home. Leaving home to *GO* to work became normal for the first time in human history.

2. It entailed significant increases in the division of labor through specialization of function. People were turned into specialists, performing very narrow and repeatable functions. This made them compatible with the machines they were paired with, and made them easily replaceable.

3. Because of this increased division of labor, the worker's relationship to his task changed radically. Being a craftsman required a lot of initiative, ingenuity, and personal motivation to keep up a good pace. In the Factory System, the craftsman gave way to the machine operator, an extension of the machine. The machine essentially told him exactly what to do, how fast, when he could take breaks, and exactly what he should make. There was no room for adding personality to a steel ingot, brake drum, or locomotive wheel.[3]

4. Work shifted from something you chose to do, like being a blacksmith, basket weaver, clay pot maker, saddle maker, etc., to something you *HAD* to do. After 1850, people began to go to work just to make money, and if there was any meaning, that was a bonus. Today, the legacy of this system leaves us with an overwhelming majority of the workforce that would change jobs right now if they could. They are making money, but not Making Meaning.

> The new system taught such narrow skills to employees that they could never open their own shops. Employees became very different workers than craftspeople.

The Factory System, designed by the giant Industrialists of the late 1800s, introduced this radical new way of work. The apprentice system, which taught people a trade so they could open their own shop, disappeared altogether. In stark contrast, the new system taught such narrow skills to employees that they could never open their own shops. Employees became very different workers than craftspeople.

## WHAT IS AN EMPLOYEE?

What makes employees of the Factory System different from workers who came before them? Three things are commonly listed:

1. an extreme division of labor,
2. a *de-skilling* of the work force, and
3. a dehumanization of the workplace.[4]

Let's take a look at the third factor first– the dehumanized workplace.

## THE GUY WHO INVENTED THE "EMPLOYEE"

In the late 1880s, the concept of *management* began to take root in factories. The most prominent management leader of this movement was Fredrick Winslow Taylor. He was the founder of "Scientific Management Theory," or what became widely and commonly known as *Taylorism*.[5] He had profoundly good ideas about efficiency, and a few much more profoundly bad ones about human beings as factory workers.

## WHY IS FREDERICK TAYLOR SO IMPORTANT TODAY?

Three people are commonly referred to as the "makers of the modern world": Freud, Darwin, and Marx. Peter Drucker, world-renowned management consultant, believes Taylor deserves to be the fourth, saying, "Taylorism is perhaps the most powerful as well as the most lasting contribution America has made to Western thought since the Federalist Papers."[6]

Taylor's ideas laid the foundation for the business practices we still use today:

1. He is considered "the Father of Scientific Management Theory."[7] Taylor was probably the first consultant and management theorist.

2. Taylorism was the centerpiece and focal point of the theory of management for decades, at least through the 1930s.[8]

3. His term *Scientific Management* and its accompanying principles were still in mainstream use in management theory and practice until at least the early '60s.[9]

4. Taylor's work still influences today's workplace profoundly. As one analysis puts it, "Many aspects of Scientific Management have never stopped being part of later management efforts called by other names. There is no simple dividing line demarcating the time when management as a modern profession diverged from Taylorism proper."[10]

Everything from Management by Objective in the 1960s, to Total Quality Management, to all the misconceptions around true Reengineering in the 1990s, have their foundation in Taylorism. A lot of that worked out great for the production floor, but a lot of it was not going to work out well for the employee. Why? Because mixed up in Taylor's very good transformational views of processes and systems were two horribly bad assumptions about people. It is these two rogue beliefs that would cause controversy to swirl around him to this very day, which have understandably distracted us from his other, much better ideas.

> "Taylorism is perhaps the most powerful as well as the most lasting contribution America has made to Western thought since the Federalist Papers." – Peter Drucker

## TAYLOR INVENTS THE MODERN EMPLOYEE

In 1903, Taylor wrote a paper called *Shop Management,*[11] and in 1911, an expanded paper called *Principles of Scientific Management*[12] in which he essentially invented the modern form of the employee as we know it today. It has morphed a lot since, but our core assumptions about employees and management can be clearly traced all the way back to these papers and Taylor's bigoted and narrow view of the world. The Factory System needed someone to recreate the human being in the image of machines, and Taylor unfortunately obliged.

Two central and devastating assumptions drove his Scientific Management Theory and are at the root of our modern view of *employee*.

## BAD ASSUMPTION #1: EMPLOYEES ARE STUPID

Taylor believed employees were more likely to be stupid than anything else. In fact, in many cases it was a requirement. "One of the very first requirements for a man who is fit to handle pig-iron as a regular occupation **is that he shall be so stupid and so phlegmatic that he more nearly resembles the ox than any other type.**" Taylor goes on, "He is so stupid that the word 'percentage' has no meaning to him, and he must consequently be trained by a man more intelligent than himself."[12]

In another instance Taylor writes, "The writer [Taylor] firmly believes that it would be possible to train an intelligent gorilla so as to become a more efficient pig-iron handler than any man can be."[13] There were some Irish, Polish, and German immigrant geniuses who could barely speak English slinging pig-iron who might have argued with him at the time. But it wasn't just pig-iron handlers he was calling stupid.

Taylor goes on to describe the *dullness problem* for a bricklayer, a ball-bearing inspector, a lathe operator in a high-end machine shop, and a steel cutter. Having shared these examples, he then applies the same assumption of stupidity to all workers: "These illustrations should make perfectly clear our original proposition that in practically all of the mechanic arts the science which underlies each workman's act is so great and amounts to so much that the workman who is best suited to actually doing the work is incapable, either through lack of education or through insufficient mental capacity, of understanding this science."[14]

> "One of the very first requirements is that he shall be so stupid and so phlegmatic that he more nearly resembles the ox than any other type."
> –Frederick Taylor

## BAD ASSUMPTION #2: EMPLOYEES ARE LAZY

Taylor assumed and believed that employees would always work at the slowest rate that would go unpunished, an idea he called *soldiering*. He believed they would do this because they are wholly unmotivated to their very core, and that over 99 percent of workers engaged in this evil laziness. Taylor said, "For every individual, however, who is overworked, there are a hundred who intentionally underwork – greatly underwork – every day of their lives, and who for this reason deliberately aid in establishing those conditions which in the end inevitably result in low wages. **And yet hardly a single voice is being raised in an endeavor to correct this evil.**"[15]

"For every individual, however, who is overworked, there are a hundred who intentionally underwork – greatly underwork – every day of their lives. And yet hardly a single voice is being raised in an endeavor to correct this evil." –Taylor

In 1911, Taylor devoted the first 15 pages of his 142-page *Scientific Management* paper to this laziness problem. The majority of the rest of the paper was about solving it by reinventing people in the image of machines, reducing them to become extensions of the machines they ran, and taking away all human choice.

Taylor knew what he was doing. He admits that this system, "tends to make the worker a mere automaton, a wooden man". As the workmen frequently say when they first come under this system, "I'm not allowed to think or move without someone interfering or doing it for me!"[16] Taylor took the formerly bright, motivated, creative, and industrious craftspeople and turned them into stupid and lazy employees.

He equated employees with and actually calls them *children* who don't have the attention span to be motivated by things like profit-sharing, but who do much better with personal attention or, stunningly, "an actual reward in sight as often as an hour."[17] He justifies calling them children by saying we're "all grown-up children," but then doesn't bother to rationalize why he himself doesn't need an hourly reward, constant supervision, and someone else to do his thinking, yet they do. He believed his trained gorilla employee would really like the hourly reward. It's very Pavlovian.

## SOUND FAMILIAR?

With all his amazing and positive impact, it would be nice to just dismiss his two worst ideas as anachronistic bigotry, except for the fact that those two bad ideas have had more impact in today's business world than any other idea he promoted. They are built into the very DNA of what we know today as the concept of a twenty-first-century employee. But those ideas will not fly in the Participation Age.

One of the unfortunate, common threads between his world in 1903 and ours in the twenty-first century is that even if employees are smart and motivated, they are not allowed to act that way. As one writer put it, "In the case of human workers under Scientific Management, they were often **able** [to be smart] but were **not allowed**.[18] In many of today's workplaces, the same conditions exist; people are **able** to be smart, motivated, creative, innovative, and problem solvers, but they are **not allowed**.

Why did these two ideas suffocate the rest of Taylor's good work? Because the Industrialists had an insatiable desire to find ways to extract more efficiency and more profit, and found their best solutions in his two worst ideas. Going forward, employees were doomed to being stupid and lazy.

## LCD MANAGEMENT VS. HCD LEADERSHIP

Taylor gave us the unfortunate foundation of the modern view of *employee*, that people are overwhelmingly stupid and lazy. No company today would affirm this as a basic tenet of their human resources practices, yet our whole management system can be summed up in one acronym stemming from these two assumptions— LCD (Lowest Common Denominator) Management.

Taylor's radical assumptions about people who previously had been smart enough to run their own businesses in centuries gone by led us to institute management practices to the Lowest Common Denominator. LCD Management is far and away the most common way to lead people at work today. But in chapters 11 and 12, we will introduce you to many companies across all industries that have rejected LCD Management in favor of HCD (Highest Common Denominator) *Leadership* (not management). They have built companies that assume people are smart and motivated and want to be regularly challenged to raise their game to the next level.

> The machine didn't need them to think, create, or solve. It just needed them to do.

Taylor, and those who followed, put in place today's common business practices in order to solve the *stupid and lazy* problem – solutions like blind obedience, passive existence, a highly directed work life, extremely narrow division of labor, exact hours in which to perform, and smothering limitations on being human or an adult at work. As we said earlier, it stripped people of their need to think, create, or solve problems, because the machine didn't need them to think, create, or solve; *it just needed them to do.* In Scientific Management Theory, "the worker was taken for granted as a cog in the machine."[19]

## I'M STUPID IF YOU BELIEVE I AM

We all live up to people's worst expectations of us. The *Saturday Night Live* character Stuart Smalley used to famously chant in his Daily Affirmations, "I'm good enough, I'm smart enough, and doggone it, people like me!" Stuart had to stare into the mirror and repeat it every day, because his imaginary parents had told him all his life what a clod he was and that he would never amount to a hill of beans.

The workplace is no different. When we treat people like children, they live down to our worst expectations of them. Much truth is said in jest. Charlie Chaplin, in his classic *Modern Times* movie, parodied the alienation and stress that the worker in a Tayloristic production plant is subjected to. It is a classic, because it is so sadly true.[20]

In an Industrial Age "managed" environment where workers have no ownership of their decisions, processes, or time, the indictment that "you are stupid and lazy" is a self-fulfilling prophecy. It's not because people are dumb or unmotivated, but because their value as humans, creators, and problem solvers goes unrewarded and unrecognized. How much brilliance did we lose from immigrant pig-iron handlers being treated like idiots? We'll never know.

## WHY HAVEN'T WE CHANGED THE EMPLOYEE SYSTEM?

This isn't yesterday's problem. The old Taylorist Factory System business practices are in full swing, and still aren't working out so hot. As we've said, the production area has changed radically since the 1970s, but the front office, and the way we treat employees in general, has evolved very little.

Business people are very in tune with anything that has a direct correlation to making a buck. I know I am. Switching out one product or service for another is a really easy choice when it's not selling, or when something better or newer comes along that will sell better. But we're much slower to see the indirect consequences of the old Factory System front-office habits. They are still there, and if you're running with these old practices, it's costing you a lot of money and your best people. Why? Because these people are beginning to find post-Industrial front offices embracing the Participation Age, where they can Make Meaning, not just money.

## IT WAS NEVER A GOOD IDEA

Treating people as extensions of machines doesn't work. In 2012, Towers Watson, an employee benefits and talent management company, completed a decade-long series of studies involving thirty-two thousand full-time workers across a range of industries and functions. It was titled the *2012 Global Workforce Study: Engagement at Risk*. They found that 63 percent of workers were not highly engaged, meaning (at best) they would do the jobs they were told to do, but not initiate anything more (Taylor's *soldiering* principle).[21]

Gallup did a similar study and pinned it at 71 percent who are *not engaged* or *actively disengaged* in their work, meaning "they are emotionally disconnected from their workplaces and are less likely to be productive." Gallup also found this was trending in the wrong direction: "disengagement with work is on the upswing."[22] One expert analyzed this data and concluded that almost 20 percent are so badly disengaged that it hurts a company to have them show up. He advised that they identify these people and pay them to stay home. If they did, companies would make a lot more money and everyone else would be happier.

LCD Management (lowest common denominator) works – people will live down to your lowest expectation of them.

This doesn't prove people are stupid and lazy. It simply proves that LCD Management (lowest common denominator) works – people will live down to your lowest expectation of them. We'll show in Part II how our company has created employee engagement, and how one client with fifty employees cut eight hours out of the average work week in two months, while maintaining the same productivity or higher (they had their best year when they did this). True Capitalists believe that championing the development of the people we work with will make them a lot more money than "ignoring the woo-woo crap," as some Industrialists have put it.

## COUNTERING THE SYSTEM

Unions justifiably arose as a counter to this degrading view of the employee and the Industrialist's abusive labor practices. But as unions also became one of the Bigs, they learned very quickly to use all the same tactics to ensure their own survival: market dominance; closed markets; job destruction by exclusive control of whole markets; maintaining the status quo (locomotive firemen were still paid for decades after locomotives stopped using firewood and started using diesel); and even destroying jobs by making it impossible to get a job without union membership; or protecting existing jobs until the whole company collapsed.

> That is the defining creation of the modern Industrial Age employee; to become narrowly skilled as an extension of a specific machine or service.

## NEW ISN'T NECESSARILY BETTER

It cannot be overemphasized how unique Taylor's new concept of the employee was for humanity. Working for someone else was not unique, but outside of slave and conscripted labor, doing so in a way that engaged very few of our human faculties was very new for the majority of people. Massive division of labor became the mantra of the Factory System.

The Industrialists were brilliant at creating efficiencies in order to squeeze every last dime out of the present market. This led them to more and more segmentation of labor into the narrowest of tasks. On the assembly line, you could be reduced to putting a nut on a bolt for ten hours a day every day. You were expected to do it with a good attitude, because there were ten other people standing in line behind you waiting for that job and a chance to feed their families. You weren't doing it because you felt you made a contribution to the world around you, but because you and your family needed to eat. You were making money, not Making Meaning.

The dehumanizing nature of the work, which stripped us of creativity and the need to make a unique contribution, was the de facto standard of the Factory System. If you didn't like it, someone else would be glad to step right into the nuts-and-bolts job in your place.

Being employed was not new. What was new was being stripped of so much of our humanness, and having the task reduced to monotonous repetition. That is the defining creation of the modern Industrial Age employee; to become narrowly skilled as an extension of a specific machine or service. A pre-Industrial Age worker was much more likely to engage his humanity at work and be rewarded for doing so. In contrast, the new *employee* of the Industrial Age was penalized for deviating from the process. Asking "Why?" and other acts of humanity were now considered insubordination. This human mindset, recreated in the image of machines, still dominates most workplaces and holds companies back from becoming as successful as they could be.

## EMPLOYEES LEAVING HOME

Another major differentiator of this new invention called the *employee* is that they were the first people to leave home en masse to GO to work. This separated work and play, as well as work and relationships. This new practice of *going* to work, and the need to respond to inflexible machines, created a nine-to-five model and a few other business diseases of the Industrial Age (which we will address in chapters 4 through 7). Leaving home to go to work was a tectonic shift in work habits, and is still one of the defining characteristics of today's employee.

## EMPLOYEES ARE "SILENT"

Employees were not hired to think, create, innovate, or improve on the process. Machines do not talk back, do not offer suggestions, and do not complain about their circumstances. The Industrialist became used to demanding that people respond to them as the machine did – with blind loyalty and silence. This peaked in the generation that entered the workforce from 1945 to1965, who were cursed with the demographic label, *The Silent Generation*.

"Good" employees continue to mimic the *Silents*. That generation is the Industrialist's ideal of how a good *company man* or woman relates to the corporation. Untold numbers of managers have built entire careers around making sure they never say anything of value, don't buck the system, and simply hang around long enough that they are the last man standing. Many insecure, upper managers love having these *brownnosers* around, and have built corporations around them. I have watched too many Silents get promoted before productive and proactive people who dare to ask "Why?" or other tough questions.

The *ideal* employee in an Industrial Age corporation is silent, even today. There's a lot of noise about getting people involved and participating, but in a majority of corporations, the ability to really make an impact from the cheap seats is next to none.

## EMPLOYEES ARE CHILDREN

Employees obediently follow orders, do what they're told, don't question authority, are blindly loyal, and live passively as others direct their lives. Pretty much what we would expect any good four-year-old to do.

The Factory System was built on processes that did not require you to bring your full game to work. The first week I was in basic training with the army, the drill sergeant barked at me, "Blakeman, the army is a system designed by geniuses to be run by idiots! Which one of those two do you think you are?!" The correct answer, of course, was the idiot. I was not hired to think, create, innovate, make a unique contribution, or build something of significance that others could learn from. I was there to be a small cog in a large, predesigned system.

## THE FIRST EMPLOYEES ACTUALLY WERE CHILDREN

The Factory System was even more constrictive. It made the army look like a very collaborative and creative environment. The Factory System would have actually run better using children, because they are less developed mentally, and a six-year-old can be taught to follow orders better than an eighteen-year-old. So, it's no surprise that what was probably the first factory was actually operated by children. The first textile factory in England in the late 1700s, which most refer to as the beginning of the Factory System, was actually staffed by orphans (more on that later). But children aren't developed well enough physically to be as productive as adults. So, the ideal employee was physically fully mature, but reduced to the cognitive faculties of a child, or better yet, a dependent orphan with no options. Remember Taylor's description: stupid, but strong like an ox.

> The ideal employee was physically fully mature, but reduced to the cognitive faculties of a child.

## EMPLOYEES ARE BOXED IN—THE DAY CARE CENTER

One defining practice for employees is that they *MUST* report to the day care center (office) every day. The children/employees must be closely managed to keep them from running into the streets or spilling grape juice on the carpets. If people are stupid and lazy, you really have no choice.

However, virtually all the evidence shows that people who work out of their homes are more productive than those who work in the corporate environment. Many Participation Age companies have places of work, just like the Industrialists. But people go there, not to be closely managed, but to collaborate, coinvent, cocreate, and cocontribute – that is, to participate and share.

## CREATIVITY IS A LONER'S GIG

This isn't a vote for never seeing each other. In our business, people see each other multiple times every week. There is no question that people working together in community regularly come up with a better result than people who rarely get together. But there is equally as much evidence that people need to get away by themselves to be creative. Great paintings, great music, great audio speakers, great buildings, etc., almost all were first conceived by one person sitting very alone.

> The modern employee was invented by the Factory System, without regard for how it impacted the people who were turned into employees.

Creativity is best encouraged when people are on their own, not when they are in a group. And new research is showing that the worst place to try to be creative is in a brainstorming session or any other type of formal meeting. In chapter 6, we'll show how a mix of working alone and in community with others creates the best environment for productivity and collaboration, as well as creativity.

## SHOULD WE STOP USING THE WORD "EMPLOYEE"?

The modern employee was invented by the Factory System, for the convenience of the Factory System, without regard for how it impacted the people who were turned into employees. It may have been a cure for the Industrialist, but it is a disease for humanity, and for the Participation Age.

The bottom line: Employees are a Business Disease of the Industrial Age, an invention that should be eradicated. The concept is tied to command and control tactics which we would employ with any four-year-old. Taylorism is so entrenched in the word *employee* that we can't even use it anymore. It conjures up a profile that is not useful in the post-Industrial Participation Age. We (and many others) are suggesting you replace the word *employee* with a term that is not tied to its Industrial Age roots.

## STAKEHOLDERS REPLACE EMPLOYEES

Use whatever word you want to replace *employee*. Participation Age companies use identifiers such as *associate, team member, staff, agent, creator, owner,* and a lot of other terms to replace *employee*. It's not semantics. Words are powerful. We believe that if labels like CEO, COO, and all the other "Os" are capitalized, Stakeholder should be as well. We don't have capital letters for "IMPORTANT" people and small case letters for *ordinary* people. Everybody is important, and we are all Stakeholders, even those who own the company.

## WHO ARE THE STAKEHOLDERS?

Anyone who touches your company is a Stakeholder. Stakeholders encompass everyone who has a stake in the future of your company: the owners or the stockholders, those who draw paychecks, your suppliers, companies with whom you partner to deliver your products or services, those outsourced functions that help you succeed, and, of course, your customers.

Stakeholders create an appropriate level playing field from which we all work together to build a better company. When I was young, I worked as a temporary employee at some companies and felt like the outsider. It was pretty obvious I didn't belong. But in the Participation Age, both your full-time and part-time staff (the Industrial Age tax people will still call them *employees* – just humor them), and your temporary staff are all Stakeholders. Everyone has a stake in making sure things go well. Some of the best input will be from temps who come in off the street with no idea about your business.

We, of course, didn't invent the term *Stakeholder*, but we like it because it directly implies ownership, the most powerful motivator in business. We want everyone to act as owners, and be owners of something, if only their work and their processes at first.

> Anyone who touches your company is a Stakeholder. Stakeholders encompass everyone who has a stake in the future of your company.

## STAKEHOLDERS ARE BECOMING THE NORM

The new generation of employees will not tolerate leaving themselves at home while the functional part of them goes to work. We've squeezed the last mile out of making people extensions of machines. Companies that ignore this and continue to treat people like *employees* will not do well in the next decade. Those that embrace Stakeholders will flourish for decades to come. Your choice.

# EMBRACING THE PARTICIPATION AGE

1. What is your mindset? What one practice can you change to begin to move away from Lowest Common Denominator (LCD) management? (Pick only one.)

_____

_____

By When? ____ / ____ / ____ : ____ a.m./p.m.

2. Who in your organization needs to be less "Silent"? What one action will help that individual make more of a contribution.

_____

_____

By When? ____ / ____ / ____ : ____ a.m./p.m.

## NOTES

1. *Most Employees Want to Change Careers,* George Brown, American Society of Employers, ASEOnline.org, July 10, 2013, http://bit.ly/14ukDHk

2. *Cornerstone OnDemand Research Suggests 21 Million Americans Are Planning to Change Jobs in 2012,* CornerstoneOnDemand.com, Santa Monica, CA, December 2, 2011 http://bit.ly/18i7UYo

3. *The Origin of Horticulture, Industrial Revolution & the Rise of Science,* (Columbus, OH: Ohio State University Press, 2004 http://www.hcs.ohio-state.edu/hcs/TMI/HCS210/HortOrigins/IndustrialRev.html.

4. *Taylorism can be seen as the division of labor pushed to its logical extreme, with a consequent de-skilling of the worker and dehumanization of the workers and the workplace.* http://en.wikipedia.org/wiki/Scientific_management.

5. *Frederick Taylor and Scientific Management Understanding Taylorism and Early Management Theory,* Mindtools.com, http://www.mindtools.com/pages/article/newTMM_Taylor.htm

6. Robert Kanigel, *The One Best Way, Frederick Winslow Taylor and the Enigma of Efficiency,* (New York, NY: Viking Press, 2005)

7. Ibid.

8. Frederick Winslow Taylor, Shop Management, (New York, NY: American Society of Mechanical Engineers, 1903), OCLC 2365572.

9. Robert Kanigel, *The One Best Way, Frederick Winslow Taylor and the Enigma of Efficiency,* (New York, NY: Viking Press, 2005)

10. Ibid, 59.

11. Frederick Winslow Taylor, Shop Management, (New York, NY: American Society of Mechanical Engineers, 1903), OCLC 2365572.

12. Frederick Winslow Taylor, The Principles of Scientific Management, (New York, NY, USA and London, UK: Harper & Brothers, 1911), LCCN 11010339.

13. http://en.wikipedia.org/wiki/Scientific_management.

14. Ibid, 18.

15. Frederick Winslow Taylor, *The Principles of Scientific Management,* (New York, NY, USA and London, UK: Harper & Brothers, 1911), LCCN 11010339.

16. Ibid, 94.

17. Ibid, 90.

18. http://en.wikipedia.org/wiki/Fordism.

19. Ellen Rosen, *Improving Public Sector Productivity: Concepts and Practice,* (Thousand Oaks, CA: Sage Publications, 1993), ISBN 978-0-8039-4573-9.

20. Ibid, 139.

21. *Does Group Participation When Using Brainstorming Facilitate or Inhibit Creative Thinking?,* Donald W. Taylor, Paul C. Berry, and Clifford H. Block, Administrative Science Quarterly 3, no. 1 (June 1958): 23-47.

22. *2012 Global Workforce Study, Engagement at Risk: Driving Strong Performance in a Volatile Global Environment,* Towers Watson, white paper, July 2012, http://bit.ly/17Bjxqo23. What Makes Employees Unhappy, Inc. Magazine (February 2013): 24.

23. *Majority of American Workers Not Engaged in Their Jobs,* Nikki Blacksmith and Jim Harter, Gallup Wellbeing, white paper, October 28, 2011, http://www.gallup.com/poll/150383/majority-american-workers-not-engaged-jobs.aspx

# Why Managers Are Always a Bad Idea, Too

*"Most of what we call management consists of making it difficult for people to get their work done."*

—PETER DRUCKER

As I was leaving the small and very remote village in the middle of DR Congo, and about to get on the bush plane, the chief pulled me in front of the couple dozen people seeing me off, and announced loudly that he would like to give me a pig to take back to the US with me. Everyone clapped and roared with approval. I knew this was a huge honor, pork is US $10-$15 a pound, and most people in DR Congo make a buck a day. A pig was a year's salary or more. I also knew that he meant a live pig; keeping them alive is the only refrigeration method that works there.

I thanked him profusely and told him I hadn't made arrangements to ship a live pig (or a dead one), and that it would take a few weeks to make that happen. We agreed that I would send him the required shipping fees if the government agreed to let me ship a pig. Fortunately, when I got back to the United States, the government said I couldn't do it. You get a lot of opportunities in life. Sometimes we are better off not having some.

Managers (not management itself) are a business disease of the Industrial Age, also. They've only been around for a little over a hundred years, and should be eliminated from business as quickly as possible. Few things are as disruptive, unhelpful, and unproductive in the workplace as managers. And the premise for needing them is especially bad.

## THE CASE FOR MANAGERS

If employees are stupid and lazy, as Taylor asserted, there is only one solution: find people who are smart and motivated to make them less stupid and less lazy – and modern management was born. As P.G. Wodehouse put it in *Carry On, Jeeves,* "Employees are like horses; they require management." The only solution to Taylor's *stupid and lazy* conundrum was to create a class of corporate citizens that had virtually not existed before the Industrial Age: people who themselves add no productive value to the company, but exist almost exclusively to make stupid and lazy people more productive.

This new class of Work Monitors justified their existence by raising the performances of workers above what it was believed they would do on their own, and the extra performance was supposed to create an increase in revenue to pay the manager and bring more profit to the company. But that's a big assumption to make – that others couldn't or wouldn't raise their performances if managers didn't exist.

## THE CASE AGAINST MANAGERS

Managers are the principal carriers of most of the business diseases of the Industrial Age. They are largely responsible for the continuing presence of archaic Industrial Age business practices in the twenty-first century.

How critical is their influence? Research done by Ethan Mollick, Wharton School of Business management professor, found that middle managers have a greater impact on knowledge-based businesses than any other factor, including the CEO, business strategies, management systems, and HR practices.[1] If you want to move into the Participation Age, you will have to start by replacing managers with leaders. And when you do, you will find you need a lot fewer leaders than managers.

Managers have an uphill battle. The hierarchical business structure we inherited from the Factory System predisposes the position of manager to be more infected with the attributes of an Industrialist than any other position. As a result, more than any other position in a company, the manager is the embodiment of the Industrialist.

> Managers are the principal carriers of most of the business diseases of the Industrial Age.

Let's review the attributes of an Industrialist from chapter 3 to see how the position of a manager feeds off these negative attributes.

## MANAGERS ARE INDUSTRIALISTS

1. Being Big – The position of manager lends itself to the Industrialist penchant for fiefdom-building. Like feudal lords, they work hard to

make their span of control as big as possible, instead of doing what helps the company meet its objective. Fiefdom-building helps justify their existence. Managers never make it their objective to work themselves out of a job and close down their department.

2. Closed Markets – Just like an Industrialist, managers are predisposed to despise anyone stepping on their territory. Managers are generally very insecure (and justifiably so) about someone going "behind their backs" directly to someone who can actually get something done. They are also not a fan of dividing their pie and giving some of it to someone else to manage. Managers love a closed market and rarely think about how they can make the other person successful, too, especially if it would cost them some span of control.

3. Resisting Progress and Maintaining the Status Quo – Managers prefer things to stay the way they are, just like any good Industrialist. They will resist any changes that threaten their fiefdom. They are not wired to think "how do we destroy our existing department to create the next better department?" Progress is *ONLY* acceptable if it expands the manager's fiefdom – who cares what is best for the company as a whole?

4. Destroying Jobs – This Industrialist practice is not a direct value of most managers, but if they personally can ensure their own survival by cutting other productive people out of their fiefdom, it's an easy call.

5. Users, Not Creators, and the Cash Cow Rule – Managers are given quotas, and the more cash they can create with the present system, the more they validate their existence. It's about fine-tuning the present, not creating a better future that could destroy the existing system. That kind of upheaval could possibly result in their becoming irrelevant or losing part of their fiefdom. Creativity is not worth the risk. Just keep the cash coming.

6. Focus on the Competitor – Other departments are viewed as competitors for budget, praise, and perceived value to the company. Marvin Weisbord, in his book *Productive Workplaces Revisited,* tells how he had to build a wall between two "departments" who couldn't get along. Managers are almost always fiercely competitive with other managers for a piece of fiefdom pie.

7. Short-Term Decision Making – An Industrialist will mortgage the future of the company to make the shareholders happy today. Managers will do

the very same thing to make the manager above them happy today. Why wouldn't they? Most likely the manager above them is hovering around demanding they make this month's quota to make the shareholders happy. This month matters more than next year. Keep the cash coming.

Can you see once again why the *Dilbert* cartoon strip resonates with us? The position of manager lends itself to exhibiting nearly all of the values and practices of an Industrialist. If you want to create a culture of participation, creation, innovation, and sharing that builds successful companies, you don't need managers; managers have to go. They should be replaced with leaders, and a lot fewer of them, too.

> Managers have to go. They should be replaced with leaders, and a lot fewer of them, too.

## PETER PIPER PACKED A LOT MORE PICKLES

The Industrialist will tell you people will not produce to the level that they could if it were not for managers and the structural constructs (time clocks, piece-per-hour requirements, etc.) imposed on them from above. The employees may not be totally lazy or completely stupid, but they're not as smart and motivated as management.

Then how do you explain our pickle factory experience?

In the 1980s, we put fifty or so college kids in a sorority at the University of Massachusetts for the summer to teach them character and leadership skills – to Make Meaning, not just money. We had them work in a local pickle factory and other common labor jobs in the area during the day, and trained them on Making Meaning at night and on the weekends. The best pickle packers (nobody there was named Peter) had packed an average of about twelve cases per day for years, making US $10-$12/hour, a very good wage at the time. You could pack as few as eight cases a day regularly and keep your job. Most did. It had been that way for decades; 8-12 cases/per day/per person was what management had decided was great production. It was what they expected, so they monitored it closely, and achieved it every day. Managers hovering over pickle-packers appeared to be working.

Our kids went to the pickle factory with a Stakeholder mentality, ignoring what the managers expected and decided to see what they could do instead. By midsummer, many of them were packing 18-20 cases a day and the superstars were packing 20-24 cases on their best days. They blew the top off the pay scale. Industrialists would say it was because they were part of the *smart and motivated* future managers' cadre. But the interesting thing is that the people who had been packing for decades at 12 cases per day (because that is what managers expected) were also now up to about 18-20 cases per day as well.

The next summer, when we came back, the company did the math and figured it made more sense to close down their California plant and truck pickles all the way to Massachusetts rather than pack them out there. They were very disappointed when we didn't come back again the third year. The factory management couldn't figure out how, after decades of "great production" at 8-12 cases a day, production had spiked so suddenly.

## DO MANAGERS KNOW BEST?

It was clear to us why. Years earlier, the factory managers, in their detached and infinite Tayloristic wisdom, had come up with a standard, imposed it on the workers, and monitored it closely to ensure they complied. Unwittingly, or merely by assumption, they treated the workers as if they were extensions of machines; and machine parts do not have the mental capacity to figure out how to improve on the managers' brilliant processes. The workers responded as machines. *They lived down to the managers' lowest expectation of them.* The managers responded with the third value of an Industrialist, which is to maintain the status quo for decades.

> The most taboo question of all, the one you should NEVER ask, is "Why?"

Were the workers stupid and lazy? No, they proved that in one summer, by doubling their performance without any expectation from management to do so. They had done 8-12 cases a day for decades because they were told what to do. And knowing that this was how they would keep their jobs, they did exactly as they were told, until some Stakeholders came alongside them and questioned the rules.

## STAKEHOLDERS KNOW BEST

If the managers had been leaders, they would have empowered the workers to figure out how to work the process better, and everyone would have made more money working the process. Instead, things were status quo for a few decades before our folks showed up and ignored the manager's unspoken expectations.

Industrial Age management takes its cue from a misconception of military management; questioning anything is considered insubordination. These workers would have never questioned the pickle-packing experts in order to come up with a different or better way. In the very hierarchical structure of an Industrial Age company, you don't question "authority." And the most taboo question of all, the one you should *NEVER* ask, is "Why?" That's the question that will get you fired. The pickle-packing employee was reduced to only asking "clarifying" questions, not questions that would attack the base assumptions developed by the geniuses known as "managers."

This inability to directly question management is another reason why Scott Adams still has so much material for his *Dilbert* cartoons. Management is very insecure in its ability to justify its contribution to the workplace. These pickle-packing geniuses had a lot of questions to answer to the owners of the company about how they had stifled productivity at nearly half the possible level for decades. I'm guessing there were a few managers in that plant who found the creativity and innovation of our workers to be very threatening to their fiefdom. In one summer, the formerly stupid and lazy employees had devalued a few decades of work by the smart and motivated managers.

## WHY DO WE HAVE TO MAKE IT THEIR IDEA?

In 1997, one of my former companies took over a difficult and complex process from one of the five largest technology companies in the world. They had struggled for years to make it work and had created a global mess instead. At that time, they had seven or eight warehouses scattered across the world delivering products, yet delivery was taking four to twelve weeks and 10 to 20 percent simply never got delivered. We took over the program and almost immediately were delivering 95 percent in fourteen days and virtually no shipments were getting lost.

A number of months into the program, I got a visit here in Denver from a division manager at the technology company. He asked how we did it. I leaned over the desk and looked both ways like I was going to tell him a big secret, smiled, and said, "We use DHL." At the time, FedEx and UPS were largely domestic shippers. If you wanted a package delivered anywhere in the world, DHL was the fastest and most reliable. We had done a few days of homework and chose them. They would show up at our dock every day, the packages would disappear, and DHL would deliver them everywhere in the world that technology company managers said couldn't be reached. Things went swimmingly. Except, our success caused us to lose the program.

The division manager frankly and directly informed me that our performance had jeopardized the positions of a few dozen high-up managers (I'm guessing he was one of them) who had communicated to him that for a decade it couldn't be done. We made the mistake of not making this their idea (hadn't read enough *Dilbert* cartoons at the time). Six months later, they took the program back and gave it to the giant vendor whom they had worked with for years. But at least now the giant vendor had a process that worked.

In Industrialist environments, when productive people on the front lines solve the problems, they threaten the authority and viability of managers back in the ivory tower. Sometimes, it's best to just play stupid and lazy. In our case, it would have been in our best interests to pull a *Dilbert* and make the managers think they came up with the idea. But we thought and acted like Stakeholders, and Stakeholders don't play silly political games to make managers feel like they are contributing.

## MANAGEMENT MAKES PEOPLE LAZY

Some (very few) people are truly lazy. But most employees wish they could be Stakeholders, and are simply adjusting themselves to our lowest expectations of them. Micromanagement is dehumanizing, strips people of their dignity, and makes them work at the lowest level that will go unpunished, because that's exactly what we're asking them to do. Frederick Taylor admitted it could reduce them to being "automatons," and it does. Management doesn't keep people from being lazy; it has the opposite effect. Management MAKES otherwise motivated people lazy.

## LCD MANAGEMENT DEMOTIVATES STAKEHOLDERS

Rather than managing to the level of the few who are inherently lazy – Lowest Common Denominator Management – those people should be let go so the adult Stakeholders in the room can get on with it. Nothing was more frustrating to me as a Stakeholder in someone else's business than watching other people work hard at doing nothing, while a few of us carried the production load. If the managers would have stayed out of the way and taken the few inherently lazy ones with them, we would have rocked the department. As it was, the good people were always the ones to leave. We all left.

## MANAGEMENT ENCOURAGES TIME-BASED REWARDS

Management is not built to reward destruction of the present system and replace it with a better one. It also isn't built to reward outsized performance by individuals. Raises are largely time-based, with a few percentage point variances on either side of the norm for people who perform above or below the required pickle-packing rate.

This kind of model discourages people from putting forth their best efforts. A friend I knew in the 1980s was hired by a giant insurance company for a fairly high-level position that took a lot of self-direction and motivation. It was a job for only the smart and motivated to perform, and he was one of the smarter and more motivated people I knew. He also knew very well from years of experience how the Industrial Age Dilbert Society works, and that a cornerstone of it is the classic annual raise.

Being smart and motivated to figure out how to succeed there, he saw very quickly what level of performance his managers expected annually. He knew that he could blow it out of the water in the first year because of his experience. But he also saw clearly that if he did that, it would not leave a lot of room to impress management in future years, which could have an impact on his annual raises. They would quickly forget how he had outperformed the whole division exponentially. So, he paced himself, always performing near or at the top of the division, but holding himself back and doling out the goods a little more each year. He got the maximum, meager raise every year and rose very high up in the company.

If the company was set up to simply reward results, they would have gotten the best out of him the first year and the company would have made a lot more money for years to come. Should he have held back because he wouldn't be rewarded for higher performance? That's another question, but the company had set up a system that made it much more rewarding for him to perform to its lowest expectation of him. LCD Management made him "lazy."

> Most people are not lazy. Management MAKES them lazy.

LCD Management is the great leveler – taking the wind out of the top performers to ensure the few lazy ones work harder. If managers got out of the way, removed the few inherently lazy people, and required people to be adults and to be self-motivated, they would be. Most people are not lazy. Management MAKES them lazy.

## MANAGEMENT ALSO MAKES PEOPLE STUPID

If we believe people are not as smart as we are, we micromanage them and strip them of their ability to create, solve problems, lead, initiate, and take ownership. All we do in the process is make them stupid.

My mother was a fantastic person, a world-class leader who had risen from the most difficult circumstances of the Great Depression to Make Meaning with her life. She and my dad were classic Industrial Age parents whom I loved dearly for all their strengths and faults, many of which I embraced and carried through with my children, while adding some strengths and faults of my own.

My mother had one annoying phrase by which I know she meant nothing negative, but which nonetheless had a devastating effect on me, not because she said it, but because I believed it. She is not at fault for my believing and embracing it. And it's a great example of how we set up environments in which people can choose to be stupid, even when they aren't.

Quite regularly, especially in situations where I had done something humorously clumsy or "dumb," she would say, "You dumb kid," and would chuckle. I would chuckle, too. A lot of times it was just plain funny. Sometimes, she said it with more frustration and more deeply when I had done something more egregious, and it would come out, "You must be the dumbest kid alive" or "How dumb can you be?" Turns out, I could be pretty dumb.

I knew she didn't mean it; many other times she would tell me how bright I was. But I decided to latch on to the "dumb" comment and run with it. And I was very successful in doing so. I graduated near the bottom of my high school class. One memorable life event found me in the principal's office a couple days before graduation, after school was already done for the year. The principal and two teachers were discussing whether they would let me graduate. They talked as if I weren't there. I felt like a character in a Charlie Brown cartoon, where all you can see and hear are adult's knees and garbled voices. We were in the same room, but two different worlds.

They let me squeak through and graduate. I had a full scholarship to attend a classical music school, but the college made me go to summer school on my own dollar to prove I wasn't as dumb as I had demonstrated during those four years in high school. And for many years after that, I was convinced that if there was one kid out of the 525 in my graduating class who would never be able to get a job, it was going to be me. I had lived down to what I had decided was my mother's lowest expectation of me.

> **Most people are not stupid. Management MAKES people stupid.**

Employees are not stupid; they just live down to our lowest expectations of them – LCD Management. If we treat them like smart and motivated Stakeholders, we'll see a whole different side of them.

Most people are not stupid. Management MAKES people stupid.

## THE MANAGER IS DEAD; LONG LIVE THE LEADER

In the middle of World War II, Kurt Lewin, a practical theorist, studied how to get people to eat more nonscarce food like fish. To get them to switch, one group of homemakers was lectured, and the other group was given the facts and the task of deciding completely on their own what they should eat. The groups who reached their own decisions were significantly more likely to adopt new food habits than those who were lectured. As Marvin Weisbord puts it, "Lewin had found a core principle: We are more likely to modify our own behavior when we participate in the problem analysis and solution, and more likely to carry out decisions we have helped make."[2]

> **The art of leadership is to know how few times the leader should actually make the decision.**

As Lewin discovered, adults don't like to be told what to do, and don't need to be told what to do. *The art of leadership is to know how few times the leader should actually make the decision.* Managers, in the grand tradition of Taylorism, exist to tell people what to do. It is assumed they are smarter and more able to direct the Stakeholders to the right way of doing things than the Stakeholders themselves. But that assumption – the need for specific direction and supervision – is what turns adult Stakeholders back into childlike employees.

At Crankset Group, we have rejected the manager model as having been built on bad assumptions. The concept of manager cannot be rehabilitated because it is flawed at its very core. So we don't have managers in our company and are committed to never having them. We don't need them. We hire Stakeholders who are self-managed adults and leaders in their own right. We practice HCD Leadership – leading to the Highest Common Denominator – which has created an environment in which everyone can reach for whatever motivates them to live their personal best, without regard to what the next person is doing or becoming.

Managers will not be tolerated in the Participation Age. To achieve rapid escape from the Industrial Age, companies will need to dump the manager role, and replace it with one-tenth as many leaders. Many existing managers have been taught to play dumb to their bosses, but would actually make great leaders if they were challenged to do so. Likewise, an awful lot of managers need to simply go back into production or be moved along if they don't want to work for a living. All the manager role is accomplishing is making people stupid and lazy with endless meetings, reports, conference calls, and other maintenance directives designed to make them look like they are adding value.

## MANAGERS MANAGE, LEADERS PRODUCE

Previous to the height of the Industrial Age and up through the 1870s, people who led other people were almost always adding some productive value of their own, instead of just managing others. This is one of the essential differences between leadership, which has existed for thousands of years, and management, which was invented just yesterday in relationship to the long history of work.

Leaders create vision and give general guidance and direction. They train, and provide infrastructure, but then they also do what they are asking others to do. Originally, the production superintendent would lead others, as well as jump in and work the line himself. He was well respected (leaders usually are) because he wasn't afraid to get his hands dirty, and did so regularly.

Managers focus on making others productive. Leaders focus on their own productivity, and inspire others to be more productive by their example. Because of Taylor's assumption that people are stupid and lazy, the Factory System leaders were turned into managers. In the modern company, that *middle layer* of hall monitors is now deeply embedded, and even in the smallest of companies, the owner believes they have to manage people instead of leading them.

> Leaders create vision and give general guidance and direction. They train, and provide infrastructure, but then they also do what they are asking others to do.

## MANAGE STUFF, LEAD PEOPLE

Management is good. Managers are bad. The fundamental flaw in the "manager as a solution" mindset is simply that people need to be managed. They don't. They need to be led, and the difference is not semantic – it is gigantic.

The Industrialist did their dead-level best to remake people into simple extensions of machines. If people are extensions of machines, we see them differently. Managing them becomes perfectly acceptable, and in fact, necessary. But if people are fully human, managing them is wholly unacceptable and dehumanizing. The simple principle is this: *manage stuff; lead people.* When people are extensions of machines, they are *stuff* to be managed. But if they are fully human, they require leadership instead.

In our company, we only manage stuff, which includes things like processes, systems, delivery of goods and services, accounting, marketing, sales, etc. These are all *things* to be managed, and everyone in the business manages stuff. We don't need someone with the title of *manager* to hover over any of us to ensure the stuff will get managed. The people manage the stuff, and we lead the people.

The simple principle is this: manage stuff; lead people.

Stuff definitely needs to be managed. It is inherently stupid and lazy. It needs to be told what to do; it doesn't have a brain of its own or any motivation to assemble itself. The packaging material and the product just sit on the counter until someone picks both of them up and puts them in the box in the appropriate packing process. Someone who is smarter and more motivated than the stuff needs to manage that process, but the smart and motivated people doing the packing do not need managing – they need to be led.

Every process, system, product, and service in a business is inherently stupid and lazy and needs to be managed.

## PEOPLE ARE NOT STUFF

Unfortunately, managers don't see much difference between the people and the process; in traditional management, people are extensions of machines or processes, and the manager believes both of them need the proactive involvement of a third party to make them work. The manager doesn't pack the box. The manager exists to closely monitor that a person doesn't just sit there like packing materials do. Sadly, the manager assumes the person is as inert as the packing materials, and must be *managed* to ensure the person will actually pick up the packing materials and put them in the box.

## LEADERS ARE PRODUCTIVE

A leader will do it quite differently. A leader will impart vision and guidance, including why we do what we do, metrics for success, and metrics for exceeding the objective. A leader will train and provide the necessary infrastructure and will create a process that requires the packing person or the process itself to proactively report to the leader regularly on how things are going.

Then the leader will do something extraordinary that the manager would rarely do – the leader will go away and be productive, too. Instead of hovering in the day care center, leaders will go somewhere and do something themselves that adds to the bottom line. Or, they might just be one of the packers on the team, and join right in being productive there, leading and motivating by example, not by threat, persuasion, cajoling, or hovering.

Managers *feel* productive – they have tons of monitoring on their plate. But a leader will lead by example, get in the trenches, and be one of the productive people. Leaders can afford to do this because the people they hired are Stakeholders, not employees, and don't need to live in a day care center where they are watched like four-year-olds. When managers are removed from the company, the work of the manager that adds no value disappears, and the few important things a manager might do get dispersed among all the adult Stakeholders. After Weisbord tore down the wall and eliminated the department managers, he was surprised at how little real work the Stakeholders had to assimilate from the former management positions.

## LEADERS MAKE FEW DECISIONS

I said this earlier, but it bears repeating: the art of leadership is to know how few times the leader should actually make the decision. A Participation Age company doesn't need top-heavy leadership, or managers who make a lot of decisions for others. The Stakeholders throughout the company are all adult leaders, and understand that if they have all the training and equipment they need, and clearly understand the objective required, they will gladly take the bull by the horns and *own* their tasks, jobs, processes, and results.

Leading instead of managing is not a new concept. A store owner prior to the Industrial Age hired someone else to stock shelves, trained them, gave them the tools needed to do it, and then that leader went back to being productive himself. If the stocker wasn't productive, he was let go and the leader got someone else who could self-manage. After training the new person, the leader went back to being productive again. Everyone produced something, whether it was maintenance, accounting, packing, new product development, or vision and leadership. No one stagnated, watching other people doing the work.

## THEORY X AND THEORY Y LEADERS

Douglas McGregor's highly acclaimed book, *The Human Side of Enterprise*, is a must read for anyone looking to bring a company into the Participation Age.[3] McGregor says there are two types of leaders. Theory X leaders assume people are largely unmotivated and therefore the manager must use close supervision, management, and clear hierarchy to ensure the productivity of employees. Theory Y leaders assume people are self-motivated and don't need the hierarchical constructs to be successful.

Too many companies have taken McGregor's Theory Y too far, creating a "Friend's Culture" model where compromise and consensus reign. McGregor never meant for such a kum-ba-yah result. There are parts of Theory X that are necessary and valid – leadership takes different forms in different situations. As an example, there is a need for strong visionary leadership when faced with decisions that affect the future of the company (new products, new processes, new people, new directions, new facilities, etc.). Strong, visionary leaders will have the courage to make decisions that may not engender support from the majority right away. Consensus is always popular, but many times ineffective. Leadership is not always popular, especially when it is being effective.

The Participation Age does not call for Theory Y compromise and consensus as the best and only way to lead. The Participation Age, and McGregor's combined Theory X/Y, call for the inclusion of everyone who will be affected by decisions in the discovery process. The Participation Age also demands that decisions, whenever possible, be made by the people most likely to have to carry them out. It also calls for unhooking people from the machine, giving everyone their brains back, and requiring that they be creative and innovative, solve problems, and stick their noses wherever they can. And it requires letting employees go who won't grow up, leave the day care center, and become Stakeholders.

> Consensus is always popular, but many times ineffective. Leadership is not always popular, especially when it is being effective.

## BUSINESS IS NOT A DEMOCRACY

Business is not a democracy at all levels. The most effective Participation Age business is a benign dictatorship, in which the founder or CEO uses his power and influence to empower everyone else to lead and make the company better. The Participation Age does not place leaders in the role of polling officers, tallying votes and making decisions based on what the majority wants. Visionary leaders regularly see things that others don't see, and it is their responsibility to move the boat of the company away from the rocks and toward new and great advances, even when few others can see it.

Participation Age leadership is based on servanthood – the willingness to use *power* for the betterment of the company and the people, not for self-promotion. Ricardo Semler's leadership of Semco in Brazil (see his wonderful book, *Maverick*) is a great example of someone who, through benign dictatorship, took a company mired in the tar pits of the Industrial Age, and in the face of ongoing objection from many around him, turned it into one of the best examples of a Participation Age company in the world, where democratic decision making now rules at almost every level, but not at the top.

> The most effective Participation Age business is a benign dictatorship, in which the founder or CEO uses his power and influence to empower everyone else to lead and make the company better.

## THE TITLE VS. THE TRENCHES

This "title" thing is another great way to see the difference between a leader and a manager. Management starts with an empty office and a title on the door. The company then goes out and finds someone to stick in that specific chair with that specific title. Because they have that title, you are now supposed to follow them, even though they have not demonstrated any reason why anyone should.

Contrast that to how leaders emerge. Leaders lead by example first – they are respected because they have done or are doing what they want you to do. They've been in the trenches. Secondly, people are following them without a title. They're being followed not because some corporate VP anointed them with an office, a chair, and a title on the door, but because they inspire, give great guidance, and help people get a clear direction where to go. They are already headed in that direction.

Very few leaders need to replace an awful lot of managers. Leaders impart vision, facilitate the development of teams, create an environment that will allow for success, champion the success of others, and use their authority to serve others in setting and reaching their own goals. When leaders lead, and employees become Stakeholders, we need a LOT fewer leaders than the managers they replace. And unlike managers, as they lead by example, these leaders will be productive and add personal value to the bottom line as well.

## LEADERS FOCUS ON RESULTS;
## MANAGERS FOCUS ON PROCESSES

Leaders help others develop their own goals, processes, and timelines. They FACILITATE the creativity, innovation, and general development of others while demonstrating how it's done, by doing it themselves. In contrast, managers set the goals themselves, tell others what they should do, how they should do it, and when they should be at work, just like Taylor preached. As a result, managers are much more focused on *processes* and how well the processes are executed, while leaders are focused largely on *results*. Leaders motivate others to develop their own great processes, and they know if the processes are good or bad because of the results they achieve.

## LEADERS GIVE OWNERSHIP

Managers get people focused on executing their processes, usually without input. Leaders motivate others to develop their own great processes, then focus on the results. When people *OWN* their processes and their results, instead of just executing someone else's process, with the leader championing them to do so, we see remarkable results. In the Afterword to this book, you will see how six hundred million people came out of poverty in China in just twenty years because people could once again own the fruit of their production and could decide how to make it happen without interference from management.

## PROFIT-SHARING IS ESSENTIAL
## IN THE PARTICIPATION AGE

To rid the world of managers, it is important to emphasize over and over again that profit-sharing is essential for creating a Stakeholder's culture. Next to owning a piece of the company, it is the highest form of ownership. If you won't profit-share, you are just another Industrialist using people for your own gain. Leaders champion the development of those around them for the sake of the whole. And leaders understand that if everyone shares in the fruit of their labors, they will take ownership of the entire process and of the company itself. You cannot preach *ownership* to people at the task, job, process, and result levels, and also not do profit-sharing. It is hypocrisy of the highest order. What you are saying is, "You can own everything except the increased profits. I'm keeping the fruit of your increased labor for myself."

> It is important to emphasize over and over again that profit-sharing is essential for creating a Stakeholder's culture.

If you do not profit-share, Stakeholders will not take over the former tasks of managers or even stay around. They will find a true Participation Age company in which to flourish and will make that company a lot of money, too.

## THE FEW, THE PROUD, THE LEADERS

In a Participation Age company, leaders are different from managers in two specific ways:

1. They lead by example. They don't get to lead because they have a title on the door they inherited. In a Participation Age company, people are called leaders only because others have decided to follow them. They come from the trenches, not from an ivory tower. They can help others because they themselves have done it. Even if they're no longer doing as much of it because they are putting more energy into leading, everyone knows that

they could jump right back in at any time to tackle a task, and many times do.

2. Leaders: you don't need many of them. Giant Corporation, Inc. is full to the brim with managers. When you replace managers with leaders, you'll find you need a lot fewer of them. The small percentage of real work that they do will easily be assimilated by the Stakeholders they used to manage.

*In a Participation Age company, people are called leaders only because others have decided to follow them.*

## MANAGERS VS. LEADERS

Here is a table of the differences between a manager and a leader. Take the test: Are you an Industrial Age manager, or a Participation Age leader?

| Manager | Leader |
|---|---|
| Makes people stupid and lazy when they aren't. | Frees people to be smart and motivated, because they are. |
| Manages by Title–Demands respect and requires submission by virtue of position. | Leads by Example–Inspires respect and attracts followers by virtue of production. |
| Oversees–Increases the production of others by measuring them. | Produces–Inspires others to be productive by being productive and showing the way. |
| Sets goals for others. | Helps others set their own goals. |
| Focuses on process. | Focuses on results. |
| Imposes accountability. | Gives ownership. |
| Pleases higher-ups. | Serves/champions the Stakeholders. |
| Engenders fear or deference to authority. | Encourages creativity, innovation, asking why, open communications. |
| Keeps people from making mistakes. | Allows people to learn from mistakes. |
| Promotes self–Becomes more important and takes credit. | Promotes others–Fades over time and becomes less important. |
| Browbeats people to make money. | Motivates people to Make Meaning, which makes more money. |
| Need a lot of them. | Need few official ones because everyone is a leader. |

If you want to know more about your leadership style, you can take our Apex Profile at http://ApexProfile.com. E-mail us at Grow@CranksetGroup.com and we'll send you a code to drop the price to US $10.00. It is a decision-making profile to help you understand the lens through which you view the business world and how you can make better decisions, who to hire to complement your strengths, and why you are having trouble or are doing well at building a business.

## SOME FINAL REASONS TO ELIMINATE MANAGERS

Jim Clifton, CEO of Gallup says, "The people picked to be managers account for the majority of variance in almost all performance-related outcomes," and says that seven out of ten managers "are not properly developing, or worse, are outright depressing seventy million of the hundred million US employees."[4]

Salary.com's research says fifteen of the top twenty reasons someone will leave your company are directly related to the managers under whom they must perform. (What a great reason to eliminate managers all by itself!) The biggest waste of time, according to 47 percent of respondents, is having to attend too many meetings. That's followed closely by having to deal with office politics.[5] If you remove managers and replace them with leaders, you eliminate fifteen of the top twenty reasons your best Stakeholders might leave you, and reduce some of the biggest time-wasters in business.

The Industrial Age is over – people are no longer stupid and lazy. Replace your managers with fewer leaders and watch your company grow.

Let's look at how some companies are doing it.

# EMBRACING THE PARTICIPATION AGE

1. What is your mindset? What one thing can you or your leadership do to move from LCD Management to HCD (Highest Common Denominator) Leadership?

   _____

   _____

   By When? _____ /_____ / _____ : _____ a.m./p.m.

2. Is there anyone in your organization who needs help moving from being a manager to being a leader? What one action is required to help that individual refocus?

   _____

   _____

   By When? _____ /_____ / _____ : _____ a.m./p.m.

## NOTES

1.  Ethan Mollick, *Why Middle Managers May Be the Most Important People in Your Company*, (in Knowledge@Wharton, May 25, 2011), http://bit.ly/1cmXDjr

2.  Marvin Weisbord, *Productive Workplaces Revisited* (San Francisco, CA: Jossey-Bass, 2004), 94.

3.  Douglas McGregor, *The Human Side Of Enterprise* (New York: McGraw-Hill, 2005).

4.  Jim Clifton, *The Chairman's Blog, Millions of Bad Managers Are Killing America's Growth*, (Gallup.com, Wednesday, June 19, 2013)  http://thechairmansblog.gallup.com/2013/06/millions-of-bad-managers-are-killing.html#comment-form.

5.  Salary.com, *Wasting Time at Work*, 2012 http://www.salary.com/wasting-time-at-work-2012/slide/11/.

# 9 to 5 Disease

> *"The day that we measured people by time clocks is long gone."*
> —RICARDO SEMLER, CEO, Semco manufacturing

Dear Father,

I received your letter on Thursday the 14th with much pleasure. I am well, which is one comfort. My life and health are spared, while others are cut off. Last Thursday, one girl fell down and broke her neck, which caused instant death. She was going in or coming out of the mill and slipped down, it being very icy. The same day, a man was killed by the railroad cars. Another had nearly all of his ribs broken. Another was nearly killed by falling down and having a bale of cotton fall on him. Last Tuesday, we were paid. In all I had $6.60. I paid $4.68 of it for board. With the rest, I got me a pair of rubbers and a pair of 50-cent shoes. Next payment, I am to have $1 a week beside my board....

I think that the factory is the best place for me and if any girl wants employment, I advise them to come to Lowell.

-Excerpt from a letter from Mary Paul, Lowell, Massachusetts mill girl, December 21, 1845.

## THE PROTESTANT/PURITAN WORK ETHIC

Working straight from 9:00 a.m. to 5:00 p.m. or 8:00 a.m. to 6:00 p.m., day in and day out, is a business disease of the Industrial Age. In the Participation Age, it too needs to go away. Fortunately, there are many companies, including some manufacturing companies with thousands of employees that are leading the way.

As with all the diseases of the Industrial Age, working with ceaseless regularity and rigid hours is a very new thing in the history of work. We didn't evolve into it because we discovered it was a better way to live. As many Participation Age manufacturing companies are demonstrating today, it wasn't even necessary for success. Quite to the contrary, it was imposed on us solely for the benefit of a very few power-hungry Industrialists building their fiefdoms.

Working this way is not natural or something we would choose, and we aren't actually very good at it. We waste massive amounts of time attempting to work nine or ten straight hours, five or six days in a row. And those who are at work the longest waste the most time.

Fortunately, as with all the business diseases of the Industrial Age, this one is fading. We're finding that even in the most industrial of manufacturing facilities, we don't need the rigid workday to build a great and lasting company. As the Industrial Age fades behind us, we are very quickly reverting back to work rhythms that served us for centuries, because these more natural work rhythms respond to our need to be human, not to be extensions of machines.

Ricardo Semler, head of the manufacturing giant Semco says, "We want people to work on a structure of their own. You don't have to show up at a certain time, and you can change your pattern at anytime. We don't want to see you at the office – we don't even have a head office. The day that we measured people by time clocks is long gone. We don't want to know when or how you're working, only if you're fulfilling your commitment."

> "We don't want to know when or how you're working, only if you're fulfilling your commitment."
> -Ricardo Semler

## THE PROTESTANT WORK ETHIC
## LEADS TO INDUSTRIALISM

Semco has come a long way from the Industrial Age and its new and strange work ethic. The spread of Protestantism in the 1600s and 1700s brought with it a shift in the classical view of work that created a perfect justification for the Factory System when it came roaring in around 1800.[1] Max Weber, the German economic sociologist, coined a term for these new beliefs about work, calling it the "Protestant ethic." The key elements of Weber's Protestant ethic were:

1. diligence
2. punctuality
3. deferment of gratification (enjoy retirement later)
4. primacy of the work domain[2]

Two of these foundational beliefs of the Protestant ethic – punctuality and primacy of the work domain – laid the foundation for Industrialists to demand, for the first time in history, that people show up for regularly scheduled, rigid workdays. The other two beliefs – diligence and deferment of gratification – supported that new demand; if you're diligent at work, you can enjoy yourself later in life after retirement. It quickly became a badge of honor to leave your home and invest the majority of, and the best of your time, at work, with regular work hours extending to as much as fourteen hours, six days a week.

## THE WORKDAY BEFORE THE AGE OF MACHINES

The primacy of the centralized workspace, and the rigidity of 9 to 5 as the central rhythm of our life, stem from these early Protestant views of work, not from observing the natural patterns of human productivity.

All you have to do is look at the thousands of years that preceded the Factory System to see that this is not normal or the best way to ensure productivity. Before the age of machines, farm, store, and shop work did not have the ceaseless regularity of the Factory System. We worked hard in spurts during the day, week, and year, revolving around planting and the harvest. Instead of a rigid workday schedule, the most important factor in the preindustrial world was the individual's dedication to accomplishing the task, or a Results-Based system of work. What mattered was if you got the crop planted, not if your tractor was in the parking lot by 7:00 a.m. and you didn't leave until 6:00 p.m.

## A SHIFT FROM THE RESULTS-BASED SYSTEM TO A TIME-BASED SYSTEM

In the 1850s, for the first time in the history of man, we shifted from measuring people based on their results to measuring them based on how much time they spent at the workplace. Thousands of years of a Results-Based work system was replaced with a very new and very strange Time-Based system. People were now being rewarded by packing a minimal number of pickles each day, in a centralized location, until the clock ran out.

## NOT THE BEST-LAID PLANS

The Industrialists didn't think this through very well. They leaned heavily on the Protestant ethic to motivate people to go to work, but another facet of that same Protestant ethic was that "by hard work the individual could be master of his own fate."[3] When we worked for ourselves on farms, in workshops, and in stores, we were masters of our own results. We could decide to bust our buns and then enjoy an afternoon siesta. But the Factory System violated this tenet of the Protestant ethic and demanded harder work for even less freedom. In the

Factory System, you were no longer master of your fate, no matter how productive you were.

So, the Industrial Age was not a natural evolution of work into a more modern and better way of doing things. Instead, it was an interruption in our age-old commitment to accomplishing the task in the shortest time possible, and was built on Frederick Taylor's broken idea that most people are inherently lazy.

The Time-Based system most companies still use today is not "the better way." It worked a lot better for tying humans to inflexible machines for the benefit of the Industrialist. Semco, the Brazilian manufacturing giant, has shown it actually was a bad idea for the factory as well (more on Semco in chapter 12). Fortunately, research is consistently showing that the faster we get back to our preindustrial Results-Based system of work, the more productive we will be as a society.

> In the Factory System, you were no longer master of your fate, no matter how productive you were.

## THIS ISN'T A GENERATIONAL THING

Don't blame the Millennials for the need to change the way we approach work. Studies show that every generation has the desire to Make Meaning at work as their highest value, with salary and other extrinsic values way down the list. Jennifer Deal has found that, "All generations have similar values; they just express them differently." We might have unique ways of getting there, but we pretty much want the same things out of work.[3]

## WHY DOESN'T 9 TO 5 WORK?

Regularly scheduled, rigid workdays, with a whistle on both ends of the day to let you know when you should start and stop shoveling, was invented by Industrial elitists. It started with the textile mills in England in the late 1700s. In 1784, the newly opened Quarry Bank Mill in Cheshire, England took kids from the orphanages and conscripted them to run the machines six to seven days a week in exchange for food and a bed. This was an extreme but classic example of Industrialist disregard for the human in favor of profit. Quarry Bank, and many others like it, continued the conscription practice for an astounding sixty-three years until the last indentured child left the Quarry Bank factory in 1847.

It is an important irony to note that this type of child abuse was where the Factory System had its roots. Where you start is unfortunately many times where you end up. The Industrialists knew the best employees would be children who had no voice of their own and wouldn't ask why. It is not an auspicious beginning, and significantly colored the development of the Factory System throughout the 1800s into the 1900s. The best employees were always childlike, submissive, compliant, and didn't ask why.

American textile mills weren't much better. The Industrial Age in America can be traced to the first textile mills opening in the Boston area in 1813 and staffed largely by single women. Mary Paul, who wrote the opening letter in this chapter, was grateful for such a wretched existence. In 1845, she went to work in the mills where eight thousand other girls and single women worked, ranging from ten years old to thirty-five. She was sixteen, and not indentured, but working conditions were no better than in England. She had to be at the mill by 5:00 a.m., got thirty minutes for breakfast, lunch, and dinner, plus two 15-minute breaks, and got off at 7:00 p.m.: a fourteen- hour day. That's seventy to eighty-four hours per week, depending on how often she worked Saturdays.[4] The good news is that she actually got paid a little, a perk the English orphans never experienced.

## THE INDUSTRIALISTS LIKED IT, BUT. . .

The Industrialists found the rigid workday served them well. It was an ideal construct of the Factory System. For the Industrialist to dominate the world and squeeze every last dime out of the existing economy, their machines had to run twenty-four hours a day, seven days a week. The most efficient way to do that was to use people as extensions of machines and put them on regular, rigidly set schedules. The humans had to adapt to the machines, because the machines were not about to adapt to the humans.

The corporation didn't think about whether it was dehumanizing. They could always get another unskilled laborer to fill in if one of them complained, slowed down, or got hurt. The Mary Pauls of the world knew it and were grateful to be one of the machine extensions who had a job.

The textile industry in the late 1700s in England was the early adapter and the model that led the rest of the world into the Factory System. Until 1850, most manufacturing was still being done in homes and barns. But from 1850 on, it gradually became the rigid 9 to 5, or more like the 5:00 a.m.-7:00 p.m. of Mary Paul's workday, and, in many cases, six days a week.

The Industrialists of the late 1800s pushed the rigid hours paradigm as far as they could. It seemed reasonable that if they could get fourteen hours out of someone, they would do it. But in 1896, Fredrick Taylor found that working a few hours less per week could actually make the stupid and lazy people more productive. People worked fifty-three hours or more per week in 1900, but thanks to Taylor and others, the work week went down over the next forty-five years to an average of thirty-nine hours a week, largely where it stands today.

This wasn't by way of being kind or as a result of anyone asking what was best for the laborer. They simply found they had pushed the work week to the point at which more hours were actually less productive. So, when companies figured out it was more profitable to hire a few more workers and shorten the shifts, they did so as quickly as they could. It was still all about the company and the best way to squeeze every last dime of productivity out of people.

That same rigid Factory System has followed us out of the Industrial Age into the Participation Age, with most employees (not Stakeholders) still punching clocks, even if they are not operating machines. The Industrialists in charge of today's front office assume they benefit from a Time-Based system, simply by default, because, to their knowledge, it's always been done that way.

## IT WAS NEVER A GOOD IDEA

But a good Capitalist understands that it was never a good idea. The Results-based structure of Participation Age companies is exposing the folly of the Time-Based system.[5] Even manufacturing companies with thousands of Stakeholders, like Semco, have discovered that their people are more productive without it. Yet, the corporate attachment to this model is so strong that companies like Yahoo are going backward and requiring everyone to show up at the company day care center during every workday.

In early 2013, Yahoo's CEO, Marisa Mayer, returned to the comfortable, time-worn Factory System model; instead of leading, she herded all of Yahoo's employees back into the office day care center because there were a lot of people goofing off at home. As a result, the few great Stakeholders remaining are being managed to the Lowest Common Denominator. The result will be that the lazy people will goof off in the office day care center instead of at home, and the Stakeholders being LCDed to death will leave.

## THE TIME-BASED VS. RESULTS-BASED MODEL

The Time-Based model doesn't work anyway. And according to a joint study by Salary.com, Microsoft, and America Online, American employees are *AT* work an average of forty-five hours, but only actually working for twenty-nine hours a week. They work three days a week and waste the other two. Yet, CEOs are convinced they can get more productivity by forcing them to assemble early at the office day care center and leave as late as possible. Various surveys blame surfing the net, going to worthless meetings (Microsoft found 71 percent of meetings aren't productive), and not having reasonable processes in place as big wastes of time.[6]

Over the years, in nonmanufacturing companies, the Time-Based model has evolved into "the car in the parking lot the longest wins," regardless of productivity. Productivity is almost an afterthought in a Time-Based company. Everyone is rewarded based more on how long they have hung around than on how much and how well they have produced.

> Productivity is almost an afterthought in a Time-Based company. Everyone is rewarded based more on how long they have hung around than on how much and how well they have produced.

This attachment to the rigid workday invented by the nineteenth-century Industrialists has resulted in the Time-Based cultural paradigm that is pervasive in the modern company, and which makes it difficult to Make Meaning, not just money. Traci Salazar, a member in one of our 3to5 Club business advisory groups, told me, "When my baby, Isabella, was born, I decided I wanted to invest in her. I worked for a major insurance carrier and was a long-term employee. I was a bit naïve; I just thought if I asked, they would give me a part-time position or at least consider it. But to my surprise, they said no. So I started my own company.

"Now that Izzy is ten years old, I'm ramping things up and building a company behind me. When I look back on it, it still amazes me how that corporation did not take the time to consider how much it had invested in me, and how much loyalty it would have received from me if it had moved toward me just a little during that time." Traci found out that Industrialists don't move toward anyone; you move toward them or you move on.

The Participation Age companies we profile later in chapter 12 work very hard to accommodate the Traci Salazars in their companies. They realize the long-term value of having Stakeholders like them on board.

## 9 TO 5—A DISEASE, NOT A CURE

The 9 to 5 "car in the parking lot" mindset is the root of many of the most ineffective practices in business. It is responsible for mindless practices like annual pay raises, which reward people for hanging around and warming a chair for another year. Holiday bonuses are another ineffective, Time-Based practice.

Easily, the worst result of the 9 to 5 Time-Based mindset is how most companies do layoffs. Most frequently, they are based on seniority. The car in the parking lot for the longest number of years wins. Laying off an incredibly productive Stakeholder who has only been there a year, in order to keep a comfortable middle manager who adds almost no value but has ten years sitting on the job, is the wrong message to send to the workforce. In the Participation Age, nobody deserves a job just because they warmed a seat longer than the next guy. When companies adhere to policies like that, they are managing to the Lowest Common Denominator, and deserve to end up with an office full of seat warmers. The Stakeholders looking for recognition of the results they produce will go somewhere else.

In virtually every case in which we have helped a company shift from a rigid Time-Based culture to a flexible Results-Based culture, the number of hours per Stakeholder spent at work have gone down, productivity has remained the same or gone up, and Stakeholder satisfaction has increased significantly. They are now able to make more meaning with their lives.

One CEO of a fifty-Stakeholder company said that after they shifted from "cars in the parking lot" to "results," he regularly had people thanking him for the transformation to a Results-Based environment. Another surprise to the CEO was that the two people he had always held up as the superstars (they worked the longest hours for years) were now the two they had the most questions about. After shifting to a Results-Based culture, these two were still working fifty-five-hour weeks while everyone else had figured out how to get the work done in thirty-seven hours a week. They may have to let them go because the Results-Based work environment has revealed that being at work the longest was their best attribute, not productivity.

## WHERE DO YOU GET WORK DONE?

Going in *to* the office from 9 to 5 doesn't work for Millennials anymore, and much less today for any other cohort group than in previous decades. Eighty-nine percent want to do work when and where they would choose, and only 11 percent would presently choose to work in an office.[7] That same survey found the two biggest motivators for Millennials are freedom and flexibility. Not surprisingly, 40 percent more Millennials are quitting their jobs to go to work for themselves than did older generations.

Jason Fried of 37Signals says he often asks people where they get work done. They mention porches, coffee shops, airplanes, an extra room, or a time of day like early in the morning. But almost no one ever mentions the office. That's because they go to work and trade a full day of work for what he labels "work moments"; bits of productivity interrupted largely by managers and meetings (the two worst culprits), conference calls, and other people tapping you on the shoulder who aren't being productive either.[8]

Yes, there are distractions at home or at the coffee shop, but they are largely distractions you can decide to ignore. At work, almost all the distractions are of someone else's choosing. And when you get into a highly productive binge at home, you can ignore the world until you've finished. That never happens in the 9 to 5 workplace. At best, we get an hour or so of uninterrupted time a few days a week. Getting into a deep rhythm of productivity is nearly impossible.

## WORK HARD, PLAY HARD

We were not made to work regular, rigid schedules with only short breaks to eat or take the traditional smoke break. It's not natural or normal and has only been around for a very short period in the history of man. Fortunately, for the most part, it's not necessary in our postindustrial world.

Most importantly, we're more productive when we don't have to. We should integrate work and play. Thorough studies of productivity show that we are more productive when we can invest two to four hours in focused work, get a big break to do something like take a bike ride, go swimming, or climb a rock wall, and then dive in for another two to three hours.

The Time-Based, 9 to 5 culture with its roots in the English textile mills is an important early business disease that caused or contributed to a lot of others. It is the core disease that causes people to waste massive amounts of time at work playing politics about whose car was there first, and it results in our inability to work and play in the natural rhythms of life that make us more productive.

> Moving to a Results-Based culture is one of the best sweeping changes a company can make if it wants to escape the gravitational pull of the Industrial Age.

Moving to a Results-Based culture is one of the best sweeping changes a company can make if it wants to escape the gravitational pull of the Industrial Age. And it doesn't have to be a slow, decade-long change. We've seen companies of fifty or more employees move from Time-Based employees to Results-Based Stakeholders in six to eighteen months, reducing work hours by 10-20 percent or more while maintaining or increasing productivity. The leader has to want to do it, then work hard to change it.

## WASTED TIME SITTING AT A DESK

The movie *Office Space* is a classic parody of the twenty-first-century Industrial Age company. Two efficiency consultants ask an employee about his workday. The employee responds by saying he goofs off playing video games, goes to a long lunch, pretends to work most of the day, and generally does just a few hours of real work. They recommend him for a management position because he appears to be "underchallenged."

A recent survey called *Wasting Time at Work* by Salary.com, showed that the average employee (not Stakeholder) wastes more than 25 percent of the workday, or 2.09 hours a day, excluding lunch and scheduled breaks, doing nothing. Why? It's not because they are lazy, but because we have set up a system that grades them on time spent in the office, not on productivity.

The Factory System model in place in most modern companies still rewards people for their *presence,* not their *production.* It's a system of mistrust based on management's belief that employees are lazy, and this survey shows the employees are living down to our worst expectations of them.[9]

> The Factory System model in place in most modern companies still rewards people for their presence, not their production.

Presence isn't a good measure of effectiveness. A *Fast Company* article in 2013 reported that the higher the number of work hours someone reported, the more likely that person was to overestimate how much he worked. People reporting seventy-five hours were actually working about fifty true hours, and fifty-five reported hours were actually forty-five.[10] People exaggerate the number of hours worked because most of them work in Time-Based cultures.

In a Results-Based culture it is quite different. In this culture, people do not work rigid hours with ceaseless regularity, and instead do so in spurts when needed. If someone claims to be working in a Results-Based culture, but works a consistent thirty-two, thirty-six, forty-two, etc. hours every single week, that should raise some concern. Stakeholders are owners, and owners never work regular hours. Stakeholders' hours will change week to week, and should look more like thirty-five hours, forty-five, forty-nine, thirty-three, forty-one, thirty-one, etc.

## RESULTS-BASED DEADLINES AND INCENTIVES

Moving to a Results-Based culture includes more emphasis on deadlines and less emphasis on rigid work hours – get this done by Tuesday; I don't care where you are in the meantime. The same Salary.com survey found that the third biggest issue with job dissatisfaction was that people had no deadlines, and, more importantly, no incentives to work harder. People who don't feel invested in the work they do are less motivated and more likely to waste time, which ultimately leads to lower productivity.

The lesson here is simple – give people clear deadlines for when things should be done, with the incentive that if they can get it done without you looking over their shoulder, they can have a more flexible work life for achieving it. If people get their work done by 2:00 p.m., they should go home and play with their kids. If they are Stakeholders, they will be even more productive going forward. If they are employees, they will abuse this a couple of times and you will move them along to find a business day care center where they can be children. Doing so will ensure that everyone gets the message that we expect they will be self-managed adults.

Mary Paul's letter to her father should motivate us to move away from the Factory System of the Industrial Age and embrace Participation Age work patterns that rehumanize work as an integral part of life.

The next chapter discusses *Separation of Work and Play*, another business disease very closely tied to 9 to 5 Disease.

# EMBRACING THE PARTICIPATION AGE

1. What is your mindset? What one thing can you do to shift from a Time-Based culture (rewards based on being "present") to a Results-Based culture (rewards for production)?

   _____

   _____

   By When? ____ /____ / ____ : ____ a.m./p.m.

2. Is there anyone in your organization who needs help refocusing on results instead of activity/presence? What one action is required to help that individual refocus?

   _____

   _____

   By When? ____ /____ / ____ : ____ a.m./p.m.

## NOTES

1. Peter D. Anthony, *The Ideology of Work* (New York, NY: Routledge, 1977, 2009).

2. Michael Rose, *Reworking the Work Ethic: Economic Values and Sociocultural Politics* (London: Batsford Academic and Educational, 1985).

3. *What Millennials Really Want Out of Work*, Adam Grant, *HuffingtonPost.com*, The Blog, August 2, 2013 1:49pm http://huff.to/15Tr6YT

4. Harriet Robinson, *Early Factory Labor in New England Internet History Sourcebooks Project*, 1883. Retrieved on August 27, 2007.

5. *The Work Ethic, Then and Now*, Seymour Martin Lipset, National Affairs Magazine, Issue Number 98 ~ Winter 1990 07/2011 http://bit.ly/16oj3GH.

6. *Global Workplace Analytics and the Telework Research Network, GlobalWorkplaceAnalytics.com,* htt p://www.globalworkplaceanalytics.com/telecommuting-statistics, October 2012.

7. *Millennials and the Future of Work, Survey* by Millennial Branding and oDesk, 2012.

8. Jason Fried, *Why We Can't Work Done At Work*, Tedx Midwest, Filmed October 2010 http://www.ted.com/talks/jason_fried_why_work_doesn_t_happen_at_work.html.

9. *Wasting Time at Work, Salary.com*, 2008 http://www.salary.com/articles/articledetail. asp?part=par1083.

10. Laura Vanderkam, *The Truth About How Much Workaholics Actually Work* (FastCompany.com, April 25, 2013).

# Separation of Work and Play

*Every day I go to work.*

*When I get to work, I park, leave myself in the car, and head into work.*

*At lunch, I always try to come back out and reunite with myself for a few minutes before I have to leave myself in the car, and go back into work.*

*I do this every day.*

*And in the evenings, I always hope I get off in time to reunite with myself before I'm gone.*

In the dark ages of blogging, back around 2005, I read the above blog post by a young kid in his early twenties. It rattled my cage and probably had as much to do with waking me up to the human carnage of the Industrial Age as any other single experience. I never bookmarked it, and a few years later I went back to find it, but never could. But it made such an impression on me that to this day I can write a pretty close reproduction of it.

He sounds a little like Mary Paul's brother (see Mary Paul's letter home at the beginning of chapter 6). But this wasn't a kid writing in 1845 about his experience in the mill. This was someone in his early twenties writing in 2005 about his experience working in the front office in modern, corporate America.

What an incredibly insightful blog post. This guy was telling us in no uncertain terms how the continued presence of the Industrial Age in the front office, the Dilbert Society, was working out for him. Not well at all. The Industrial Age had given him a standard of living unparalleled in human history, but it hadn't improved his life. Instead, his work experience was actually dehumanizing his life. Mary Paul could have written something very similar, just not with a computer.

## WHAT WOULD LEAD TO THIS VIEW OF WORK?

For centuries, community was built around work and small markets. The kids ran and played, learned and worked, the grandparents helped out – everyone was involved. When work was slow, people played more, and when it picked up at harvest time, or in the mornings when the cow needed milking, they put their hands to it. Barn raisings, quilting bees, and even harvest times brought everyone in the community together as families to work, play, and socialize.

## THE OLD (AND RETURNING) NORMAL

Frederick Taylor's quote opening this chapter made it clear how we would change all that to work in the twentieth century: we should "work where we work and play where we play, and not mix the two."[1] Taylor may have considered it "a matter of ordinary common sense" to separate work and play, but it's not normal, it's not human, and it doesn't help productivity in the Participation Age. Separating work and play is another business disease instituted during the Industrial Age as a cure that ended up being the disease itself.

The Industrialists interpreted Taylor as saying we needed to clean up the human being and make him as much like a machine as possible. Getting people to leave play at home was one of those smart, dehumanizing tactics that Taylor believed would get people to work better as extensions of machines. The machines didn't play; we shouldn't, either.

Who did this bit of Taylorism benefit? The Industrialist. Remember, one of the main attributes of Industrialists is that they are users, not creators. They use people and resources to pull money and power up through a cash cow hierarchy to themselves. Separating work from play was one more step that stripped people of their humanity so the Industrialist could use them to create more money and power for himself.

## AN EVOLVING DISEASE

As with all the business diseases of the Industrial Age, this trade-off wasn't some kind of grand conspiracy; it just evolved over time. The machines needed to be run twenty-four hours a day, and the company needed people to be there on a regular schedule to make them go. People needed money, and the money was only available by trading the best time of our day, year, and life to get it.

So we did, and over time, it just became *normal*. But in the Participation Age, separation of work and play doesn't fit anymore.

## TIME IS THE NEW MONEY

As the Industrial Age grows more distant in the rear-view mirror, something else has changed radically; time is the new money, just the opposite of the Factory System.

The Industrialist says, "You give me the best time of your day, the best time of your week, and the best forty-five years of your life, and I'll give you some money." He gives you a nearly infinite resource, money, in exchange for your very finite one, time. The carrot at the end of the stick is that you'll get time later, when you retire . . . if you're still alive, of course.

In the Participation Age, when you give people their time back, they will make you money. Time is the new money.

Over 150 years of continually accepting this trade-off actually has us believing that money is more valuable than time. But the younger generation, less affected by Industrial Age nonsense, isn't buying it. For them, Making Meaning is more important, and having the time to do it is the answer. Time is the new money. In the Participation Age, when you give people their time back, they will make you money.

## AT WORK, BUT NOT WORKING

In today's office, we are *AT* work more since the advent of the Factory System, but are also wasting more time there. Bob Kustka, founder of Fusion Factor, says, "The longer you work, the less efficient you are. Working energy, like physical energy, is best used in spurts, where we work hard on a few focused activities and then take a brief respite." To an Industrialist, those *respites* are wasted time. These intermingled "spurts" of work and respite are not encouraged by our leftover Factory System model. We are taught to buckle down for nine hours straight, then go home and blow off steam. Yet, all the research and thousands of years of human history tell us that we don't function well that way.

"Working energy is best used in spurts, where we work hard on a few focused activities and then take a brief respite."

Louis Efron says, "Defining work in such a traditional manner doesn't make sense to employees in today's constantly interconnected and fast-paced world. For businesses, this means that attracting, engaging, and retaining top talent depends on reinventing their work environments, blurring the line between work and play.[2]

Participation Age companies are figuring that out. And they understand that it is not so much *WHEN* work gets done, but, as Kustka said previously, *IF* it gets done. In 2013, the billion-dollar online retailer Zappos announced it would move its headquarters from Henderson, Nevada to the Old Las Vegas City Hall in downtown Las Vegas. Tony Hsieh's reason, "I want to be in an area where everyone feels like they can hang out all the time and where there's not a huge distinction between working and playing."

## RESULTS-BASED: GET DONE. GO HOME.

In an article questioning the prevalence of the forty-hour work week, David Cain expressed what a lot of people feel. "Under these working conditions (forty hour work week), people have to build a life in the evenings and on weekends. The last thing I want to do when I get home from work is exercise. It's also the last thing I want to do after dinner or before bed or as soon as I wake, and that's really all the time I have on a weekday… our free time is so scarce."[3]

A Participation Age Capitalist will help people understand that if their work is done, they should go home. An Industrialist will instead introduce "time creep." They will figure out how to immediately increase the metrics, with the reasoning that if the worker can now get "X" done in six hours, I'll just increase the workload so they get X+2 done in eight hours. A Participation Age company won't do that.

## TOP MOTIVATORS—MAKING MEANING

Three things motivate people more than money in the Participation Age.[4]

1. Flexible work schedule – let me decide when I work.

2. Praise and Recognition – catching people doing something right helps them Make Meaning, not just money. It's one of the most effective, non-monetary rewards around.

3. Breaking up the workday – studies show productivity goes up if we take a break in the middle of the day and do something unrelated to work – take a walk, ride a bike, go for a swim, visit an aquarium.[5]

Fortunately, more recent generations don't have the baggage of having grown up in the Industrial Age and are leading a peaceful revolution against separation of work and play. They expect their lives to be fulfilling, meaningful, significant, and enjoyable *RIGHT NOW* – not when they retire. It's mystifying to their parents because it looks like they're not willing to "settle down and get a job."

Time is indeed the new money, just like it used to be before the Industrial Age interrupted our normal patterns of life. Stakeholders expect to integrate work and play, not unnaturally separate the two.

## PRESENCE VS. PRODUCTION

In 2002, a young web designer friend of mine who was just one year out of college was given a huge pay raise by a very small branding agency, from a great starting salary to almost double that. Not a bad raise for one year of work. The company saw him as indispensable and didn't want him going anywhere else. A few months later, as winter approached, he quit. Why? Because they wanted him there for a full, uninterrupted, Industrial Age workday, and as a committed cyclist, the only time in the winter to ride was in the afternoon.

> Stakeholders expect to integrate work and play, not unnaturally separate the two.

He could have worked in the evening, and that would have had no impact on the company, but it was stuck in the Time-Based, Industrial Age construct that valued his presence more than his production. It was otherwise a very forward-thinking company, but the front office was still insisting on the same tired "money for hours" deal that was dominant in the Factory System. My friend now runs his own successful company and goes for a run or bike ride in the middle of the day, any time he wants. The small company he had worked for that demanded the separation of work and play is still focused on cars in the parking lot.

## YOU GIVE ME TIME, I'LL MAKE YOU MONEY

Imagine if the company above had encouraged my friend the young web designer/bike rider to ride his bike during the afternoons and work at home in the evenings. He might still be making them a lot of money with his world-class work. Instead, he created his own world where he didn't have to trade time for money, and now he gets to keep more of both. He now frequently works from places like Amsterdam, New York, San Francisco, and the coffee shops around his home. And he rides his bike during the day.

Sara Sutton Fell, CEO of FlexJobs, says people want workplace flexibility over a promotion. "Today, more and more top-level talent are foregoing promotions in favor of what really matters most to them -- work-life balance.[6]

## WEALTH (FREEDOM), NOT RICHES (MONEY)

Getting rich is an Industrial Age construct. Being wealthy is a much more evolved mindset. Riches equal money, but wealth equals freedom – the ability to choose what to do with my time and my money. In the Participation Age, we understand that money does not give us freedom, only the combination of money and time can do that. The Industrial Age couldn't afford to offer us both. But today, companies that are giving people time are now making more money. Give them more money and they will leave. Give them time, and Stakeholders will make you more money.

McKinsey & Company reports that 25 percent of all work can now easily be done from home.[7] Telework Research Network says at least 40 percent of work can be done part-time from home.[8] The amount of work that can easily be done from home is growing rapidly.

*CNN Money* reported in February 2012 that 70 percent of PricewaterhouseCoopers' Stakeholders telecommute, as do 80 percent of Intel's staff and 90 percent of Cisco's.[9] And years of solid research show that people are more productive working from home in an environment that does not separate work and play.

The Center for Talent Innovation (CTI) cites that flexible work arrangements are highly desired by 87 percent of Baby Boomers, 79 percent of Generation-Xers, and 89 percent of Millennials. Their research supports our belief that time is the new money: "*Companies that treat time as currency — through remote work options, staggered hours, and reduced-hour arrangements — are also more likely to attract and retain high-caliber employees.*" And productivity goes up – a win-win.[10]

> Riches equal money, but wealth equals freedom – the ability to choose what to do with my time and my money.

Fortune Magazine says many technology experts are convinced most people in the near future won't need offices as we know them. Our company, Crankset Group, typifies that. We have a good-sized space leased at an office complex for workshops and meetings with clients, and we rent other spaces around town, but at the writing of this book, all of our Stakeholders, including me, work from their own house – there isn't any "office space" at our office.

Virgin Group founder Richard Branson said employees are often more productive when you give them freedom and flexibility. "We like to give people the freedom to work where they want, safe in the knowledge that they have the drive and expertise to perform excellently, whether they are at their desks or in their kitchens," Branson wrote. "Yours truly has never worked out of an office, and never will."

## COMPANIES THAT GET IT

I started this book with a story about one of my many trips to Africa, and have sprinkled stories about our company in Africa here and there throughout this book. I'm sure many readers immediately assumed that I could do that because I owned the company. In the Industrial Age mindset, that kind of flexibility is only available to the guy who owns the business. But Mayur Singh, a vice-president of HSBC, one of the largest banks in the world, spends six months of the year working at an eco-conservation project (a lot more time away from work than I take as an owner), and six months in the HSBC office working.

He's not alone. In India, HSBC launched its Flexible Work Arrangement initiative, allowing any employee to participate like Mayur Singh. The result? Productivity has shot up in 88 percent of the participants, and has not declined at all in those who have decided not to participate (nobody's whining about Singh not being in the office – they are all adult Stakeholders).[11] In a Results-Based culture, Stakeholders are all motivated to make the company more money by having more wealth – freedom to choose what to do with their time.

Patagonia, a manufacturer of pricey athletic clothing, encourages its thirteen hundred Stakeholders to take off during any work day to ride a bike or go surfing. It also gives them two full weeks of paid leave if they will use it to serve a nonprofit of their choosing. They understand that separating work and the rest of someone's life is an artificial and unhelpful separation. The company is better off recognizing the natural daily rhythms of life.

A Portland-based management consulting company called Point B, with over four hundred Stakeholders, offers the same vacation time and paid holidays as our company does – none. They do it differently than we do, though. We pay salaries, whereas Point B pays only for time worked. One Stakeholder gushed, "I've never worked anywhere that was as committed to helping employees realize what the work-life balance means to them individually."[12]

Many of the Bigs are getting in on the action. At IBM, 40 percent of their entire workforce has no office. Sun Microsystems saved US $400 million between 2006 and 2012 with 50 percent of its workforce at home. Nearly 33 percent of AT&T managers don't have an office address, either. And 85 percent of big company executives expect a big jump in the number of people working without an office over the next five years.

## IT'S NOT OPTIONAL

Too many people reading this through an Industrialist's eyes are going to say they just won't play in the new Participation Age sandbox and don't need to; there will be plenty of stupid and lazy people left over with which to squeeze the last dime out of the existing matrix. They are wrong. The Millennials are a much smaller workforce than their predecessors, and true to Capitalism, they will make their own rules.

A recent PricewaterhouseCoopers report says:

> The idea that companies would source talent needs from an unlimited supply of workers from emerging markets has not materialized. Talent

shortages are just as critical in China, India, Eastern Europe, and parts of South America. **By 2020, we believe the people supply will be the most critical driving factor for business success.** Companies may go to extreme lengths in their search for talent, and once they have it, they will take measures to keep people 'locked in' to their organizations. Without this talent, they will be unable to compete.[13]

The work world is changing. In the Age of Participation with a shrinking workforce, Stakeholders will decide for themselves which organizations are desirable and which are not. They will use measurements such as culture, employer brand identity in the world around them, and the company's willingness to engage in Making Meaning, not just money, to make that choice.

We are beginning to see a dramatic shift in the employer-employee relationship. As the PricewaterhouseCoopers study said, "The employee may call the shots in tomorrow's world. Competition for good people will be higher than ever in the coming years."[14] In the Industrial Age, the company held all the cards. In the Participation Age, the shoe is on the other foot, even in weak recoveries like the one that started in 2009.

> With a shrinking workforce, Stakeholders will decide for themselves which organizations are desirable and which are not.

## TIME IS SCARCE, MONEY IS NEARLY INFINITE

The Industrial Age practice of trading time for money has been exposed as a disease, not a cure. Going forward, the shrinking workforce will put the Stakeholder in charge, and what the Stakeholder wants is to Make Meaning, not just money, and to do it all the time.

A Capitalist who is always thinking about the long-term health of his company will understand that helping people get back to a normal blend of work and play will be the best for the company in the long run.

In the Participation Age, time is the new money. Companies that figure out how to compensate Stakeholders as much with time as with money will do well going forward. The Industrialists will cling to the status quo, and future books will report last seeing them rearranging the deck chairs around their factories on the way down.

# EMBRACING THE
# PARTICIPATION AGE

1. What is your mindset? What one thing can we do to encourage the reintegration of work and play?

   _____

   _____

   By When? ____ /____ / ____ :____a.m./p.m.

2. Is there anyone in your organization who needs specific assistance reintegrating work and the rest of his world? What one action is required to help that individual refocus?

   _____

   _____

   By When? ____ /____ / ____ :____a.m./p.m.

## NOTES

1. Frederick Winslow Taylor, *The Principles of Scientific Management* (New York, NY, USA and London, UK: Harper & Brothers, 1911), 87 LCCN 11010339. http://en.wikipedia.org/wiki/Frederick_Winslow_Taylor

2. *Six Reasons Your Best Employees Quit You*, Louis Efron, Forbes.com 6/24/2013 @ 10:40PM, http://onforb.es/1f54aex

3. *Your Lifestyle Has Already Been Designed*, David Cain, *ThoughtCatalog.com*, January 24, 2013, http://thoughtcatalog.com/2013/your-lifestyle-has-already-been-designed/

4. *Attract and Keep A-Players with Nonfinancial Rewards*, Sylvia Ann Hewlett, http://blogs.hbr.org/hbr/hewlett/2012/05/attract_and_keep_a-players_wit.htm.

5. Dr. Toni Yancey, *Instant Recess: Building a Fit Nation 10 Minutes at a Time* (Berkley, CA: University of California Press, 2010).

6. *Employees Want Workplace Flexibility Over a Promotion*, Sara Sutton Fell, HuffingtonPost.com, 08/01/2013 5:18 pm ,http://huff.to/1bX9ocS

7. McKinsey & Company, http://www.mckinseyquarterly.com/Preparing_for_a_new_era_of_knowledge_work_3034.

8. Telework Research Network http://www.teleworkresearchnetwork.com/.

9. *100 Best Companies to Work For, CNN Money*, 2012, http://money.cnn.com/magazines/fortune/best-companies/2012/full_list/

10. *Attract and Keep A-Players with Nonfinancial Rewards*, Sylvia Ann Hewlett, http://blogs.hbr.org/hbr/hewlett/2012/05/attract_and_keep_a-players_wit.html.

11. *HSBC Offers Flexible Working Hours to Staff*, http://articles.economictimes.indiatimes.com/2010-06-28/news/27604529_1_hsbc-first-hsbc-bank-flexi-time.

12. *Oregon Business*, The 2012 List: Top Companies to Work for in Oregon. *OregonBusiness.com*, March 2012, http://bit.ly/17tVCer.

13. *Talent Mobility 2020, The next generation of international assignments*, PriceWaterhouseCoopers, white paper, 2010, http://pwc.to/16iKChH

14. Ibid.

# Retirement—A Bankrupt Industrial Age Idea

8

*"Retirement at sixty-five is ridiculous. When I was sixty-five I still had pimples."*

—GEORGE BURNS

Went into the heart of Kinshasa for the first time today, with my Congolese partner and Chief, to dream about what will be.

Mobutu Sese Seko ruled this nation for thirty-two years, from 1965 to 1997, and turned it into a "kleptocracy." For decades, joining the government to steal money and possessions was the only viable business strategy, if you can call it that. Mobutu ruined this country, and they are still recovering, but with a real desire to do so.

Kinshasa is a city of eleven million people with electricity that works only a few hours a day, no working traffic lights or waste disposal, and almost no inside running water. Everything is covered in dust—everything—the roads, the businesses, the houses, even the dirt itself is covered in a layer of dust. It reminded me of an old African saying I learned in Kenya: "Once the dust of Africa gets into your blood, you will always come back."

My Chief and I walked the downtown. He showed me many buildings that had once been in great shape but had fallen into various states of disrepair. We sat and talked for a few hours. We talked about vision--if you see "what is," everything is hopeless, but if you see "what can be" or better yet, "what will be," you see incredible potential in the midst of immeasurable suffering. It is very easy for the Chief to see "what will be"—he is wired to see life this way.

We were amazed at all the potential in this great city. We stood quietly for a minute and looked around, then the Chief said, "In a few years we will stand on the hills above Kinshasa and look out over this and say, 'this is what we and God have done together. Let's get started." He is a man of great vision who understands life is short. He is not waiting until the future to do something significant with his life or for his country.

## LIVING LONGER – A BRAND NEW THING

Two-thirds of the people who have ever reached the age of sixty-five in the history of man are alive today.[1] Living longer is a brand new thing, and we are profoundly unprepared to deal with it. The Industrialists found it extremely inconvenient, so they invented this dumb idea called *retirement*. Thankfully, it is an early stab at dealing with old age and will itself die away.

Retirement is a really bad, bankrupt, Industrial-Age idea that was never a good idea in the first place. It is a core business disease of the Industrial Age and will not be welcomed by future generations. Besides the fact that it was invented to get creepy old people off the assembly line during the Industrial Age, it makes a mockery of the more than forty-five years that come before it. And as proof, it's already being rejected by a majority who grew up in the shadow of the Industrial Age.

As with all the business diseases of the Industrial Age, the concept of retirement is invented and not natural. It was first conceived in 1889 so the Industrialists could discard us when our best and most productive years were all behind us. But this bad idea is being exposed as the disease it is, and as we learn more about how caustic it is to us, we are returning to the more natural rhythms of life that we followed for centuries, before the Industrialists invented retirement.

> Retirement is a core business disease of the Industrial Age and will not be welcomed by future generations.

## WHERE DID RETIREMENT COME FROM?

For centuries, people revered the elderly. But by the Industrial Age, they were starting to get in the way, and hostility toward them became commonplace. As the Industrial Age matured, so did the guys who installed the machines thirty years earlier. The machines had replaceable parts and still worked great, but the guys running them were getting a little long in the tooth and slowing down. Their slower production, coupled with their pay increases over the years, compounded the problem for the company. These geezers, slowly trudging into work, were not what the Industrialist wanted to see first thing in the morning. I can't begin to top the humorous, yet cutting way Mary Lou Weisman says it in her book, *The History of Retirement, From Early Man to A.A.R.P.*:

> Retirement came in very handy in the United States, where large numbers of aging factory workers were wandering around the Industrial

Revolution, dropping things into the works, slowing down assembly lines, taking too many personal days, and usurping the places of younger, more productive men with families to support. It was one thing when an occasional superannuated farmer leaned on his hoe in an agrarian culture – a few bales of hay more or less didn't matter. But it was quite another when lots of old people caused great unemployment among younger workers by refusing to retire.

The Great Depression made the situation even worse. It was a Darwinian sacrificial moment. Retirement was a necessary adaptation and everybody knew it, but the old guys were not going quietly. The toughest among them refused to quit, even when plant managers turned up the conveyor belts to Chaplinesque speeds.[2]

Weisman is, of course, referring to Charlie Chaplin, who released probably his best movie, *Modern Times,* in 1936 as a protest of the Factory System, and who starred as a cog in the Industrial machine. That funny, satirical movie made a lot of Industrialists very angry.

## STICK A FORK IN ME, I'M DONE
Dumb assumptions about "old people" helped further this campaign to institute forced retirement. William Osler, the world-renowned physician and one of the four founding faculty members of Johns Hopkins, gave the 1905 valedictory address at the Johns Hopkins Hospital and said, "It is a matter of fact that the years between twenty-five and forty in a worker's career are the fifteen golden years of plenty." He said workers between ages forty and sixty were barely "tolerable," but certainly those above sixty should be put out to pasture.

In that valedictory speech at Johns Hopkins, he quoted Anthony Trollope's 1882 Industrial Age novel *The Fixed Period,* which recommends that the elderly be chloroformed by the age of sixty-eight. Osler later died of the flu at the age of seventy, having sucked up two extra years of oxygen someone under forty could have used to be more productive.[3]

## BISMARCK MAKES HIS MARK
Because we were born with it in place, we assume retirement has been around for centuries. But the German Chancellor, Otto von Bismarck, invented retirement in 1889. That's right – invented it. It didn't exist before that, anywhere, at any time, in the history of the world. It is an Industrial Age construct invented to solve a problem that has itself become a disease.[4]

Otto and the gang set the age of retirement at seventy when the average German was dying at forty-three.[5] The United States followed suit in 1936 by setting retirement at the age of sixty-five when the average American died at fifty-three.[6] Not that everyone died that young – if you made it into young adulthood you were likely to make it to the retirement age, but rarely much past it. So, sixty-five was a safe bet for the Industrial Age factory that could squeeze every last ounce of life out of you, then set you "free" like an elephant going to the bone yard to die.

## GET OFF THE BUS, GUS

When Otto invented retirement, it wasn't something people jumped at, but were more forced to do. There were riots and massive resistance to the idea. But as Weisman so eloquently stated, we needed to get the "old guys" out of the way so the Industrial Age could chug on without them. Remember, Industrialists are about the here and now, and what they can accumulate in the present. They weren't worried about what some geezer would do for the remainder of his life, especially since he wasn't of any perceived value to the company anymore. Is it any wonder that young people don't respect the elderly like they used to? That's an Industrial Age issue as well. Retirement sends the message that they are no longer of value, when, in fact, the "Gray Hairs" are our most valuable source of wisdom and experience.

After decades of resistance, in the 1950s, at the peak of the Industrial Age, people began to discover that they could replace work with play, and retirement finally began to catch on as an attractive idea. This is an odd discovery, considering the two (work and play) had lived side by side in full integration for centuries. But during the Industrial Age, we separated work and play and did our best to eliminate the play part. The Puritan ethic reigned – a good man works himself to death.

## NO LASTING MEANING FROM LEISURE

The debates of the 1950s and '60s as to whether leisure could replace work as a source of meaning in people's lives have been clarified by today's experts. Surveys show that most people prefer continuing to put their hand to Making Meaning over holing up on a golf course in their later years. Leisure is very attractive as a change of pace, but most of us reject it as a source of meaning. People want to *participate* and *share,* even in their later years.[7]

Retirees who bought the lie that play could fully replace work are returning to the workforce in droves today. The majority have gone back to work in some form, and less than 18 percent say it has anything to do with insufficient retirement income, even after the great recession of 2009.[8] Every six years since 1992, people have been surveyed and asked again when

> A couple of generations have now had a go at retirement, and we're learning it's not what it was cracked up to be.

they expect to retire, and each time the expected age at retirement has gone up significantly, with over 40 percent now expecting to work full-time after age sixty-five, not to make more money, but because they don't want to be "done."[9] A couple of generations have now had a go at retirement, and we're learning it's not what it was cracked up to be. People are deciding to *CHOOSE* (a very powerful thing) to stay in the workforce and are doing it to Make Meaning, not just money.

## THE NEW NORMAL
There are actually two of them, closely related.

**The first new normal:** For those who are already on the Industrial Age retirement track, the new normal is to continue to work past the traditional retirement age. Just playing is not as interesting as we thought it would be. The overwhelming majority of Americans nearing retirement, about 75 percent, do not like the idea of an abrupt retirement at fifty-nine, sixty-five, or any other age.[10]

If you have the Industrial Age mindset of work, this sounds awful. Why would I trudge off to the salt mines every day in my seventies if I don't have to? You shouldn't, and you don't have to. Work, as defined in the post-Industrial Participation Age, is fulfilling, meaningful, and something you CHOOSE to do because you are Making Meaning along with money. Your *significance* comes from knowing you are still contributing to the world around you.

Companies that are still stuck in the Industrial Age aren't interested in giving you both meaning and money. Don't work for them. There are plenty of companies that are beginning to provide both. Seek them out because they are looking for you, too.

The young are working hard to Make Meaning and money, both at the same time. We can learn a lot from them.

Those in their later years can actually leave the salt mines and find something to put their hands to that is meaningful to them – things like running or working at a day care center because they love kids, starting a cooking school, writing music, working at a bike shop, throwing themselves into a nonprofit, designing clothing, inventing a cure for a disease, opening a dive shop. All those things you wished you could have done when you were working for "The Man" but couldn't.

**The second new normal:** For those who are just entering the workforce today, they will ignore the Industrial Age mantra to focus first on the *Ozzie and Harriet* bucolic life thing, and will find ways at a very early age to make money while Making Meaning, too. The young are working hard to Make Meaning and money, both at the same time. We can learn a lot from them.

## WHAT MAKES RETIREMENT SO WRONG?

There are three major problems with retirement:

### 1. **A goal realized is no longer motivating.**

Retirement is a goal that can be realized, and once it is realized, it's no longer motivating. That is not what we were promised by the Industrialists who invented it.

In 1900, if a male made it to age twenty, he could expect to die at sixty and a half years of age. In 1935, when the age of retirement in the United States was set at sixty-five, males who had entered the workforce at twenty could expect to die at sixty-four, and females at sixty-seven. For most people, the joy of retirement simply wasn't joyful.[11]

An isolated German study said retiring early might actually increase your longevity (if you have something meaningful to do in retirement).[12] But many more studies, both before and since that one, say the opposite. Recent research looked at mortality for people who retired at fifty-five vs. mortality for those retiring at sixty-five. If someone retires at fifty-five, they are 89 percent more likely to die before they turn sixty-five than is someone retiring at sixty-five to die at seventy-five! A Greek study with similar results showed that variations in the health of the subjects was not a factor.[13] The researchers said it had nothing to do with how much money the retirees in the study had, or what work they had done. The simple control in the study was that the older people are when they retire, regardless of their socioeconomic class, the longer they will live.[14]

Do you really want to take the chance that the German study was right and all the others weren't? Do you need to? The point isn't whether we should stop going to the office or the shop. We must replace them with some other way to Make Meaning. Just about every study shows that when we stop engaging ourselves in Making Meaning, we deteriorate. Those who replace going to the office with other equally or more meaningful pursuits are healthier and live longer. Although recreation is a big part of our lives, it is not, by itself, a meaningful pursuit, and there is no study that supports the idea that it will make you live longer.

There is a second reason why retirement is a bad idea.

> We are made to be and to do something significant.

### 2. **We are made to be and to do something significant.**

Not just for the first two-thirds of our lives, but for every living day we draw breath. Retirement teaches us that there is no reason to keep going once The Man cuts us loose. The only thing we're good for after that is drinking beer and playing golf. No longer useful. Out to pasture. Stick a fork in us; we're done.

The National Opinion Research Center (NORC) posed this question to Americans: "If you were to get enough money to live as comfortably as you like for the rest of your life, would you continue to work or would you stop working?" In 1982, an average 70 percent of respondents said they would continue working. However, in 1982, very few Americans had been able to fully experience retirement yet and give the rest of us feedback. But by 1988, the average had already jumped to 85 percent.[15]

As the first few generations retired, we got to watch the results, and the further we get from the Industrial Age, the more we realize retirement is just a dumb Industrial Age idea that was foisted on us, once again, to help the Industrialists make money, but certainly not for our own good.

Besides being unmotivating to the point of causing death, and the fact that we are made to do and to be something significant all of our lives, there is one more reason why retirement is a bankrupt Industrial Age idea.

3. **Retirement teaches us to put off doing anything really meaningful and substantial with our lives until "later."**

I heard it hundreds of times growing up, from future pasture-geezers still in their forties, "When I retire, I'm going to . . ." (fill in the blank.) What a horrible way to live, always hoping for a future time when you're actually free to do something with your life.

Retirement teaches us that we should pursue money first and meaning *later* – if you happen to live that long. The Industrialists had to do it that way. They needed our most productive years tied to a machine running at Chaplinesque speeds. Then, when we could no longer keep up, they needed us out of the way.

In the Participation Age, and with the help of the newer generations who never experienced the Industrial Age, we will turn off retirement and replace it with something much better, much sooner in life that will cause us to live longer, better, more meaningful lives.


## THE "IDEAL LIFESTYLE"

I'm not an advocate of going to the office or the shop until you simply can't get out of bed anymore. Our traditional view of work has us thinking that is our only option for Making Meaning. But, in fact, too many of the traditional workplaces don't allow you to Make Meaning at all, just money. Our Crankset Group Facilitators teach business leaders and others to pursue a substantially different path, which we call the Ideal Lifestyle. The assumption the Industrialists want us to make is that it takes forty-five years to become financially secure enough to leave their employment. We suggest replacing retirement altogether with The Ideal Lifestyle.

Business owners have an easier path to this. They can build a business that makes money when they are not around and can do it in three to five years. Our company has shown thousands of them how to do it. They may not be able to fully disengage in three to five years, but with the right mindset, they can be getting regular time away from their business in that amount of time. I built my present business to allow me to have every Friday, the last week of every month, and one month a year to get up in the morning and ask myself, "What should I do today?" That adds up to almost 55 percent of the work year. We got there in four years from the printing of a business card, with no experience in our industry (and other businesses are doing it even faster). With that kind of freedom, and a business that continues to grow quickly, we don't ever need to retire.

Does this mean I spend 55 percent of my time at the beach? Not hardly. But I do love goofing off – going to places like New Zealand to ride my bike, drink wine, and see the sites. We do that kind of thing regularly. But I found that recreation is simply a great way to change my mental and geographical scenery and give me more fuel for being productive. I take a lot of those fourth weeks – I call them Freedom Weeks – to travel and do workshops with business leaders on how to escape the need to retire at sixty-five and instead get to an Ideal Lifestyle when they are thirty, forty, fifty, or whenever they first realize retirement is a dumb idea.

I use other time away from my main business to work on my second business in Africa, and to work with business leaders there. I've been to Africa many times and still without a day's vacation while there. In all my trips there, I've seen one wild African animal, a wildebeest. Someday, we'll do the safari thing, but eight-hour trips on the back of a dirt bike at night to visit an important chief and see how we can grow the economy is a much bigger draw to me right now. That's a trip no tourist will ever be able to recount. I want to Make Meaning, not just goof off and risk early death by golf.

But you don't have to be a business owner to be able to live the Ideal Lifestyle. Stakeholders can also do this. They have to find Participation Age companies that will help them Make Meaning, and they have to be intentional about their finances. Fortunately, the number of Participation Age companies is growing quickly, as we gain more and more distance and separation from the Industrial Age. We'll show some examples of Stakeholders living out their Ideal Lifestyles later in chapters 11 and 12.

*If you don't have a vision for your own life, you will become part of someone else's vision for theirs.*

I don't intend to coast or even slow down. I intend to go out accelerating, with a blue flame coming out of my backside that will keep me from sitting down for decades. Right now, I can't see dying until I'm at least 120. I have way too many things to do to create significance in the world around me before I go. And I'm setting up people and systems to keep going once I'm gone, so I'm not even necessary for the task. We should all live like fighter jets accelerating on the way up. And boy, am I having fun doing it.

If that sounds tiring to you, I would suggest you take another look at your vision for your life. The pejorative definition of *employee* is this: If you don't have a vision for your own life, you will become part of someone else's vision for theirs. Read my first book, *Making Money Is Killing Your Business,* to get a handle on how you can use your business and your life to create Meaning in the world around you. Get a handle on your "Big Why" and how it ties to your Ideal Lifestyle, and watch what happens. Every decision you make in business will be filtered through it, and you will find yourself getting out of bed with an urgency to contribute to the world around you, when before you were tired. And going out to pasture will no longer look attractive.

## FREEDOM IS WEALTH

Riches are money, but freedom is wealth. Riches only capture one of the two great resources in life – money. Wealth captures both of the great resources – time and money. If you have money, but not time, you are not wealthy, just rich. If you have time and no money, you are neither.

Wealth is the freedom and the ability to choose what to do with my time and my money. There is no greater freedom, but most companies today are still stuck in an Industrial Age model that gives you only money, no freedom. The retirement game teaches us that we won't be free until we retire. It's nonsense. We need to stop living for a future that never arrives. Don't be that person who, when you're gone, others say about you, "Too bad he didn't get to enjoy his retirement."

> We need to stop living for a future that never arrives.

Companies that are moving away from the Industrial Age are figuring out how to provide both time and money, not just money. I'm not talking about two weeks of vacation, but an ongoing regular mix of the two – being able to go for a two-hour bike ride in the middle of the day, or walk your dog, or go to your fourth-grader's play. And also take two weeks off. Or every Friday.

CEOs using an Industrial Age filter might be concerned reading this, thinking that productivity will go down. But in chapter 12, we'll show how we have helped companies make more money by increasing production while their staff worked fewer hours. In a Participation Age company, this works quite well.

Life should be meaningful, fulfilling, and satisfying today. But most people are not *Making Meaning,* they're just making money. Fifty-five percent of all employees are unhappy and unfulfilled in what they do, and up to 64 percent of them are under twenty-five.[16] Putting up with unfulfilling work for over forty-five years before you can retire is not how we were meant to live.

## DEATH BY GOLF

Retirees have replaced work with play, thinking that it will make them live longer. But a thorough ninety-year study of 1,528 Americans called The Longevity Project shoots big holes in the retirement dream. Turns out goofing off for the last thirty years of our lives is a really bad idea if we want to keep living. This massive study proved what we've been saying for years now – we should get up every day asking how we can Make Meaning in the world around us.[17]

## KNOW WHERE YOU'RE GOING

The Longevity Project found that people with the most focused, long-term paths in life were the least likely to die young. Looking at the participants in the study who were in their seventies, those who had not retired had much longer lives than their golfing counterparts: *"The continually productive men and women lived much longer than their laid-back comrades."* There is nothing wrong with golf or any other kind of play. They are great components of a rich life and give us needed diversions. But when all you do is play, and that play is not adding *significance* to the world around you, the study says you're in for a short ride.

## FOCUS, FOCUS, FOCUS . . .

Also, those who moved from job to job without a clear progression were less likely to have long lives than those who went deep and long in a focused direction with their business lives. Your personal vision for what you want out of life, and sticking to it, is very important to living a meaningful and long life.

Fully 75 percent of those interviewed planned to continue to work in their retirement years, largely because they didn't think recreation or just hanging out would be fulfilling enough. It's a little ironic that this ninety-year study calls working in retirement "A Twenty-First-Century Phenomenon," since the idea really hasn't been in full swing for even ninety years yet here in the United States. It's not really a twenty-first-century phenomenon at all. People are figuring out that retirement is a dumb Industrial Age idea. It just took a couple generations for it to come to light.[18]

> We shouldn't sacrifice the first sixty-five years of our lives getting to the last thirty.

## WHAT IS WORK?

We shouldn't sacrifice the first sixty-five years of our lives getting to the last thirty. These discoveries about retirement make it all the more urgent that we put our hands to something now that creates more than just the *Ozzie and Harriet* mirage offered by the present day giant Industrialists. We need to be fully committed to finding work that creates significance for us and in the world around us.

A man walks into a bar and sees a sign: "Free Beer Tomorrow." He orders a beer, comes back tomorrow, and sees the same sign, and orders another beer. A week passes before he realizes he's been had.

Tomorrow never comes. Neither does *later*. Carpe freaking diem already. Don't let the Industrial Age idea of retirement lull you into waiting to do the things that you've always wanted to do *later*. Later never comes. You just might not get to them.

## EMBRACING THE PARTICIPATION AGE

1. What is your mindset? What one thing can we do to seize the day? Should you put dates on your bucket list and start getting to them, even if you're just thirty years old?

_____

_____

By When? ____ /____ / ____ :____a.m./p.m.

## NOTES

1. *Unlocking the World's Potential*, HSBC research and ad campaign

2. *The History of Retirement, From Early Man to A.A.R.P.*, Mary-Lou Weisman, Article in NYTimes.com, March 21, 1999.

3. William Osler, Wikipedia, the free encyclopedia, http://en.wikipedia.org/wiki/WilliamOsler.

4. http://www.ssa.gov/history/ottob.html.

5. http://www.jbending.org.uk/stats3.htm.

6. http://www.ssa.gov/history/lifeexpect.html.

7. A. J. Veal, *The Elusive Leisure Society 4th ed.* (Sydney, Australia: University of Technology, 2009).

8. *FWI's National Study of the Changing Workforce,* Sloan Center on Aging & Work (2008).

9. *Growing Older in America, The Health and Retirement Study* (National Institute on Aging, National Institutes of Health, U.S. Department of Health and Human Services, 2011), 51.

10. Ibid, 53.

11. *Mapping History* (Eugene, Oregon: University of Oregon Press, 2012).

12. *Time to retire–time to die? A prospective cohort study of the effects of early retirement on long-term survival,* H. Brockmann, R. Müller, and U. Helmert, Soc Sci Med. 69, no. 2 (2009) 69(2):160-64.

13. *Age at Retirement and Mortality in a General Population Sample, The Greek EPIC Study,* Christina Bamia, Antonia Trichopoulou, Dimitrios Trichopoulos, American Journal of Epidemiology, (October 23, 2007).

14. *Age at retirement and long-term survival of an industrial population: prospective cohort study,* British Medical Journal (October 27, 2005): 331:995.

15. *Work Ethics; Productivity,* OFTC, http://www.oftc.edu/academics.aspx?id=1454.

16. http://www.nypost.com/p/news/business/poll_most_in_us_don_like_their_jobs_4iRFvxrVqLk3mxtMVmCULO.

17. Howard S. Friedman and Leslie R. Martin, *The Longevity Project: Surprising Discoveries for Health and Long Life from the Landmark Eight-Decade Study,* (New York: Hudson Street Press, 2012).

18. Working in Retirement: a 21st *Century Phenomenon,* 2008 National Study of the Retiring Workforce: (NSCW, 2008).

# PART II

EMBRACING
the Participation Age

# Stakeholders—
# A New Model for the
# Participation Age

**9**

"*Pick yourself. Don't wait for someone to pick you. The shift is that it doesn't matter if you own a company. You can make an impact if you want to.*"

—SETH GODIN, from his book *Linchpin*

The Industrial Age created the modern concept of the employee, and did it on such bad assumptions (you're stupid and lazy) that the whole concept is simply broken. Our own company can't use the word *employee* anymore, because we all internally know we mean something different by it.

Words are very important, and the word *employee* is not redeemable. It's not like it had great roots, then got sidetracked by Industrialists, and can simply be brought back to its former greatness. The word was defined at its core by the Industrial Age and is built on too many deeply flawed notions. It is one of the most significant diseases of the Industrial Age. We have to move on from this word, and more importantly, the business practices it represents, or risk never making progress in pulling the front office out of the Industrial Age and into the Participation Age.

## EMPLOYEES ARE REPLACED BY STAKEHOLDERS

Our company doesn't hire employees; we have replaced them with Stakeholders, and we are working with many companies that have decided to do the same thing. Our Stakeholders "live well by doing good." That vision is what drives us to be transformative in helping other companies build a Participation Age culture, where everyone makes more money in less time, so they can all get off the treadmill and get back to the passion that brought them into business in the first place. It's not woo-woo crap, but hard-core, Capitalist intention to be the best company in the long-term, making great profits, and adding tremendous value to the world around us.

Stakeholders are first and foremost *owners* who are self-motivated adults who take initiative, make decisions, carry responsibility, take ownership, and are creative problem solvers. Stakeholders can be left home alone, employees (children) can't.

## STAKEHOLDERS ARE ADULTS

Our Stakeholders are all adults. *Employee* is a four-letter word for us. Adults don't need someone to keep them from running into the streets or ruining the carpets. Adults ask questions, most importantly, "Why?" Unlike the Silent Generation, they don't live passively but are self-motivated, self-directed, creative, and problem solvers. They make waves, question everything, and are highly visible. And they don't expect the company or other adults to take care of them.

## STAKEHOLDERS ARE OWNERS

First and foremost, Stakeholders are owners. Stakeholders are different than stockholders. Stakeholders don't have to physically own any of the company, but at a minimum, they own their work and the results it creates. It is a requirement of being a Stakeholder. They will also own profit sharing, and may even go on to own stock or a piece of the company.

Twenty-first-century Industrialists replicating the Factory System model in the 2000s will not be able to have Stakeholders because they will never let them be owners of their work or their results. A Participation Age company requires it.

Adults own stuff, so Stakeholders own their work as a natural part of being an adult. In contrast, employees use their positions to either make money, get a promotion or both. Like children, employees are users. Kids don't think in terms of ownership. When they are done with their toys, they just drop them on the floor right where they are, and move on to find the next thing they can play with. Employees exhibit a lot of non-owner behaviors at work.

> Stakeholders are first and foremost *owners* who are self-motivated adults who take initiative, make decisions, carry responsibility, and are creative problem solvers.

But Stakeholders own their tasks, processes, and jobs, and they own how they work within the system. They don't see themselves as users, but as owners. Most importantly, they own their results, something employees rarely think about. The most powerful motivator in business is ownership, and when you find people who view life as owners/Stakeholders, they will rock your business.

## STAKEHOLDERS BRING THE WHOLE PERSON TO WORK

The Industrial Age taught employees to leave their *humanness* at home and to only bring the part of them to work that could be productively tied to a machine. In contrast, the Stakeholder brings the whole messy person to work, not just the extension of the machine.

That sounds counterproductive, except that the messy parts are what help us think, ask why, create, solve problems, innovate, and inspire others to do the same. You don't get to have your cake and eat it, too. If you want people who will regularly bring great ideas, creativity, problem solving, and innovation to work, you have to not just *allow* the whole person to show up, you have to *require* it.

Stakeholders don't need to be taught this. They bring the whole person to work by default because a Stakeholder would never think about dividing themselves into "Work Bob" and "Play Bob." It's unnatural and keeps us from contributing as we are required to do in the Participation Age.

## STAKEHOLDERS REQUIRE LEADERSHIP, NOT ADULT SUPERVISION

If you hire Stakeholders (adults) instead of employees (children), it changes the way you direct people. We have taught employees that they are stupid and lazy, so they will wait for us to tell them what to do, then they need to be closely supervised to make sure they actually clean their room, not just pretend to. Stakeholders don't need management; they just need leadership. Simply put, Stakeholders need a leader who will give them vision, give them the tools they need, train them, and point them in the right direction, and the Stakeholder will take it from there. Employees need to be hovered over during the whole process to make sure they get it done.

> Stakeholders need a leader who will give them vision, give them the tools they need, train them, and point them in the right direction, and the Stakeholder will take it from there.

## STAKEHOLDERS DON'T REPORT TO THE DAY CARE CENTER

There is nothing wrong with an office. We have one. Ours happens to exist to serve clients, meet with them, and to hold workshops and 3to5 Clubs. But we don't have office hours, vacation time, or personal days. We're not interested in whose car was in the parking lot first or who left last. Stakeholders work from wherever they can be most productive. All of our people work from home. If it served them to have an office desk, we would get them one. But employees are different. They need to be herded daily into a day care center masquerading as an office. They can't be trusted to work as adults on their own without direct and close supervision.

The difference isn't whether you regularly come to a central location – it's why. If you come together to collaborate, build a better mousetrap, or serve your customers, that's great. But if you come to the central office because that is where the manager can supervise you, that means you are being treated like an employee, not a Stakeholder. Our Stakeholders come to an office at various intervals during the week because it serves our clients and our team for them to do so. But none of them would find a manager there. We don't have any managers. We don't need them – we have Stakeholders.

## STAKEHOLDERS FOCUS ON WORK, NOT PROMOTION TO THE NEXT TITLE

Stakeholders have very different motivations than employees. For instance, being upwardly mobile is not a goal of a Stakeholder. In our company, upward mobility is not even available. Every adult who works with us has a title that includes the word Chief: Chief Results Officer, Chief Connecting Officer, Chief Transformation Officer, Chief Operations Officer, Chief Development Officer, etc.

We don't have supervisors, managers, directors or VPs – just Chiefs. None of us will ever need to be promoted; we all came in at the top. The only place to grow is laterally. We'll just grow into more responsibilities as we become better at things. As our influence and impact grows, that will be recognized and somebody might change our title (there is no centralized title giver).

Because Stakeholders are owners, they understand all of this. Owners of companies don't get promoted; they just make more money because they expanded their value to the world around them. Stakeholders own their jobs and their results. Stakeholders make more money than employees because they are always thinking about how they can add value, and thus, they make more money.

If you are a Stakeholder who is making a bigger impact, and they tell you they have to continue to pay whatever everyone else is getting in that position, leave. You're working for an Industrial Age company. Someone else will pay you what you're worth, and is avidly looking for you.

## STAKEHOLDERS CREATE BETTER TEAMS

We believe in working together as a Committed Community to get results for each other and for other business owners. Children/employees come along for the ride but don't proactively build community. Stakeholders proactively build community among themselves and do so because they understand the economic value of being on one page, building relationships, and knowing what makes each other tick. Stakeholders live in a world of abundance, not scarcity. They believe making other people successful will make them successful, so they work much better together. In contrast, employees have trouble playing in the sandbox without adult supervision.

## STAKEHOLDERS LIVE IN A WORLD OF ABUNDANCE

One of the assumptions of the Industrial Age is that business is a zero-sum game with a finite market. I need to get mine before the next guy gets his, and if I can get it all so that no one else gets any, that's the highest form of business. That's very much how children (employees) view the world.

Stakeholders understand clearly that the best way to become successful is to champion the success of their customers and coworkers first. When a culture is filled with Stakeholders, everyone is better off, enjoys their work more, and is more productive. And the company always makes more money. The companies that are annually chosen as the "top companies to work for" are also the companies that make the highest profits every year.

> Stakeholders live in a world of abundance, not scarcity. They believe making other people successful will make them successful, so they work much better together.

## STAKEHOLDERS PARTICIPATE IN PROFIT-CREATION AND PROFIT-SHARING

Stakeholders are owners who own their jobs, processes, systems, and their results. They function as if they have actual equity ownership in the business, which means they need to be rewarded like an equity owner. When an equity owner achieves a result, the company grows, and the equity owner also makes more money personally. In the Participation Age, with *sharing* as a principal hallmark, Stakeholders MUST participate in profit-sharing. Without it, all the rest of the talk about Stakeholders is just that – talk.

Every full-time Stakeholder will take part in profit-sharing. Why wouldn't they? They're all adults who own their work, so they should own some of the profits from their work as well. No equity owner would work harder just to see the profits given to someone else. Stakeholders will find another place to work if you do that to them.

Profit-sharing is critical to creating a culture in which Stakeholders thrive. If this single element is missing, the Stakeholder concept will not fully unfold within your organization. Nothing will make you more of a hypocrite than to preach ownership to your Stakeholders of everything *EXCEPT* the fruits of their labor.

> Stakeholders are owners who own their jobs, processes, systems, and their results.

Broil King, Inc., makers of gas barbecues, instituted a profit-sharing program that put some money in a pot for every barbecue that ships. If one comes back for repair due to being shipped incorrectly, or missing parts, etc., money comes out of the pot to pay for that. Broil King put up an electronic sign to show everyone the money in vs. the money out. At regular intervals everyone in the plant, from the plant leaders to the shipping clerks, receives an equal distribution from that pot. After the program was instituted, mis-shipments and quality control issues were reduced to next to nothing. Everyone now takes ownership of anything they see that might keep a unit from shipping correctly, because if it doesn't, the money to fix it comes right out of their pockets. Ownership is a very powerful thing. Which brings us to bonuses.

## STAKEHOLDERS NEVER GET BONUSES, ONLY REWARDS

Stakeholders in our company do not receive bonuses at the end of the year for having occupied a chair for another twelve months. In the comedy movie *National Lampoon's A Christmas Vacation*, Clark Griswold put a deposit down on a big swimming pool before he could pay for it, because year-end bonuses were simply an extension of the paycheck for everyone. If you hung around for a whole year, the next bonus was automatic, so much so that everyone was indignant when the predictable annual extra paycheck didn't happen.

Stakeholders in our company don't get predictable annual bonuses. They get rewarded when they do things well. A friend and president of one of our 3to5 Clubs, Alan Wyngarden, instituted a program for his Stakeholders in which they regularly "catch someone doing something right." It's easy to catch people doing things wrong, but Alan's company decided to reinforce proactive adult behavior instead. When someone is caught doing something right, they receive things like simple thank yous, gifts, and monetary rewards. We work under the same principle. People get gifts, money, gift cards, weekends away, and other rewards for having performed well. It's ad hoc and requires that we pay attention to people. And that's a good thing, because then we see their great value.

Stakeholders make more money through performance rewards and broadening their value to the organization than they ever would through bonuses, and those making the greatest contribution get the biggest rewards. Nothing irks Stakeholders like the 2.5 percent across-the-board bonus that goes to both disengaged employees and Stakeholders, regardless of their contribution. Any equity owner would reject a system that paid every business owner in their industry the same amount, regardless of how well they had grown their businesses. Stakeholders are no different.

## A CAUTION ABOUT SHORT-TERM DECISION MAKING

Profit-sharing will be one of the biggest challenges to many giant corporations, because shareholders will resist the possible risk to short-term profits. But I haven't found one Participation Age company that isn't doing profit sharing, because as we've said, ownership is the most powerful motivator in business. In too many companies, shareholders have been taught it's not good to share with Stakeholders. They don't realize that in the long run, it is better for their wallets. The traditional shareholder system is built around the seventh attribute of Industrial Age companies – short-term decision making. They will gladly forfeit much more profit later for some profit now. CEOs of giant corporations are going to have to change decades of Industrial Age, shareholder thinking to make this critical adjustment.

## STAKEHOLDERS ARE SELF-MOTIVATED

Stakeholders are self-motivated, which is why we don't need managers, a day care center full of cubes cleverly disguised as an office, or a lot of the other trappings of an Industrial Age company. In the Participation Age, Stakeholders are proactively working to make the company better all the time.

## STAKEHOLDERS MAKE YOU AND THEMSELVES MORE MONEY

Do Stakeholders make a difference? We believe they do. We're still small, but we have Stakeholders on four continents now. Our business grew 61 percent in 2010, 41 percent in 2011, 66 percent in 2012, and is on track to grow 60 percent in 2013 at the writing of this book. Why? Because every Stakeholder is an adult, taking responsibility, creating, problem solving, making it happen, and taking ownership of whatever needs to be done to bring our clients the best experience and the most tangible results possible. And everyone is a lot happier because they all work with adults who pull their own weight.

Going forward in this book, if we use the word *employee*, we're describing an Industrial Age, front-office worker. When we use the word Stakeholder, we're talking about self-motivated, self-managed adults who own their processes and their results.

In the following chart, we contrast an employee with a Stakeholder. You will notice, not surprisingly, that an Industrial Age employee shares many of the same attributes of an Industrial Age company.

| Employees | Stakeholders |
|---|---|
| **Require Adult Supervision** (Management). Closely monitored throughout production. | **Require Leadership** – Give me vision, guidance training and resources. I'll take it from there. |
| **Assumed to Be Like Children** – Need lots of boundaries, constructs, direction, supervision, scolding or coddling, a parent, and protection. | **Assumed to Be Adults** – Need vision of what is possible, support, a champion, a community, tools, and space to create, innovate, and produce. |
| **Users/Renters** – I use stuff the company gives me to get the job done. | **Owners** – I own my task, my job, my processes, my computer, my desk, my hallway, my team, my department, and my company. |
| **Rewarded for Time in Their Seats** – I've sat here a year now; I should be getting a 3.25 percent raise. | **Rewarded for Results** – Is my customer happy today? If I keep that up, I'll make a lot more money. |
| **Scarcity Mindset** – There's only so much to go around, I better get mine before others do. | **Abundance Mindset** – Zig Ziglar – If I help others get to their goals, I'll get to mine, too. |
| **Do What They Are Told** – Don't question authority. | **Investigate and Question Everything** – Authority is only as good as the soundness of its position. |
| **Teamwork** – To get the task done, but I want to keep the ball as long as possible myself. | **Community** – Serve, to accomplish both the task and building relationships. |
| **Hoarding Knowledge** – Unshared knowledge is power; it keeps me employed. | **Making Others Successful** – Serving others is power; it keeps me employed. |
| **Passive/Reactive** – Tell me what to do and I'll do it. | **Proactive** – Tell me what to do and I'll figure out how to do more of it, better. And then I'll figure out what isn't being done and do that, too. |
| **Focused on the Next Title (Promotion)** – I'm waiting for someone above me to quit; If I do that long enough, I'll make more money. | **Focused on Expanded Competence** – No promotions, ever. Not needed or wanted. I make more money by expanding my competency and contribution to the company. |
| **Expect the Company to Take Care of Them** – Focused on benefits. | **Expect to Take Care of Themselves** – focused on contributing. |
| **Extensions of Machines** – There's a lot of HR policy stuff discouraging me to be human at work. I leave myself in the car when I come in each day. I just try to get by. | **The Whole Messy Person at Work** – All of me comes in to work every day. I get involved in community at work. It makes me more productive. |
| **Making Money** – I'll work longer hours if I have to in order to make a little extra. | **Making Meaning** – This is rewarding stuff; I make both money and meaning. I should get home – it's late. |
| **Time-Based** – I get here early and leave late – I'm a good employee. | **Results-Based** – I get a great result quickly and go home. I will be rewarded because I do more work in less time. |
| **Needs Benefits and Vacation Time** – Sacrifices the flexibility of mixing work and play for the certainty of benefits and fixed vacation time, even if it would be less than in a Stakeholder environment. | **Needs a Work/Reward Environment** – If I work and get the result, I will get more and better time off than an employee. Loves the ambiguity of being an owner and taking time off in the ebbs and flows of working together with others to get a result. |

Some people might look at the previous table and say, "The person on the right is not a Stakeholder, just an ideal employee." From an Industrial Age point of view, you're right. The employee research we've quoted extensively in this book shows that about one out of five people might fit the bill for the right column today – the buzzword being "highly engaged."

If you want to build a post-Industrial Age company, you don't put up with a workforce that is 80 percent employees and 20 percent Stakeholders. As we've said, most people live down to our worst expectations of them. If the company believes they are, in any measure, lazy or stupid, the company will set up a system designed to artificially make them smarter and more motivated by external means (management), and people will respond by becoming the automatons that Taylor admitted the Factory System created.

A call center can create automatons or attract adult Stakeholders. Zappos has Stakeholders in their call center. I ran a few of these, and call centers are manic about measuring the length of a call and ensuring people stick to a carefully contrived script from hello to goodbye. Zappos has no scripts and doesn't measure call times. Zappos knows that confining them to quick, pre-scripted calls demonstrates implicit distrust in their ability to deliver great customer service – or as Zappos and Tony Hsieh puts it in the title of his book, *Delivering Happiness: "The phone staff can also give away free overnight shipping without asking or reading [a script]."* And as we mentioned earlier, there is no phone center manager. They all rotate weekly to take on the more general duties of a call center that go beyond fielding the calls.

The result? Zappos doesn't have automatons in their call center. This results in some of the most passionate customers in retail, who consistently say their phone experience is unlike anything they've ever experienced outside a small, family-run operation. It's no surprise they went from startup to nearly a billion dollars a year in just ten years, due largely to their amazing customer service.

## WHICH DO YOU BELIEVE?

Either 80 percent of the workforce is lazy, or we've made them that way with systems that were set up to account more for the lazy than for the motivated. My experience is that if we set up a company culture and system that encourages people to be adults, 80 percent of the people will respond as adults. The other 20 percent will then have to work at a company stuck in the Industrial Age, where the company and the employee deserve each other.

The concept of Stakeholders isn't new. There are a fast-growing number of businesses in every industry, of every size and age, which have already cashed out of the Industrial Age, both in the production area and in the front office, and are fully embracing the Participation Age. To do so, they proactively create company cultures that are conducive to celebrating Stakeholders, while twenty-first-century Industrialists create cultures that mirror the Factory System of the mid-1900s. Culture matters deeply. In the next chapter we'll see why.

## DO I HAVE STAKEHOLDERS OR EMPLOYEES?

1. STAKEHOLDERS act like ADULTS, taking responsibility and being motivated to create, solve problems, initiate, and improve in order to get a specific result.

2. Employees act like CHILDREN, waiting to be told what to do, coming to you with problems instead of solutions, deflecting responsibility, blaming, etc.

3. Stakeholders are VICTORS (always looking for a way to make something work); and

4. Employees are VICTIMS (always looking for an outside circumstance to blame).

5. Stakeholders are RESULTS-ORIENTED; Employees are PROCESS-ORIENTED (What do you want, I did my job? Not my fault it didn't work out, etc.).

# EMBRACING THE PARTICIPATION AGE

1. What is your mindset – What one thing can we do to encourage Stakeholders to take ownership, and encourage employees to become Stakeholders or move on?

_____

_____

By When? ____ /____ / ____: ___a.m./p.m.

2. Is there anyone in your organization who needs specific assistance moving from *employee* to *Stakeholder*? What one thing can you do to help them make that transition? Are there others who are refusing to make the transition and need to be moved on?

_____

_____

By When? ____ /____ / ____: ___a.m./p.m.

# Why What You Believe Matters So Much

*"Culture eats strategy for lunch."*

—PETER DRUCKER

Most of the Congolese government officials learned from dictator Mobutu's legacy that the role of government is to provide income and a lifestyle for the bureaucrats, and that extortion and stealing are the right of those that govern. He ruled from 1965 to 1997 and institutionalized extortion and stealing to the point that his government became known as a "kleptocracy."

The problem in the Congo today is there isn't anything left to steal, so bribery is the only remaining form of supplemental income. For low-level government workers who haven't been paid in six months to three years, it's their only income, so most people don't even see it as bribery, just direct payment to the people actually doing the work.

For the upper levels, it's a lot more sinister and is used to supplement their existing regular income and siphon off large sums of money whenever possible. My friend the Chief and I personally know quite a few government officials who refuse to take part, and would give their lives for DR Congo – quite a stance in that environment. But for the most part, honor, integrity, and a person's word are simply not closely held values in the government of DR Congo.

The Chief system is entirely different. Throughout DR Congo, the Chief system runs on honor, integrity, and a person's word. If a Chief says he will do something, you don't question it. He will do it, or nearly die trying. There was an instance when my Chief was not able to make a very important meeting with another Chief, so he sent me instead. He told the Chief, "Chuck is me," which means that who I am, and whatever I say, represents my Chief's word. That was good enough for the other Chief, who had never met me, but invited me to his remote area, even though he had rejected all European and American invitations for years.

These two systems, existing side by side, are clarion examples of how our backgrounds influence our values, and how our values determine our daily actions.

## CULTURE, A FOUR-LETTER WORD FOR INDUSTRIALISTS

Culture is a four-letter word to the purest of Industrialists, both today and in the early years of the Factory System. Andrew Carnegie prized his public reputation, so he was publicly complimentary of his workers. But in the privacy of his business, culture was irrelevant. He was an avid believer in social Darwinism and therefore saw his workers as fully disposable.[1] So he turned over his steel empire to be run by Henry Frick, a ruthless tyrant.

Frick had one great ambition, as do all Industrialists, including Carnegie – to build an empire. In Carnegie and Frick's cases, the empires were demonstrated not by conquering and ruling countries, but by conquering and ruling the steel industry. Neither Frick nor Carnegie had any affinity for steel. Building an industrial empire was their core driving ambition, and steel was simply the means by which they would build it.[2] They went on to control most of the steel industry, making Carnegie one of the most powerful men on earth, at any human cost necessary.

## REACHING THE MELTING POINT

Work hours and work conditions were widely documented as inhumane and intolerable. Men worked twelve-hour shifts, seven days a week. Sweat filled their shoes and they often drank a couple buckets of water a day. They got one day a year off, July 4. Fatalities in Carnegie's mill accounted for twenty percent of all deaths in Pittsburgh in the 1880s. For this, they made five hundred dollars a year, just above the poverty line, and usually quit working by age forty because they were simply unable to go on.[3]

On June 30, 1892, Frick reduced wages by twenty-two percent at a time when the steel industry was booming. Carnegie's workers and the townspeople finally rose up together to protest the conditions at the Homestead Steel Works. In the month prior, anticipating a rebellion, Frick had installed a high barbed wired fence and sniper towers. The place more resembled a prison than a factory. The workers went on strike, and five thousand or more worked in shifts surrounding the factory to keep Frick from bringing in cheap labor from out of state. Frick, with Carnegie's blessing, did them one better. He brought in three hundred heavily armed Pinkerton Detective agents by barge in the middle of the night.

Accounts of the conflict read more like a civil war battle than a union stoppage, with sixteen men dead and twenty-three wounded. But the Pinkertons were held at bay. Carnegie turned to his good friend, the governor of Pennsylvania, who had been elected by Carnegie and his friends. The governor sent in two thousand troops to rout the townspeople and the workers from the plant.

The rebellion was put down, the battle lost, and wages reduced significantly, with no improvement in working conditions. Union movements were destroyed nationally and were not a factor for the next four decades, as the Industrialists built their Factory System empires in near impunity. Carnegie, always guarding his public reputation, directed and supported Frick's actions from the shadows, both verbally and in writing. After Homestead, he could no longer feign any detachment, and spent the rest of his life attempting to rehabilitate his image by building libraries, schools, and museums. But make no mistake, these men were cold-blooded Industrialists to whom the idea of *culture* would have simply been laughable.

## CULTURE AND THE BOTTOM LINE

As the Internet encourages the spread of the Participation Age, it gets harder and harder for companies to hide the hypocrisy of a public face that is inconsistent with their office face. Too many twenty-first-century Industrialists see culture as woo-woo crap, simply because they don't see a direct and immediate connection between culture and the bottom line.

One of the easiest ways to identify if a company is more Industrialist or Capitalist is to look at the top executive's true view of culture. Not what the executive says the culture is, but what is lived out in the trenches of the company. Most executives assign the task of "creating a culture" to Human Resources so the CEO and other leaders can do the "real work" of being productive. Heavy reliance on an HR department for this is almost always a sign the company is practicing twenty-first-century Industrialism. As Jason Fried of 37Signals said, "You don't create a culture. Culture happens. It's the by-product of consistent behavior. If you encourage people to share, and you give them the freedom to share, then sharing will be built into your culture. If you reward trust, then trust will be built into your culture. Don't think about how to create a culture, just do the right things for you, your customers, and your team, and it'll happen."

> "You don't create a culture. Culture happens. It's the by-product of consistent behavior. Don't think about how to create a culture, just do the right things for you, your customers, and your team, and it'll happen."

For any twenty-first-century Industrialist, culture is one of those annoying "talking points" they have to use when they hit the speaking circuit or talk to the press. The twenty-first-century Industrialist practices the public face of a Carnegie, usually much better than Carnegie did. But how their companies are structured – to make money without regard to Making Meaning, and to USE employees instead of championing Stakeholders – is the real belief system. What we do speaks louder than what we say.

## CULTURE IS A BIG DEAL

Great culture doesn't come from the HR department, but from how the leadership lives inside the business. If you don't think it's important to run your company on sound beliefs, values, and principles, take a look again at Enron, Bernie Madoff, Fannie Mae, ongoing government scandals, and many other organizations that violated fundamental cultural values. Some get away with it longer than others, but there is no future in running a company without a solid belief system. The less obvious examples are those that limp along for decades – like GM, United Airlines, and a lot of Wall Street – regularly mortgaging their futures for the highest profit today.

## WHAT YOU BELIEVE IS YOUR CULTURE

As Fried said, you don't create a culture. Your culture is your belief system, and your belief system is your culture. Your beliefs, values, and principles will determine how you make every decision, and the outcome of those decisions is your culture. If you don't like what you see in the company, the thing to change is your belief system about what is true.

We at Crankset Group worked for a very short time with a company whose CEO had come to us in desperation. He was ready to throw in the towel and sell the business in a heartbeat to anyone who would buy it because he couldn't extricate himself from the day-to-day operations and was working twelve-hour days relentlessly. We interviewed a number of his staff who all said they felt underappreciated and grossly underutilized. And they all said waiting on the CEO to make decisions and finish tasks were the biggest bottlenecks in the business.

Without knowing anything about Frederick Taylor, the CEO actually said to us that from his experience, his people were a little stupid, and in many cases lazy, reflecting Taylor's two basic assumptions about employees. We attempted to get this twenty-first-century Industrialist to transfer some of his power to his staff, to empower them to build a great business for him, but to no avail. His belief that people are stupid and lazy IS the company's culture. In fourteen years in business, he has never had an employee stay more than two years.

He fired us after just six weeks, acknowledging that he did not believe in our attempt to move responsibilities off of him and onto the staff. He really should sell the company, because he's miserable and so is everyone else. But he won't, because then he would have no power. Industrialists love power.

If your culture is constructive and permeates everything you do, Stakeholders who can help you build a great business **will come running to you.** We NEVER recruit people to become part of our business; we simply post the open positions. Stakeholders find us and are personally compelled to jump on board.

## WHAT IS YOUR COMPANY CULTURE?

*If your culture is constructive and permeates everything you do, Stakeholders will come running to you.*

In working with companies on four continents, we have seen seven common types of company cultures. There are probably more, but these are the main ones we have seen as we advise businesses. Surprisingly, there isn't much variation from country to country. Some countries have more of one type than another, but we see all these business cultures everywhere we work.

Five of these seven cultures support a twenty-first-century Factory System culture stuck in the Industrial Age. One of the cultures, the Friends Culture, is reactionary to the Industrial Age Factory System. But only one of the following company culture types will strongly encourage Stakeholders to stay with you for the long haul – the Community Culture – which we describe last.

### 1. **Inmate Culture**

In Charles Dickens' *A Christmas Carol,* Scrooge barks at Bob Cratchit, "Christmas is a poor excuse for picking a man's pocket every twenty-fifth of December!" This classic Industrial Age culture epitomized Andrew Carnegie's steel mills, and is still in use today, thankfully in far fewer companies than in those days. In the Inmate Culture, you aren't "borrowed" from your family or your friends; you belong to the company. And if you don't buy that, you belong on the street. Period.

The inmate model assumes people are more stupid and more lazy than all the other models. All processes are set up to box them in, remove the need to think or make decisions, and to treat them like prisoners, so they learn that the company is their only hope.

This is the harshest reflection of Scientific Management, or Taylorism, but was extremely common in the late 1800s through the 1930s. If you don't like unions, you can blame the Industrialists for inventing the Inmate Model, which required a very organized response to get any kind of relief. The Industrialists hate labor unions, but they created a model that dehumanized people, and the necessary response was labor unions.

## 2. Axle-and-Spokes Culture

This one is creepy, but we've seen it enough to name it. It's more like a cult than a workplace. Imagine an old wagon wheel with a big axle and wooden spokes. Then imagine there is no wheel attached to the spokes. That's the Axle-and-Spokes model, and it works about as efficiently. In this culture, all the important communication is done to and through the leader, and the culture is set up to actually mitigate against people talking amongst themselves. The leader doesn't want people "talking behind his back;" it all has to come through him. He divides people and pits them against each other (no wheel; everyone is a spoke attached only to the axle – the boss). The guy at the top of this culture is very insecure.

Sometimes, it's a fear-based culture, but not always. In some cases, it is built around someone who thinks he is indispensable. People who end up staying in this kind of culture are usually codependent in some way. They deserve to be here because they are willing to put up with propping up the boss and making him the center of everything.

## 3. Hired-Hand Culture

We see this Industrial Age model a lot in smaller businesses, not so much in big businesses. People are a necessary annoyance in the business. The business leader or CEO views the people like ranch hands, reluctantly giving away annoying tasks like riding the fence and replacing barbed wire. They give away the most undesirable jobs first, and only give away things they like doing if they absolutely have to. In this culture, the leader abdicates. Once the job is in someone else's hands, they don't want to hear from them. Go ride the fence and leave me alone.

The leadership of this business might not believe employees are stupid or lazy, but since they're pretty sure no one else is as good as they are, or that they are indispensable, they communicate just that. Only Industrial Age employees will be attracted to a Hired-Hand culture. Stakeholders who want to Make Meaning, not just money, will get on their horse and ride away from these businesses.

## 4. Family Culture

I'm the adult, you're the children. I will take care of you and protect you and burn myself out doing things that you can't seem to get done. You will depend on me for everything. It makes me feel valuable. My door is always open for you to come to me to solve your problems for you. I can't expect you to bring solutions, just bring me the problems. I'm the adult in the room.

This kind and gentle parent/child approach assumes that everyone else is a child, and since an Industrial Age employee has childlike characteristics, people who have been taught to be stupid (and maybe lazy) will love working here. We see this in everything from "mom and pops" to fairly large companies where the department heads function as the only adults in the department.

Do you really want kids at work? Some business owners and company leaders apparently do. Stakeholders won't stay here because they tire very quickly of seeing how much the ineffective people are coddled, while the Stakeholders shoulder the majority of the work. People rarely get fired from this type of office day care center.

### 5. Allies Culture—The Main Culture in Business Today

This is the most predominant Industrial Age cultural model still in practice in the twenty-first century. It got its wings in the 1940s, but is still directly descendent from Taylor's *stupid and lazy* principle. In the Allies Culture, the focus is largely on the task, and relationships are only a necessary inconvenience to help us get the task done. Like England, Russia, France, and the United States in World War II, we don't have to like each other; we just need to focus on the task at hand. This is the most advanced form of Industrial Age culture. Some of its tell-tale signs are:

- hiring for skills and experience, not for culture. Companies with an Allies Model make the mistake of regularly hiring for skills and experience, which is all a resume will tell you, when they should hire first for culture, which you will never get from a resume. In chapter 14 we'll tell you why we think hiring for skills and experience is such a bad way to hire.

- culture is something HR does. Culture is either disregarded or if it is taken more seriously, employees attend a class in which they learn about the company's vision, mission, green compliance, and the nonprofits that the company supports.

- task orientation. The Allies model says just focus on the task. Get the job done and go home to your next-door neighbor if you want friends. Every company should be focused on making sure the task of producing a great product or service is accomplished every day. But an Allies Culture will focus almost solely on the task. Relationships exist to accomplish the task.

Companies built on the Allies Culture love resumes. They hire the most skilled and experienced people with little regard for cultural fit, because again, we don't need to be friends here, just allies in accomplishing a task.

Companies operating on an Allies Culture have it backwards. If you create a great business culture, people will be much more free to focus on the tasks, because the *allies* aren't carrying on endless side-skirmishes that the company has to mediate. Office politics are most prevalent in an Allies culture, and research shows that people invest as much as 50 percent of their time in *managing up* (brownnosing). The *Dilbert* cartoon exists because of the Allies Culture model.

### 6. Friends Culture

This culture is a reaction to the Industrial Age and its corresponding Factory System. All authority is bad because the Industrialists abused it.

We see the Friends Culture a lot in smaller companies that have been bought out by employees, or by one employee who has worked there a long time. We also see it in larger, but very new companies started by Millennials. But the Friends Model is actually an unintentional extension of Industrial Age employment, because nobody wants to be the adult Stakeholder and make decisions on their own. They need to get everybody involved, and everyone in the group makes the decisions. Kum-ba-yah – can't we all just get along? Good luck with that.

> Anything with two heads belongs in a sideshow.

Initially a product of a 1960s reaction to the Industrial Age, this is also called the Hippie Culture model or communal living. Everyone is on a level plane. No one person is in charge. Everything is decided by committee or consensus. Everyone is in charge of everything (therefore, in reality, nobody is in charge of anything). "We're all friends here, right?"

Wrong. Anything with two heads belongs in a sideshow. Imagine something with five or ten or twenty heads. It sounds great on paper, but in a world where change is the only constant and the pace of change just continues to accelerate, companies that rely on consensus decision making will have a hard time keeping up. And usually they will end up with something very vanilla because the only way to please everyone is to make a decision that offends no one. Consensus eventually, if not quickly, leads to something unremarkable that is "okay" with everyone and stretches no one.

> The hallmark of the Participation Age is sharing, not consensus.

The hallmark of the Participation Age is sharing, not consensus. The decision making role needs to be shared. There are people all over the organization making decisions, usually with a lot of input (more sharing). Some decisions are made democratically – majority vote. And yes, there are some decisions that are made by consensus, but very few.

In chapter 5 about managers, we talked about Douglas McGregor's Theory X hierarchical structure, and his Theory Y nonhierarchical structure. He was disappointed that people who adopted the Theory Y model threw out the baby with the bath water, attempting to build a completely flat business with no hierarchy at all. The Friends Culture is the result.

## THE BENEVOLENT DICTATOR

Because he was willing to exhibit Theory X leadership when it was necessary, he ironically has been able to build a great company full of Theory Y, nonhierarchical decision making. It takes a strong leader willing to occasionally and continually practice Theory X leadership to ensure that a Theory Y company emerges from the Industrial Age and thrives. The best form of business leadership is not pure democracy, which is the Friends Culture, but a benevolent dictatorship whose responsibility is to serve and empower everyone else to act like owners and make decisions.

The Friends model is a falsely safe narrative in the short term. If we all make the decision, none of us individually have to be adults and make the decision, or be responsible for the result. The Friends Culture is not a timeless way of doing business, but a recent reaction to the heavy-handedness of the Industrial Age. I predict it will fade as we get further away from the Industrialists.

### 7. The Community Culture

This is the Participation Age model. The Community model is not a size-dependent or age-dependent model. It is already being practiced by companies of all sizes and ages, with three to thirty thousand Stakeholders, and in businesses that are just beginning or over a half century old.

To most Industrialists, the Community model may look a little fuzzy and confusing at first. To those tracking with the Participation Age front office, it will look very familiar and will clearly resonate with the cultural direction great companies are taking today. Many companies, such as W. L. Gore, Semco, TI Industries and others have been using it for decades. We'll profile a number of them in chapter 12.

## THE PARABOLA— CLEAR HIERARCHY, BUT NOT TOP-DOWN

Clear hierarchy does not mean a heavily top-down hierarchy. We'll use the image of a satellite dish to demonstrate the Community model that is taking hold in companies of all sizes.

> In the Community model, leaders are on the bottom as servants, not a privileged class, but hierarchy is deemphasized by giving leadership and decision making to a much broader group of individuals – really to everyone.

Unlike most Industrial Age cultures, hierarchy is not a core focus of a Community Culture. The Community Culture exists to serve the business purposes of the organization, not to create layers and a management ladder to climb. It's not pyramidal like an Industrial Age hierarchy is, but more parabolic, like the broad bowl of a large satellite dish.

Some newer management models have reacted to the top-down hierarchy by showing the exact same pyramidal model, but upside down, with the CEO at the bottom. It's still a many-layered, top-down (or bottom-up) hierarchy full of managers. It improves on the old Industrial Age model by emphasizing that the leaders should be servants, but most of these models are just a fashionable tweak to the steeply hierarchical Industrial Age model.

The satellite dish more accurately reflects the type of leadership and business culture of the Participation Age. In the Community model, leaders are on the bottom as servants, not a privileged class, but hierarchy is deemphasized by giving leadership and decision making to a much broader group of individuals – really to everyone.

In his great book, *Productive Workplaces Revisited,* Marvin Weisbord advocates a new workplace in which "everyone improves whole systems," not just leaders. This approach is a clear example of a satellite dish and Stakeholder approach to leadership and culture.

The satellite dish allows for leadership and decision making to move from one person to the next as needed to accomplish the objective. Remember, in a Participation Age company, leaders and decision makers are not people with titles who hold corner offices. Leaders and decision makers are the experts in the middle of whatever business issue is being addressed. So leadership swishes around on the parabola as needed to get the job done.

> Effective leaders know when to get out of the way.

Sometimes, the founder or leader of the company finds himself way out on the edge of the satellite dish, with someone else dead center in the middle of it, making some decision. And then leadership swings back to the company leader when their leadership or expertise is needed to make a decision. This works very effectively in our company. I'm not in the middle of the parabola very much any more, and will be there less in the future.

Effective leaders know when to get out of the way, and do it as often as they can. They also understand that the best leadership is to champion the development of others. An inverted, parabolic, leadership paradigm, like a satellite dish, reflects the fluidity of such an environment. There is always someone in charge of every result or decision, but in the Community model, leadership changes and moves around from person to person, depending on who has the most expertise and who people find the most reliable and competent on that issue.

As an example, 37Signals swaps the leadership of their call center every week, with everyone in the call center taking turns being the leader. That makes everyone more alert to the issues, and everyone leads from whatever chair they occupy.

Traditional Industrial Age business cultures require that the further up the hierarchy people are, the more they should know and the more comprehensive their decision making should be. They feel great responsibility to make all the decisions because the title on their door says they are the guru. Ego is a very big part of Industrial Age front office culture.

Capitalists do not need to express their big egos by dominating those around them and by having the biggest title. Capitalists who work inside a big company express their big egos very differently. A healthy big ego can be expressed in wanting to solve big problems, being transformative in the world around them, having big ideas, and knowing that they were instrumental in pushing others and the company forward.

> The parabolic Community model lays the foundation for building a culture of inclusion, within which people can demonstrate the main hallmark of the Participation Age – sharing.

## COMMUNITY ENCOURAGES SHARING

The parabolic Community model lays the foundation for building a culture of inclusion, within which people can demonstrate the main hallmark of the Participation Age – sharing. If the structure is wrong, it will be very difficult to build a culture in which people will be adults, take ownership, and share in the creation of something great.

In the Community Culture model, leaders work hard to get out among the people and find out what they want and need. Making unilateral decisions without input from those who will be affected is a bad idea. And the more someone will be affected, the more it makes sense to get their input. The Community culture leader will invite a LOT of input and feedback, and the best ones push decisions across (not down) to those who will live with those decisions. Sharing the decision making is a critical component of the Community model.

## BASKETBALL, SOCCER (FOOTBALL), OR HOCKEY

The satellite dish is a good visual for us. Soccer, basketball, and hockey also provide good visuals for the right structural underpinning of a Community Culture. In these games, at different points, everyone is the most important player. They are constantly either positioning themselves strategically to receive the ball or puck, or are in possession of it, and must make a good decision what to do with it. You can see *leaders* swishing around the playing surface like on the satellite dish. Whoever has the ball is now at the center of the parabola and needs to be equipped to make a great decision as to what to do with it next. The coach is over on the sidelines, not parading around in the middle of the field interfering with play.

The analogy only breaks down because in business there are multiple balls or pucks in play all the time, with multiple people constantly moving to the center of the parabola and off to the edges. Whoever has the ball is holding the company's future in their hands at that moment, even if only in a small way. They must be trusted to make a good decision, which requires training and thorough immersion in the company culture, vision, mission, and direction. It is the responsibility of the coach to make sure the players have all been trained, equipped, and put in the right positions to make the company more successful. If they are well equipped but still can't make a decision, the ball must be pulled away from them as quickly as possible and given to someone able to do so.

## HEAVY-HANDED LEADERSHIP IS OVERUSED

Theory X leadership (I'm the boss, I'll make the decision) should be used very sparsely. It is not the job of the coach to run out on to the field and make the plays or grab the ball and give it to someone else, which is the normal response of top-down, Industrial Age hierarchies when they see something they don't like. In the typical Industrial Age Factory System, very few people in the company even get their hands on the ball. The managers feel it is their responsibility to make all the decisions and ensure that the stupid and lazy people are more productive. That is the *value* of the Industrial Age manager – to be the smarter and more competent person who makes the decisions. (Again, *Dilbert* cartoons start racing through my head.)

The great companies are already immersing themselves in the Community Culture, pushing decisions not down, but across the satellite dish parabola to those most competent and to those who will be most affected by the decisions. Giving ownership and responsibility to Stakeholders is one of the most powerful ways to provide them with the ability to Make Meaning, which is a much higher motivation for Stakeholders than just making money.

Committed Community is the basis for getting the task done in the post-Industrial Age company. We're committed to both the task and the relationships that accomplish them. Community imputes trust and creates an environment in which everyone is encouraged to take ownership and make a contribution. Community members play clearly defined roles, but as part of a team, not behind *siloed*, cubical walls.

## SHIFTING TO A RESULTS-BASED CULTURE IS CRITICAL

This is a very important cultural change. Shifting from a Time-Based culture to a Results-Based culture is a critical cornerstone of bringing a company out of the Industrial Age. Without this shift, it is nearly impossible to enter the Participation Age. It may sound radical, but we have to remember that results-based work dominated for centuries.

The time-based pay system was only instituted to serve the Factory System in the late 1800s and is largely unhelpful to us today. In chapter 12 we'll even show you a manufacturer of heavy machinery with thousands of employees that does not dictate work hours to the Stakeholders who make the machines. They are a very successful company.

An Industrialist's day, week, and month revolve around Time-Based activity. Industrialists believe that unless you are sitting at your desk for the appropriate "shift," you can't possibly be as productive as you should or could be.

## THE ANNUAL PAY RAISE—"TIME IN GRADE"

But it gets even worse. Industrialists actually give people raises for having hung around another year. It's really a stunning thing when you think about it. The army calls it "time-in-grade." Your next promotion is determined by how long you have been at that pay level, not how competent you are. Sure, guys here and there get promotions a month early because they have an extra tenth of a point on their annual evaluations, but there is no true variance at all for having done real work or goofing off like mad.

I expect that kind of thing from the army and government bureaucracies, which have no bottom line to measure their effectiveness. But I have never understood why anyone would be given promotions for having sat in the same chair for a year, as if time has somehow made them more valuable. The Community model rewards results, not time.

## SEVEN CULTURES AT A GLANCE

Here's a quick table showing these seven common business cultures side by side:

| Inmate | Axel/Spoke | Hired-Hand | Family | Allies | Friends | Community |
|---|---|---|---|---|---|---|
| We own you | We scare you | We put up with you | We are the adults | We give you a task | We all do everything | We all lead |
| The most stupid and lazy | We don't trust you | You are a necessary evil | You are helpless and needy | You focus on the task | We all make every decision | We all have responsibilities |
| Most restrictive – you are boxed in on all sides | All commun-ications go through the boss | You do only the things that aren't fun; I do those | You don't have to think (it makes me valuable) | Skills, experience & resumes – go home to Make Meaning | Everyone is in charge; therefore no one is really in charge | Decisions are made at the level they will be carried out |
| You will make no decisions | You will not talk to your peers | You will not bother me | Come to me for every-thing | Politics + time = rewards | Personal metrics are unhelpful | Own your results = rewards |
| Prisoner – we are your only hope | The boss holds all power | You're out of the loop on everything | The parent thinks; I just "do" | ALWAYS make it "their" idea | No hierarchy; slow group decisions | Question everything; expand, learn, grow |
| Adversarial | Cultish | Ignored | Co-dependent | The Dilbert Society | Group Hug | Ownership |

## HUMAN "RESOURCES" AND THE SOFT SKILLS

The Human Resources department grew out of the Industrialist's need to compartmentalize the human side of business and move it as far away from the production line as possible. In the Participation Age, the *soft* skills more directly related to human beings are being rediscovered as more important and more rare than the *hard* skills, and leaders are now paying direct and personal attention to *The Human Side of Enterprise,* as Douglas McGregor called it in the title of his book. As a result, many Participation Age companies are finding that having an HR department is no longer necessary or needs to be radically redefined.

## THE WAVE IS BREAKING

A Community Culture model may seem a little avant-garde to some right now, but many Community Culture companies have been in the Participation Age for decades, and it is a tidal wave breaking over us today. In a few short years from now this will be a big "Duh," as the younger generation builds businesses in the Participation Age that encourage people to share in the creation of great companies.

# EMBRACING THE PARTICIPATION AGE

1. What is your mindset – which type of culture do you have today (Inmate, Axle-and-Spokes, Hired-Hand, Family, Allies, Friends, Community, or a mix of them, or your own!)? What is one way your culture is impacting the way you do business today, positively or negatively?

_____

_____

By When? ____ /____ / ____:___a.m./p.m.

2. What one thing can you do in the next four weeks to improve your company culture? (For example: write our beliefs/values and meet as a company to discuss; develop a company *significance* plan (nonprofit, etc.); let an employee go; hire a Stakeholder; stop micromanaging; empower somebody to make a decision; create a vision for how people can be significant as the company grows; have a beer or a weekend away with some Stakeholders; send a thank-you note; CATCH SOMEONE DOING SOMETHING RIGHT!)

List a maximum of **two** actions (when we list ten things, we do none).

_____

_____

By When? ____ /____ / ____:___a.m./p.m.

## NOTES

1. *Andrew Carnegie: Pittsburgh Pirate*, no author cited, *The Economist*, January 30, 2003 http://www.economist.com/node/1559629

2. *American Experience: Andrew Carnegie*, PBS, http://www.pbs.org/wgbh/amex/carnegie/sfeature/m_partner.html.

3. *Andrew Carnegie: Pittsburgh Pirate*, no author cited, *The Economist*, January 30, 2003 http://www.economist.com/node/1559629

# The Results-Based Business: Our Story

*"Executives need to include the interests of all the stakeholders, not just shareholders; but also the employees and the citizens of our communities."*

—SIMON MAINWARING, best selling author of *We First*

How does all this work its way out in a real company? What are the practical applications that can move a company away from the archaic business practices of the Industrial Age to the Participation Age? Is this for all companies, or just for companies that want to be different?

## THE NEW NORMAL

This isn't about those wild-eyed exceptions to the rule that happened to get lucky doing business in a quirky way. Nor are we advancing the idea that embracing the Participation Age is optional and something you should do if you just want to be different. This is about the new normal, which is really the old normal.

In his best-selling book, *Drive: The Surprising Truth About What Motivates,* Daniel Pink says our whole system of business rewards and punishments is upside down. Our carrot-and-stick rewards system inherited from the Industrialists ignores the deeply human need to direct our own lives, to learn and create new things, and to do better by ourselves and our world. He says we are all driven by three things – autonomy, mastery, and purpose – all of which point to the deepest of human needs: to Make Meaning, not money.[1]  Pink's work further challenges us to run full-speed into the Participation Age if we want to be successful in the coming decades.

## THE PARTICIPATION AGE: IT'S FOR EVERY COMPANY

First, we'll look at our very small but fast-growing seven-year-old company, with eight full-time and twelve part-time Stakeholders. Then we'll look at a twenty-year-old company with fifty Stakeholders that was steeped in the Industrial Age and is just now embracing the Participation Age. In the next chapter we'll look at some larger companies, including two multinational companies with three thousand and ten thousand Stakeholders respectively, which have been fully engaged in the Participation Age for decades.

All of these will encourage you that any company, of any size or age, no matter how deep its roots are in manufacturing or Industrial Age practices, can trade in its Industrial Age, front-office practices for a place in the Participation Age.

## CRANKSET GROUP: A SMALL, YOUNG COMPANY IN THE PARTICIPATION AGE

We incorporated Crankset Group in October 2006, but started operations in March of 2007. We grew slowly but steadily at first like most companies, and started to show healthier growth after about three years. From 2009 to 2010, our business grew 61 percent. Growth in 2011 was 41 percent, 75 percent in 2012, and at the writing of this book we are on pace to grow nearly as quickly in 2013. Today, although we're mucking around in seven countries on four continents, we're still a very small company with eight full-time Stakeholders and twelve part-time Stakeholders, many of whom are working their way into full-time positions with Crankset Group.

We are adding new full and part-time staff regularly and have a very large company on our hands at maturity. That's with what we can see now. But our plan is to Make Meaning in every city and larger town in the world over the next twenty years, and the company will grow in whatever way it needs to in order to meet the needs of our customers.

In the past, I've started and grown companies myself with up to 120 staff members and have also been in leadership with a few other companies that had up to 1,000 employees. My clients in those bigger businesses were almost exclusively giant technology and pharmaceutical companies. This background with the Bigs will serve us well as we grow. We are just shy of US $1 million a year in revenue at the writing of this book, having grown slowly without outside capitalization.

I personally do a lot of speaking, workshops, and nonequity partnership engagements helping companies embrace the Participation Age, but the Crankset Group's main offering is peer advisory groups, called 3to5 Clubs. They are focused on the forgotten core of every economy, which is businesses with one to twenty Stakeholders. 3to5 Club peer advisory groups (http://3to5Club.com) are now being rolled out across the globe to serve small and local business owners everywhere.

## OUR GROWTH

All of our growth nationally and internationally to date has been organic. We have done no advertising, marketing, or recruiting of any sort. We don't recruit, and actually expend a great deal of energy trying to talk people out of joining us, because this is *missional work*, requiring a deep dedication to Making Meaning with small and local business owners.

Many times we have passed on great people simply because the culture match was not there. If we ignored our culture, we could grow much faster, but we feel strongly it would compromise our future. How you start has a lot to do with how you finish, and we are in it for the long haul worldwide, so starting well is extremely important to us.

We've grown over 400 percent since the start of the *Great Recession* in 2009, and our growth is expected to accelerate in the coming years. Why? Because every Stakeholder at the Crankset Group is an adult, taking responsibility, creating, problem solving, making things happen, and taking ownership of whatever needs to be done to bring our clients the best experience and the most tangible results possible. We didn't attract these people by accident, nor do we believe they are rare.

## YOU GET WHAT YOU INTEND, NOT WHAT YOU HOPE FOR

When we started Crankset Group in 2007, I had twenty-five years of experience always doing something a little unconventional, but never addressing all of the core business diseases of the Industrial Age head on. This time, I had a very different picture in my head of what I wanted. This time I intended to build a Participation Age company that would make both money and meaning and have a very rewarding time doing both. Just as importantly, I wanted to prove that others could do it in any business of any size, and that we could build something that invited the next generation to celebrate work, not avoid it. I believe we have built that company, and now we will focus on growing and expanding it around the world.

## WE'LL BE BIG, BUT BIG IS NOT THE OBJECTIVE

Even though our projections show a company with thousands of Stakeholders and a potential billion or more in revenue, we have no focused intention of growing to that size. I tell business leaders all the time, "You get what you intend, not what you hope for." Our intention is to create great products and services, build value in the world around us, and make our clients into Raving Fans. Our offerings, and therefore our clients, will determine how big we get. For a Capitalist, being Big always comes as a result of building something great. Being Big is never an end in itself for Capitalists.

## CULTURE IS KING

As Peter Drucker said, "Culture eats strategy for lunch." Industrialists think it's something you pawn off on an HR department so you can do the "real" work of the business. Capitalists see culture as the greatest strategic tool available to them for building the business of their dreams.

Next to making sure we create and deliver the best products and services possible, we've worked harder at building the right culture than anything else. It is integrated directly into delivering those great products and services. We wouldn't put anything out that didn't reflect who we are to our core. We've had a lot of opportunities to take on products or services that didn't fit our culture but could have led to faster growth, but we passed because we're Capitalists who are in it for the long haul, not Industrialists trying to make as much money as we can right now on the status quo.

> Capitalists see culture as the greatest strategic tool available to them for building the business of their dreams.

Great companies do not *have* a company culture. They work to *be* what they say they are. At Crankset Group, we do not motivate or train people to learn the culture. It is who we are at our very core and oozes out of our products and services into every relationship we build.

## BELIEFS FIRST

To us, culture is our set of beliefs, values, principles, and assumptions about work and life by which we make every decision in our business, and by which we structure everything we do. (See appendix.) Our beliefs guide all our choices regarding culture, the products and services we create and sell, the clients and partners we want (and who want us), and the Stakeholders who will join us. Culture is not something we teach; it's who we are. Our lives and our business practices teach everyone around us our culture. This starts with articulating our beliefs.

Culture stems from your belief system. Every business owner and CEO runs their company on a set of beliefs. The problem is that most of them do it using the "Random Hope" strategy of business. They've never written down what they believe and are just winging it as each shiny object passes before them.

> Culture is our set of beliefs, values, principles, and assumptions about work and life by which we make every decision in our business, and by which we structure everything we do.

Our beliefs are written down, and they guide the development of our vision, mission, and operating principals. All of this is in the appendix at the end of the book. Not all of these beliefs will fit your business, but in principal, they should give you an idea of what kinds of core beliefs drive Participation Age companies of all sizes.

Most small companies our size would not see the value in writing down what they believe, which has a lot to do with why they aren't successful; they're too busy making widgets to ask why they are making widgets. We wrote down our beliefs because we want what we describe as "Utter Clarity" on how to make decisions on which to build a lasting company.

The following are just a couple of our beliefs. As you review the appendix with a more complete list of our beliefs, I strongly encourage you to write down what you believe, then turn it into a vision statement, a mission statement, and principles by which you will operate your business.

# CRANKSET GROUP BELIEFS

*We believe in the Worth of the Individual.* That all Stakeholders are made to do and to be something significant. If we help Stakeholders Make Meaning, we will make more money.

*We believe in Ownership.* It is the most powerful driving force in business. Everyone must own something, including their tasks, their processes, their jobs, their futures, their results, and profit-sharing. Stakeholders are owners.

*We believe in Abundance.* You either live in a world of Abundance or in a world of scarcity, and whichever one you choose affects every decision you make. We choose abundance over scarcity and competition. Stakeholders serve others before themselves.

*We believe…etc.*

**Culture Always Comes First**

When we look for a new Stakeholder, the first part of the ad is a statement of the full version of our beliefs (see chapter 14 on how to hire). People come to work for us because we know what we believe and it's what they believe, too. That matching process is tremendously powerful and removes many of the problems created by the common "Allies Culture" of the Industrial Age.

## VISION AND MISSION

Defining our Vision and our Mission statements would be impossible without first clearly identifying our beliefs. Size has nothing to do with the importance of vision and mission statements lighting our way through the daily maze of business. Small businesses need them every bit as big ones. (See my previous book, *Making Money Is Killing Your Business*, for a thorough discussion of Vision and Mission statements.) Our vision is:

> To Live Well by Doing Good.

I can unpack that for two or three pints of Guinness as to what it means throughout our business and in everyone's personal lives. We can show how it affects the metrics by which we judge our success, and even how it has caused us to start an unrelated business in Africa. Our vision is the compass for everything we do, whether it's buying a computer or opening up a business in a new country. It is our true north.

*Our vision is the compass for everything we do. It is our true north.*

## YOUR VISION EXPRESSES YOUR CULTURE

This is where culture begins. If people want to join our business, they will have to be compelled to live well by doing good, whatever that means to them. If they aren't, there is no room at Crankset Group for them, no matter how skilled and experienced, or how much they could help us in the short run. We're in it for the long haul, and our vision statement helps keep us focused on that.

Our vision statement is all about us, but our mission statement is not about us in any way; it's all about our customers. Customers want to know what you will do for them. Our mission statement is all about the outcomes we will get them. It is:

> To provide tools for business leaders to make more money in less time, get off the treadmill, and get back to the passion that brought them into business in the first place.

We have that hanging prominently in our Business Transformation Center in Denver, CO. In a Participation Age company, the mission statement is about the customer, not about the company.

Our beliefs, vision, and mission work together to express our culture. These are not words we came up with during a leadership retreat, but

*Our mission statement is not about us in any way; it's all about our customers.*

Culture is not a statement you make; it's who you already are.

an expression of who we already are. We didn't throw this stuff out there to try to attain it; we are already living it as best we can. Culture is not a statement you make; it's who you already are. Nobody can copy who we are, only what we do, and for that reason alone, we are transforming businesses and growing exponentially.

## CRANKSET GROUP STRUCTURE

In chapter 10 on the subject of culture, we identified a number of cultural models (or structures that resulted from culture). The last one we identified was the Community Culture model. It is the one that helps us build a Participation Age company that attracts Stakeholders and maximizes profits in the twenty-first century.

We call our Crankset Group business structure "Committed Community" because we're focused on both the task and the relationship. As a result, we expect the whole person to come to work every day, even the icky parts that don't directly help someone *run the machine*. We've all got icky parts and barnacles along with the brilliant and wonderfully productive parts, and if we let people bring the whole person to work, the parts that we might think of as barnacles just might help solve problems no one else could address. At the Crankset Group, nobody leaves parts of themselves at home or comes into work as an extension of a machine.

That doesn't mean we have a lot of mandatory company fun to *create* community. We don't mandate lunch or happy hour or anything else together. But because we're all in this together, it happens when it should.

## GET OUT OF THE WAY

Our Committed Community is like the parabola (satellite dish), basketball team, or soccer team, not a pyramid hierarchy. As people swish around on the parabola, there is clear leadership all the time, just not always from the same person.

While I was gone on one of my trips to Africa, some Stakeholders back in Denver identified a property they felt we should lease, sent me some info on it, then went ahead and signed the lease, bought furniture, had the place renovated to meet our needs, and put it all together while I was gone. When I got back, I was driving to it for the first time and had to call and ask if it was on the north side of Orchard Avenue, or on the south side. Others were definitely in the middle of the parabola for that whole transaction. I was swishing around on the edge in Africa at that point.

The satellite dish view helps us in other ways, too. In our company, my job, and the job of every leader, is to continually get out of the way, decrease my own visibility, and increase that of others. In chapter 5, in the section on managers vs.

leaders, I said, "The art of leadership is to know how few times the leader should actually make the decision." To do this, I have to believe there are others who are better than I am, and who can regularly move to the center of the satellite dish. Not surprisingly, because we believe others are better, I believe we have already found some people who are better at everything I do (or used to do).

The Capitalist does not have an insatiable ego that requires that all recognition must flow back to them. 3M Corporation has built a great history on leaders who are servants, not limelighters. At Crankset Group, this upside-down parabola has gotten me kindly excused from meetings and even revenue-producing activities that I created. Others have taken the center of the parabola and gently – or not so gently when I didn't get the hint – kicked me out. That leaves room for others to grow, and allows me to invest in things I'm better at that will help us all grow the business. If we let them, people will help us find the highest and best use of our time.

An Industrialist finds this all very difficult. From having grown up on the edges of the Industrial Age, I have to check my motives all the time to see who I'm championing, and all too often it's me. If I'm at the center of the hierarchy as the founder and principal owner, it's better for me to see life as a satellite dish than as a pyramid. It's good for my ego, and it's great for the future of the company.

## THREE FUNDAMENTAL PRINCIPLES
## OF A PARTICIPATION AGE COMPANY

You will see three principles emerge as I outline how our business lives in the Participation Age. Our model is built on sending the following three messages very clearly and with everything we do:

1. **We are all owners.** Owners don't get stuff handed to them. If they want more time and more money, they figure out a way to make that happen, and most importantly, are *empowered* to make it happen. Ownership of task, job, process, team, community, result, time, and even extra money are critical to attracting and keeping great Stakeholders in the Participation Age.

2. **We are all adults.** Adults don't need caretakers holding their hands as they cross the street, or telling them what to do all day at work. Stakeholders are adults; employees are children. Adults identify problems, create solutions, and implement them. Children wait for others to come up with a solution and tell them what to do. Children need managers (a lot of them), and adults need leaders (few of them). We are all adults at Crankset Group.

3. **We are results-based.** We won't institute any policy or process that compromises being a results-based organization. As an example, we do not reward people with raises or bonuses for having hung around another year. We reward results, not time spent sitting in a chair.

The following sections discuss ways in which we see these three Participation Age principles worked out in our business.

## OUR SATELLITE DISH

Crankset Group hierarchy is pretty flat, but the division of responsibility is also very clear. As on a soccer or basketball team, we all have clear roles and responsibilities that might not be crystal clear to those in the stands, but they are to us. And as with these team analogies, there is a lot of overlap. At times, one person steps in and takes over the functions of another if an individual is caught at the wrong end of the field when the ball is advanced. It's never perceived as "stepping on each other's toes," which is what children and employees do. We cover for each other and support each other, which is what adult Stakeholders (and teammates) do.

## EVERYBODY'S A CHIEF—NO FIRE HYDRANTS ALLOWED

As a way of living out a culture of Committed Community, we don't have hierarchical titles that create fiefdoms and territory – Vice President of This Fiefdom, Manager of That Subfiefdom, etc. The last thing we want is to build fire hydrants for Industrial Age dogs to mark as their territory.

Departments and the titles that come with them are two of so many Industrial Age constructs that lead to stifling bureaucracy. And it's that hierarchical bureaucracy that causes us to waste up to 50 percent of our time just playing politics. It's what some nicely call *managing up*, and what others describe less delicately as *brownnosing*. We eliminate a lot of that by just not having a traditional reporting structure. People know who their principal mentor or leader is, but people get what they need from anyone. Nobody *owns* a specific relationship.

To eliminate both unnecessary hierarchy and the "promotion game," everyone at Crankset Group comes into the company as a Chief Officer, no matter their position: Chief Transformation Officer, Chief Relationship Officer, Chief Results Officer, Chief Development Officer, Chief Connecting Officer – you get the idea.

Roles and titles are fluid. Krista Valentine came into the Crankset Group as the Chief Results Officer. But after a while, she expanded her role, and it made much more sense to see her as the Chief Relationship Officer. I think that was decided over a beer, not in an office. She performs an entirely different function than when she came to the company, and she has a much broader impact on what we're doing.

When titles are *flat*, it communicates a great deal to those in the organization – that they are all expected to perform and proactively lead at the highest levels of the company. There is no lower level. We need to work hard at being leaders, not managers. It works in all sizes of companies.

Putting *Chief Officer* in everyone's title is not frivolous; it's a very serious thing for us. It allows everyone to swish around in the parabola and grab the lead when the ball is in their hands. And it communicates something very important about promotions. We don't have them.

## PROMOTIONS AREN'T PROMOTED

Nobody will ever get promoted at Crankset Group. Ever. As noted above, everyone comes in at the top – Chief "fill-in-the-blank" Officer. That may sound demotivating to some of you, but we believe it is the opposite – extremely motivating and humanizing.

Promotion gets people thinking about being promoted to *management* so they won't have to be productive anymore, so they can sit around and make others productive. In the American knock-off of the British TV comedy, *The Office,* Darryl finally gets promoted to warehouse manager, gets an office and a desk upstairs in the front office, and you never see him working in the warehouse again. He just sits behind a desk and *manages* the warehouse from afar. He loves it because he has arrived at a level of management where he no longer has to lead by example, or actually even work. Crankset Group will never have a Darryl.

Jason Fried and David Heinemeier Hansson, coauthors of *Rework,* a great bestseller full of Participation Age business advice, run a company called 37Signals. Jason wrote a magazine article in 2012 explaining that someone in his call center wanted to be promoted to manager after having been there for a number of years. 37Signals does not have a call center manager, but rotates the leadership very regularly between every person in the call center. Without the possibility of promotion, Jason and the call center employee came to an agreement that she would move on. Living in abundance and not scarcity, Jason, David, and 37Signals helped her find her next place to work. We share the same view of promotions that 37Signals embraces.

## NO MANAGERS—ONLY LEADERS

None of the people at Crankset Group are stupid or lazy, so there is no need for unusually smart and motivated managers. All of us are smart and productive and bring direct value to the company, not through managing others.

*Dilbert* has made big mileage out of what I call "Seagull Management" – the manager flies in, squawks a lot, craps all over the place, flies out, and leaves the mess for others to clean up. For the reasons we talked about in chapter 5, we don't have seagull managers or any other type of manager, just leaders.

Does that mean it's anarchy at the Crankset Group? Not at all. We simply replaced supervisors, managers, directors, VPs, and CEOs with leaders. Leaders are responsible for people, processes, and outcomes, but they do it much differently than managers.

> Leaders at the Crankset Group are all personally productive, not productive through managing someone else.

Leaders at the Crankset Group are all personally productive, not productive through managing someone else. Everyone in our business will always have a personal result they need to achieve that can be tied directly to delivering our products and services to the client. People do not have other people they "report" to on a daily basis whose job it is to watch them work. And by the way, our Millennials do just great in the environment as do our Xs, Ys, and Baby Boomers. Being a Stakeholder isn't a generational thing. It's a human thing.

## NO TITLES ON THE DOORS

We don't have leadership roles for which we go out and hire someone. Everyone is encouraged to be a leader, and leaders are recognized as such only when people start following them. In a traditional management model, whoever gets picked by the higher-ups to sit in the office can, by fiat and virtue of a title, demand that people obey them. No one is actually following, which is what people do voluntarily with leaders. They're just obeying, because the hierarchy requires it, and they'll lose their job if they don't. (Again, is it any wonder that Scott Adams has been so successful turning all this into *Dilbert* cartoons? It's easy pickings.)

> Being a Stakeholder isn't a generational thing. It's a human thing.

## TIME-BASED VS. RESULTS-BASED CULTURE

This is THE big one. It is one of the best and most practical sweeping changes a company that desires to escape the gravitational pull of the Industrial Age can make. And it's really quite simple – simple, but sometimes hard to implement.

In chapter 13, we talk about the best way to foment change – change everything at once, in a very small controlled environment, after months of preparation. Then do the same around the company, until it's all changed. Moving from a Timed-Based culture to a Results-Based culture is a great way to change everything at once, but starting in small pockets in the company. Nothing will get people to see the world as Stakeholders better than ownership, and in a Time-Based culture, Stakeholders own their time.

Our Crankset Group culture is results-based, not time-based. We don't have office hours. While we do have an office, we use it largely for workshops and training for our clients. Everyone at Crankset Group presently works from home.

We're not against offices; we're just against doing things that aren't effective. If someone were more effective with an office, we'd get them one. But so far, all of our Stakeholders like working from home and just meeting at the office for events, collaboration, and very rare meetings.

At Crankset Group, people are not rewarded for whose car is in the parking lot the longest, but for the results they achieve. We have metrics for everyone. Some metrics are very obvious – setting up workshops and breaking them down on time, getting the right materials where they need to be, selling the right number of seats to fill our venue, getting information where it needs to be on time, keeping the library out on the cloud organized and posting new materials quickly, getting great reviews at the end of our workshops, etc. Other "metrics" are more about the intangibles – serving and championing others to make them successful; exhibiting initiative, innovation, creativity, and leadership; lessening burdens instead of creating them; etc. We're not afraid to compensate for those intangibles.

## NO PAY SCALES

We don't have a *range* of money we pay for a certain job. Everyone is treated equally, not by paying them within a certain pay range for a specific job, but by paying them for the result they get. Compensation for the same job can vary widely, based on the added contribution a Stakeholder is making that the next person beside her is not.

When we post an ad (we don't take direct references, we'll show why in chapter 14), we almost never put a salary amount in it. The great Stakeholders who respond don't usually ask until we're in the final stages of the interview process, which can take a month or more. Most of them assume that a company with this kind of culture is, of course, not going to treat them cheaply. Employee-minded people who live in a world of scarcity will ask very early in the process.

We also don't do annual pay raises, which are tied to a time-based culture. We do them when someone is adding value, increasing the breadth of their impact on the company, or when people start to follow them, etc. It would drive most traditional HR people to drink because it's not predictable and doesn't look *fair*. But it is actually quite easy when you have a laser-like focus on who is producing like a Stakeholder and who is occupying a chair like an employee. And you'll get a lot of help from everyone around that person who is not pulling their weight.

## NO VACATION TIME OR SICK DAYS

Owners don't get formal vacation time or sick days. Stakeholders are owners, so they get the same deal as an owner. We encourage people to take off at noon to walk the dog or 3:00 p.m. to ride their mountain bikes and work later if they need to. But if they're done for the day, they should go home rather than sit and pretend to be productive. They'll be a lot more productive tomorrow if we encourage them to enjoy life today. We've had people work through weekends, too. That's what owners do.

Our objective is that our Stakeholders would have more time off than they would in any Industrial Age company that *gifts* people a couple weeks off each year, and then maybe increases it by another week each year because they stuck around for five years (time-based).

Most of our people have to be kicked out to take time off. It's important to do that. Owners don't know when to quit, and the work is never done. We need to be a Committed Community for each other at times and get people to walk away from what we call "The Tyranny of the Urgent." We enjoy getting them to leave, and training them on how to know it will never all be done. Stakeholders cover for each other and are glad to do so, because everyone is pulling their weight all the time.

## NO BENEFITS

Owners of businesses don't get benefits handed to them. Stakeholders are owners, so there are no formal company benefits at Crankset Group. Instead, we pay a mutually agreed-upon salary, then we add enough in for Stakeholders to go get their own health, life, and retirement plans, so their salaries are actually higher.

Is that just sleight of hand? Aren't we doing the same thing as the Industrialists? No, it's a very powerful message to all of us. Industrial Age companies prefer to keep benefits in-house because they want you to see the added value they are bringing to your life. Without the company, you wouldn't have health insurance, life insurance, eye care, a retirement plan, etc. It's a way of making you falsely grateful and dependent, and it's mildly cheaper for them, too. Our folks can take their benefits with them if they leave.

## NO BONUSES

Bonuses are time-based. Congratulations, you hung around another year; you deserve a bonus for warming the chair for another twelve months. We will never do holiday bonuses or other *expected* payments. Owners don't get holiday bonuses. They get more money when they produce better results. We give results-based rewards throughout the year, and people get raises when the company makes more money and when they contribute to that growth.

## AD HOC REWARDS INSTEAD

On top of results-based rewards, we will here and there simply give an ad hoc reward for intangibles, everything from a restaurant card to a wad of cash. One good friend, Alan Wyngarden, calls it "catching people doing something right." We're all quick to catch people doing things wrong, but we want to catch people being adults and doing things right. We think doing that allows us to spend less time catching people doing things wrong.

## NO ANNUAL REVIEWS

Annual Reviews are also a time-based thing and create the expectation of a pay raise for having sat it out for another year. We review processes, results, and performances all year long, train as we go, and reward as we go. We don't clean our garage once a year; we pick away at it all year long. Doing it once a year is convenient for the company, but doesn't serve a Stakeholder who might bring greater value a third of the way through the year.

## NO DEPARTMENTS

Departments are created so managers have a fiefdom to control. We believe that being able to go directly to whomever can get you an answer is a better way. Should you go to someone in the company and recruit him off his team without talking to the team first? Of course not. But if he has information that will solve your problem, have at it.

The lack of departments also keeps the classic *silos* from forming, where one department is stymied because the next department isn't responding, or one won't let the other use its resources, etc. Departments, just like managers, create politics, and politics in the office is probably the biggest time waster we have.

## PROFIT-SHARING AND STOCK

If a company is not willing to do profit-sharing, this whole model will fall apart on them. This is another in a long list of reasons why it will be so hard for giant corporations to move their front offices out of the Industrial Age and into the Participation Age. Shareholders are not going to want to *share* with Stakeholders. The Crankset Group starts profit-sharing in the January after the Stakeholder's first year. It's not a time-based reward, but recognizes that everyone who has been with us for over a year has proven they are Stakeholders (or they wouldn't still be with us) and need to be reaping the results of their contribution like an owner.

For us, there is no profit-sharing scale, any more than there is a pay scale. We assign it based on how much people contribute as owners of their jobs and the system. They know exactly what the percentage is, but it's different for everyone. Someone doing administrative assistant-type work could have a higher percentage than someone with what would traditionally appear to be bigger responsibilities. It all depends on how widely they contribute to the organization, and accounts for their leadership, creativity, innovation, problem solving, etc.

Not everyone will get stock in the Crankset Group or be able to buy it. The only difference between stock and profit-sharing is that when the company is sold and you're a stockholder, you get a share of the sale,

The bottom line – since ownership is such a powerful motivator, profit-sharing is nonnegotiable in a Participation Age company.

and you can take it with you when you quit. A percentage of profit-sharing is just as good as long as you are with the company. As the company grows, more people will get involved in these decisions to keep them from being subjective and unwarranted. The bottom line – since ownership is such a powerful motivator, profit-sharing is nonnegotiable in a Participation Age company.

This is a glimpse into our Committed Community model. We didn't invent it. In chapter 12, we'll show you other companies of every size and age with similar business practices that are flourishing in the Participation Age.

# EMBRACING THE PARTICIPATION AGE

1. What is your mindset – Are there any Community model business practices identified above that could be immediately useful to continue to build your Participation Age company? What one thing can you do to bring that practice into your business?

_____

_____

By When? ____ /____ / ____ :____a.m./p.m.

2. Is there anyone in your organization who needs specific assistance embracing your Participation Age business practices? What one thing can you do to help them get there? (Is there anyone who has clearly opted out who needs to be moved along?)

_____

_____

By When? ____ /____ / ____ :____a.m./p.m.

NOTES

1. Daniel Pink, *Drive: The Surprising Truth About What Motivates Us* (New York, NY: Riverhead Books, 2011).

# Companies Thriving in the Participation Age

> *"It appears that bosses would rather be in control than have organizations work well."*
>
> —MARGARET J. WHEATLEY, bestselling leadership consultant

> *"If we do not let people do things the way they do, we will never know what they are really capable of and they will just follow our boarding school rule."*
>
> —RICARDO SEMLER, CEO of Semco manufacturing

## IT'S FOR EVERYONE

The Participation Age isn't just for smaller companies like ours, or newer ones without a lot of Industrial Age baggage. In this chapter, we profile companies with twenty Stakeholders to over ten thousand, even some that have made a full recovery from an Industrial Age legacy. These companies have returned to the fundamentals of Capitalism to embrace creativity, innovation, and growth by adding to the world around them.

## A BIGGER (BUT STILL SMALL) EXAMPLE

We recently worked with one US $15 million service-based company with fifty employees to move them from a traditional twenty-first-century Industrial model to a Participation Age model. The company is owned by two partners who in twenty years had always taken the traditional two weeks a year or so to go on what we call *crackberry* vacations – they ran the company off their computers and *crackberry* cell phones while their families enjoyed the vacation. As part of a move to the Participation Age, they decided to change that pattern dramatically, and did so quickly. In fifteen months, they had moved the entire company from a Time-Based culture to a Results-Based culture.

For the founders the work involved exchanging management and close supervision for leadership, setting up metrics for a results-based reward system, and helping everyone move from working as employees to contributing as Stakeholders. To make the transition, they changed everything at once, but only after months of preparation, and in one small environment at a time. The process of total change in a small environment was repeated until the whole company had transitioned.

The announcement was made that everything would change, starting with one area of the company, at a future date many months away; then we all got to work preparing for the change. The two founders took the lead and set to work completing their move from managing to leading. The founders wrote out their beliefs, values, principles, vision, mission, and strategic plan (two pages maximum).

To assist the employees in their transition to Stakeholders we focused on Freedom Mapping, a version of process mapping that maps not only the processes, but the Stakeholder's relationship to the processes. This ensures we're helping everyone get off the treadmill, so as Stakeholders/owners, they can all get back to doing things that are the highest and best use of their time.

It took about eight months to complete enough of the process (you're never done) to start to transition the first two teams. During the eight-month preparatory transition, about fifteen of the fifty people, or about 30 percent, realized they did not want to become Stakeholders, and left. A couple others were moved along by leadership. The rest took the challenge to move from employee to Stakeholder as an opportunity to Make Meaning, not just money.

When the company switched over the first couple functional groups, the initial results were as anticipated. Before the switch, the average employee in those departments was working forty-five and a half hours per week, but within one month after moving into the Participation Age, the average was down to thirty-eight hours per week, with the same or higher overall productivity.

People began taking that new seven and a half hours of freedom at various times during the week. Some began coming in at 9:00 a.m. or 6:00 a.m., or taking three hours in the middle of the day to go to their kids' plays or ride a bike. Some of them started coming in early and leaving early or coming in late and staying late. This may not seem like a big deal in companies that are already offering flex time, but it is a major transition for a company that has had strict office hours for a couple decades.

For many more months, people had to be reminded regularly that the culture had changed and that with freedom came responsibility. Leading a results-based culture doesn't mean the leadership or the Stakeholders get to coast. Some people (few) still goof off and need to be reminded they must be adults or they will be moved along.

## FLEX TIME IS NOT RESULTS-BASED

It's important to note that a Time-Based culture is very different than flex time, which has been available for decades, even in some otherwise very Industrial Age companies. Flex time usually requires the employee to pick a specific start and stop time each day and stick to it; it still requires the presence of managers to ensure everyone gets their work done; and pay is not related directly to results. In a Results-Based culture, Stakeholders have no regular hours, no managers hovering over them, and results dictate pay. And it can be as broad as defining their own work and productivity requirements, and deciding which peers get to stay and which must go. That is very different than flex time.

## THE RESULT

How did this company do? The company finished the year with its best revenue and profit in years, and the new Stakeholders regularly went to the founders and thanked them for changing the culture in their company. Productivity went up, while the average work week went down by seven and a half hours. And in the new year, fifteen months from the beginning of the transition, the two founders each began taking almost two weeks off every month, or five and a half months a year, including a full month each and every summer.

Has it been clean and easy? Of course not. The founders still find themselves looking at e-mails and answering calls at times when they are on their two weeks away from the office. But they have been gone for long stretches without doing so, which they never could have done before. They are enjoying being with their kids more and having time to smell the roses. Just as importantly, they are thinking and acting much more strategically about their roles in the company. Along with a better quality of life, they are now achieving things they had put off for years – like writing books, becoming industry speaking experts, and even starting some complementary businesses.

This new focus on leading is not surprising. When we get out of the trenches and have time to relax, recharge, and be in an environment completely away from work, we start thinking and acting more strategically. We have worked with a lot of business owners who, when finally able to get away from the day to day, were able to solve strategic issues that had been standing in their way for years.

This small, twenty-year-old company with fifty Stakeholders is a great example of one that is making the transition from an Industrial Age culture to a Participation Age culture. It is evidence that traditional companies can enter the Participation Age quickly when the leaders see the benefits. The founders (and now leaders) of this company would not tell you it was easy. Developing a Participation Age culture is simple, not easy. But commitment to the end result proved to make this a successful transition for them.

## A BIG THAT FIGURED IT OUT DECADES AGO

Big businesses can do this, too, including giant manufacturing companies.
Some people are pioneers. Bill Gore was just that. In 1958, at the height of the
Factory System, he created a company that foretold the Participation Age. It is
a magnificent example of a big manufacturing company that gets it and ignored
the Industrial Age altogether.

W. L. Gore & Associates (makers of Gore-Tex) is a $3.2 billion company
with ten thousand employees. In 2013, and in every prior year since the list was
begun, W. L. Gore & Associates, Inc. has earned a position on *Fortune Magazine's*
annual list of the US' "100 Best Companies to Work For." Only thirteen companies have made the list every year, putting W. L. Gore on a special *Fortune*
"All Star" companies list. The company also makes the "Best Places to Work"
lists everywhere in the world it has facilities. W. L. Gore is simply one of the best
places to work in the world.

## WHAT IS W. L. GORE'S SECRET SAUCE?

W. L. Gore's Participation Age culture is consistently identified as the number
one contributing factor to their success. *Fortune Magazine's* annual ranking gives
the following reasons why W L. Gore is always on the list and is an "All Star"
company:

**Ownership of their work,** 2010 – "Associates (they never call them 'employees')
are in charge in a culture remarkably free from structure. One associate said, 'If
you tell anybody what to do here, they'll never work for you again.'"

**No hierarchy,** 2011 – "No hierarchy or traditional job titles. Applicants are interviewed by five to eight associates, who look for 'people with a high tolerance
for ambiguity.'"

**Company ownership and self-evaluation,** 2012 – "No bosses, just small teams
whose members evaluate one another. Every employee is a shareholder of the
company after one year."

**Leaders as servants, no managers,** 2013 – "Eschewing hierarchy and bosses,
W. L. Gore encourages a team-based environment – and there are no executive
perks. 'At Gore, we don't manage people,' wrote founder Bill Gore. 'We expect
people to manage themselves.'"

W. L. Gore has had it figured out for decades. They expect people to be adult
Stakeholders, so they only hire Stakeholders, not employees. In 1967, Bill Gore
described their culture as a *Lattice Structure*.[1]  Following are some high-level

excerpts from that model. As you read them, remember, that Bill Gore wrote this in 1967, and the company had already been doing these things for years. This wasn't a paper he wrote, it was a life he lived out through his company. (Anything in brackets [ ] is my clarification.)

---

### The Lattice Organization

*"A lattice organization involves self-commitment and natural leadership, and lacks assigned or assumed authority. . . . Every successful organization has a lattice organization that underlies the facade of authoritarian hierarchy. It is through these lattice organizations that things get done, and most of us delight in going around the formal procedures and doing things the straightforward and easy way."* – Bill Gore

**Attributes of the Lattice Organization**
• No fixed or assigned authority
• Sponsors (mentors) not bosses
• Natural leadership defined by followership [Not titles]
• Objectives set by those who must make things happen
• Each person in the Lattice interacts directly with every other person [No managers]

**Principles**
• Fairness
• Freedom
• Commitment
• Waterline [Any decision that creates risk for the company, has to be made in the context of the team, not by yourself.]

**Leaders**
• Focus on business objectives
• Coordinate activities
• Align teams to meet goals

**Leaders Offer Associates:**
• Assistance in problem solving
• Acknowledgment of team accomplishments, encouragement
• Help in strategy formulation
• Explanation of business practices

- "Big picture" viewpoint
- Role-model behavior

The title *leader* is earned by gaining followers.

Sponsors [they mentor newer associates]
- Engage in a one-on-one relationship
- Focus on the development and growth of the associate

Each associate has at least one sponsor; some have more than one.

**Work Teams, Titles, and Leadership**
In the lattice [organization], individual authority and credibility are based upon proven skill or a history of contribution rather than an assigned title. All employees are known by the same title, *associate*.

Leadership evolves based on knowledge, skill, experience, or capability in the particular activity in which a team is involved. Leaders are associates who have developed followers. Each associate self-commits to projects or responsibilities.

**Communications—Direct, not Through Managers**
There is no hierarchy of communication. Associates are free to go directly to whomever they believe has an answer.

**Keep Teams Small**
Small teams facilitate direct communication. Any single Gore plant contains a number of small teams (business teams, functional teams, etc.) that enable associates to interact and pursue common goals.

**Salaries Set by Peers**
Associates rank each other twice a year on contributions to the success of the enterprise, and functional committees assign pay according to the rankings. This method was designed to be as internally fair as possible. Benchmarking with other companies ensures external competitiveness.

Again, the fact that the above was written pre-1970, and that W. L. Gore practices it at every level even today, are both astounding facts.

All of these principles are still deeply embedded in the culture and practices of W. L. Gore today. That is remarkable transference from theory to practice.

W. L. Gore's current CEO, Terri Kelly, sounds just like Bill Gore from forty-five years ago: "In more traditional management settings, people can feel confined by narrowly defined titles and roles. However, at Gore, we encourage associates to actively define their own commitments by matching their skills and interests with business needs. This type of work environment creates a strong sense of ownership, promotes ingenuity, and ultimately enables us to bring unique, high-value products to market."

Since it's founding in 1958, Gore has avoided the traditional hierarchy of the Industrial Age, opting instead for a team-based, Participation Age environment with ten thousand Stakeholders. If most companies worked like Gore, *Dilbert* would have never been popular.

## SEMCO—ANOTHER TRADITIONAL MANUFACTURER ESCAPES THE INDUSTRIAL AGE

I've chosen to highlight manufacturing companies because the perception is that they would be the least likely to benefit from moving into the Participation Age. W. L. Gore debunks that. So does Semco. Semco makes things like washing machines, meat slicers, and heavy industrial machinery.

The difference between Semco and W. L. Gore is that Gore was a Participation Age company from its inception. People could excuse W. L. Gore by claiming they didn't have to make a transition – the company operated in the Participation Age from the start. But Semco spent thirty years as a traditional, top-down, Industrial Age manufacturing company before transitioning to the Participation Age. If the most traditional of manufacturing companies like Semco can escape the Industrial Age, it encourages the rest of us to believe we can do it, too.

In 1980, Ricardo Semler took over his father's manufacturing business, Semco, which was founded in the 1950s as a shipbuilding company in Sao Paulo, Brazil. They went on to be a mixer and agitator supplier. Today they offer more than two thousand products and services, among them dishwashers, digital scanners, and even banking. In 1980, when Semler took over, Semco's revenues were US $4 million. In 2012, they were over US $250 million. Semco has grown almost 40 percent a year and grew 600 percent during the worst ten years of the Brazilian economy in the late 1900s. Semco now has over three thousand Stakeholders, with an unheard of turnover of less than 1 percent.

When Ricardo Semler took over this highly traditional manufacturing company in 1980, his first act was to fire 60 percent of the management team. The rest of the management people followed them out the door over the next few years.

Semco was a deeply Industrial Age company that, through Semler's leadership, has become one of the best examples of a Participation Age company.[2] At Semco, the two ruling assumptions are very much the opposite of Fredrick Taylor's two *stupid and lazy* assumptions:

1. **"Trust in adult behavior"**—assume that the basic human drive is to be productive, to build something lasting, and to contribute to something bigger than themselves; and

2. **As adults, every person's rhythm is different** when it comes to when, where, and how they do their best work.

As such, there are no employees in the day care center at Semco who must be looked after by day care providers/managers. Semco is a Brazilian company and exists in one of the strongest union climates in the world, yet they have managed to fill thousands of positions with Stakeholders who approach work the same way they approach it at home – as self-managing adults. A few years ago the unions said that Semco was the only company in Brazil they could trust.

Some of the practical results that have evolved from Semco's two ruling assumptions demonstrate why writing down your beliefs is so important to building a great company. Everything Semco does stems from those two core beliefs:

1. **No HR department**—The leaders at Semco do not abdicate their responsibilities to the Stakeholders in order to focus on operations and making money right now. They see operations and people in an integrated way, and not a function to be segmented out to HR professionals.

2. **No policy documents**—None anywhere in the company. Adults will figure out together what matters.

3. **No headquarters**—There are various facilities in many locations. None of them reports to a flagpole at some "most important" location.

4. **Six or more leaders take on the function of "CEO"**—and pass it around every six months. A Participation Age company is not a consensus/hippie/feel good kum-ba-yah culture – there is clear division of responsibility, without the need for managers or multiple layers of hierarchy.

5. **No job titles**—Everyone is just an associate – no senior, junior, or part-time labels.

> The day that we measured people by a time clock is long gone.

6. **Stakeholders all decide their own working hours**—and find teams of people to work with that share those life rhythms. Ricardo Semler says, "We want people to work on a structure of their own. The day that we

measured people by a time clock is long gone. We don't want to know when or how you're working, but only if you're fulfilling your commitment." Be reminded, this is a manufacturing environment, not a service environment where flex time is a lot easier to institute.

7. **All three thousand or so Stakeholders regularly receive the company's financial statements**—Classes help them understand how to read the reports.

8. **Each small team is fully self-governing**—and has to figure out how to best contribute to the larger picture at Semco. Stakeholders choose and regularly reaffirm both their teammates and their team leaders by a vote, and post the results publicly, most on a six-month cycle. Because most of them are Stakeholders, people rarely get voted out for not pulling their weight.
*NOTE: In my opinion, this is one of the key reasons Semco's model works. Imagine if you could vote on the ten to twelve people working around you every six months, with no interference from a manager as to who stays or goes. The corporate world would change very quickly. W. L. Gore uses this same model.*

9. **All meetings are voluntary** and the first two people there become *board members* with a bigger say during the meeting.

10. **The responsibility for reviewing and setting targets falls squarely on every employee** for themselves. No one else sets an employee's targets or reviews them. Everyone knows very clearly how they are doing at all times. If you have consistently demonstrated you can't contribute at the levels required by the team, you'll be voted off the island in the next semiannual Stakeholder election. As a result, there aren't "probationary periods" during which the children get threatened for ninety days if they don't stop finger-painting the walls. People will do a lot of extraordinary things with a gun to their head, but how do they do when the threat is not present and they must be self-managed? We show who we are when no one is monitoring us.

As you can see, there is a remarkable level of independence, interdependence, and responsibility placed on each person at Semco. People can even start their own businesses using company resources, and many have. All of this flows from Ricardo Semler being clear on his beliefs, and writing them down (see chapter 9 again on *culture*). To get the full story, read Ricardo Semler's book *Maverick, The Success Story of the World's Most Unusual Workplace.*

Following are some more of Ricardo Semler's beliefs that have resulted in one of the most remarkable companies in the world:

1. **Quality is more important than quantity.** A fourteen-hour day is not valued, and people who work the longest hours at Semco will often be left behind when it comes time for their team to determine pay raises, reward pay (results-based bonuses), or leadership roles.

2. **Leaders will always give away their power, not collect power.** (An attitude that is thoroughly anti-Industrialist.)

3. **Never fear being replaced. Get results,** and because you are unique, no one could ever possibly replace you. There is no fear of reprisal for speaking your mind at Semco. Asking "why" is encouraged, not seen as an attack on the leadership, as it would be to any twenty-first-century Industrialist.

4. **Trust is fundamental.** Semco starts with and assumes trust in its Stakeholders. If Stakeholders prove (rarely) that they can't be trusted, they are gone. This ensures that Semco is managing to the *highest common denominator* – the best people – so the great people are not suffocated by having to live within a day care center mindset.

5. **Rules destroy creativity.** Creativity is more important than rules. To that end, Semler encourages the regular use of the "Three Whys" – before finalizing any decision, ask at least three different "why" questions.

6. **Encourage people to rotate jobs regularly.** Learn new things, broaden your expertise. It makes the company better, while making the person better. As a result, people are cross-trained throughout Semco.

First, you must drive out the Industrialist from within.

You can see how Semler's beliefs led him directly to building a Participation Age company from what had been a traditional environment for decades. The ironic thing is that for the last couple decades, CEOs and managers have been streaming through Semco's factories looking for how they, too, could build a Participation Age company. The secret isn't in those factories; it's in Ricardo Semler's beliefs, which resulted in those innovative processes and systems.

We rarely understand that processes and systems are a result of a belief system. If the CEO's belief system is not in line with building a Participation Age company, no amount of touring any Participation Age company – Semco included – will help. First, you must drive out the Industrialist from within.

## PARTICIPATION AGE COMPANIES IN EVERY INDUSTRY

Following are a few more great Participation Age examples from a wide cross section of industries. If one is in your industry, contact them and ask to learn from them.

### TD INDUSTRIES

Founded in 1946 near the peak of the Industrial Age, TD Industries is a construction company that now has sixteen hundred Stakeholders and approximately US $320 million a year in revenue. Similar to W. L. Gore, it is also one of the thirteen companies to be named an All Star Company and make *Fortune's* "100 Best Companies to Work For" list every year, a rare achievement.

TD Industries makes the list because of its *servant-leader* culture. It is a Committed Community that uses the parabola or satellite dish organizational structure outlined in chapter 10, "Why Culture Matters." The company is 100 percent owned by its sixteen hundred Stakeholders and no one leader owns more than 5 percent. Management as a whole owns only 12 percent. The Stakeholders hold elections to choose the Board of Directors, something you would never see in a twenty-first-century Industrial Age company.

As a construction company, they also do not hire on a job-by-job contract basis, but retain their Stakeholders full time. Everyone is called a "Partner" (with a capital 'P'). There are no *employees* (lower case 'e') at TD Industries.

As part of their Committed Community model, leaders and construction worker Stakeholders have regular meetings to discuss and share ideas on where the company is going. Everyone is a leader at TD Industries.

Industrial Age companies love to hang pictures of their CEOs in rows on a Wall of Fame. At TD Industries, if you have worked there for five years, your picture goes up on their "oak wall," and if you stay for twenty years, that picture remains forever. CEOs aren't any bigger deal than any other Stakeholder – they value everyone the same.

### WHOLE FOODS

Founded in 1980 by John Mackey, Craig Weiler, and Mark Skiles, Whole Foods is a US $10 billion company with sixty-four thousand Stakeholders. It is also one of the thirteen companies to be named an All Star Company and to make *Fortune's* "100 Best Companies to Work For" every year the list has been published. Companies making this shift can take great encouragement from seeing Participation Age companies so profitable and so highly regarded.

John Mackey often says that Whole Foods' "Higher Purpose" (belief) is at the core of all the company's practices. He openly puts this higher purpose above making money, and as a result of that higher focus, runs a very profitable company that also Makes Meaning.

As with all great Participation Age companies, ownership is the most powerful driving force. At Whole Foods, everyone can own the result of their work by sharing in the profits, beyond their regular salary. All Team Members, including part-timers, are eligible for stock options.

In *Fortune's* "100 Best Companies to Work For" review, Fatima Kone, a Whole Foods Team Member, reflected on how the culture at Whole Foods impacts her. "I've worked for a lot of companies, and I have to say that this feels more like a family than a group of coworkers. Everyone gets credit for what they do, not just leadership." Fatima's feeling that they are not just coworkers (the Allies culture), reflects the satellite dish culture of the Committed Community.

Whole Foods Participation Age model also emphasizes transparency. Every Team Member can vote on new hires, go on field trips to meet suppliers to see where the food comes from, and view everyone's salaries. This abundance mindset does not work for Industrial Age companies who feel secrecy is the best way to protect the scarcity mindset.

## WEGMANS

Wegmans was founded in 1916 in the middle of the Industrial Age. It is a US $6 billion grocery store chain with forty-four thousand Stakeholders and is our fourth *Fortune* 100 All Star Company to make the "100 Best Places to Work For" list all sixteen years, only one of thirteen companies to do so.

In the glory days of the Industrial Age, giant corporations prided themselves on employee retention and vowed they would never lay people off. Now, the twenty-first-century Industrialists do it as one of their perceived best (but short-sighted) cost-cutting measures. In contrast, this grocery giant has never laid off a single Stakeholder in its ninety-four-year history. CEO Danny Wegman says the company's success comes from sticking to its principle of "doing the right thing" – encouraging employees and managers to lead with their hearts rather than calculations. In this way, the company regularly avoids cuts in pay, benefits, or product quality. Again, it's their beliefs that drive everything.

Not surprisingly, Wegmans' turnover is exceptionally low at 3.6 percent, compared to an industry-wide average of 38 percent.[3] And the Stakeholders are encouraged to build Committed Community by rewarding one another with gift cards for providing good service. Stakeholders love the place so much that they recruit relatives to the point that one in five employees are related. This Committed Community recruits and retains itself.

Wegmans is fanatic about employee health. More than two thousand Stakeholders have enrolled in a free smoking-cessation program since 2009, and in 2013 they opened a new 24/7 health hotline for Stakeholders, and rolled out free yoga classes in each of its stores. This level of caring makes Wegmans a close-knit community. When opening two new stores recently, Wegmans chartered jets to fly all the newcomers to Rochester to be welcomed by Danny Wegman himself. It would have been a lot cheaper to bring Danny to the stores, but the Stakeholders will remember it the way it happened a lot longer.

Of Wegmans's Stakeholders, 11 percent have been with them for more than fifteen years, an amazing statistic in today's transient workplace. It's no surprise that Wegmans is regularly rated in the top ten best companies to work for every year.

## NEWER COMPANIES ARE DOING IT, TOO

There are thousands of companies either already fully adapted to the Participation Age or rapidly moving toward it. Some were born that way; others have made radical shifts so as not to be left behind. But the examples are legion and growing. Zappos (Tony Hsieh) and 37Signals (Jason Fried and David Heinemeier Hansson) are newer examples of Participation Age companies that were born without Industrial Age barnacles.

I would highly recommend you read Hsieh's book, *Delivering Happiness,* and Fried and Hansson's book, *Rework.* They are both great examples of the mindset of Capitalists building Participation Age companies. These business owners can help you develop a Participation Age mindset.

The WorldBlu List of Most Democratic Workplaces showcases fifty-one companies from all industries, with five to fifty thousand Stakeholders, that are parabolic *satellite dish* companies which practice a Community model of business. See www.worldblu.com/awardee-profiles/2013.php for the complete list.

Davita, Inc. is one such company. It was started in 1999 from the ashes of a nearly bankrupt Total Renal Care (founded 1994), and is a health care services company that says, "We are a community that just happens to be organized in the form of a company." Their website reveals a company driven by a belief system – www.davita.com/about. All of the company's teammates developed the company name and their beliefs together in 1999. Davita makes *Fortune's* World's Most Admired Companies list every year. Now a Fortune 500 company, Davita has no central division, titles like *Chief Wisdom Officer,* and no symbols of hierarchy, and they openly declare that every teammate must buy into their premise of creating a village-like community, or they should not stay at Davita.

## THIRTY FORTUNE 500 COMPANIES
## EMBRACING THE PARTICIPATION AGE

A broad look at the Fortune 500 reveals a number of other Participation Age companies among those giants. In their book *Firms of Endearment*,[4] Raj Sisodia, David White, and Jagdish Sheth take a look at the Fortune 500s and ask if there are any of them that put a higher priority on passion and purpose – Making Meaning – than on making money. That would be a tough sell among the Fortune 500, since the number one priority of publicly traded companies is to increase shareholder profits – to make them money.

But he found thirty that had raised their hands and told investors that they were about something bigger than making money. They include companies like Container Store, Costco, Harley-Davidson, Honda, jetBlue, Johnson & Johnson, New Balance, Patagonia, Southwest Airlines, Starbucks, Timberland, Trader Joe's, UPS, Wegmans, Whole Foods, and others.

Here we contrast the seven main attributes of *Firms of Endearment* with the seven main attributes of a twenty-first-century Industrialist, as covered in chapter 3.

# FIRMS OF ENDEARMENT VS. INDUSTRIAL AGE COMPANIES

| Firms of Endearment | Twenty-First-Century Industrialists |
| --- | --- |
| A broader purpose than revenue generation. Being Big is a by-product of being great. | Being big is a higher priority than being great. |
| Exemplary corporate citizens in the communities in which they work and live. | Actively work against free markets to keep them closed so others will not enter and become threats to their dominance. |
| They consider their corporate culture to be their greatest asset and primary market advantage. | They resist progress and work hard to maintain the status quo; their legacy systems are focused on the last great idea, not the next one. |
| They carefully hire people who are passionate about the company and are great cultural matches. | They destroy jobs by a focus on growth by acquisition, not by organic growth stemming from invention or innovation. |
| Leaders are servants and champions of any new ideas that will help their Stakeholders and their customers. | Users of ideas, resources, people, and the world around them to create cash cows for their investors. |
| They promote work-life integration and live in a world of abundance. | They focus on destroying, mimicking, or buying perceived competitors, not on inventing the next best thing; a scarcity world-view. |
| They consciously humanize the company environment for customers and employees. Decisions are made based on what is good for the company in the long term. | They focus on short-term decision making to support the above six attributes, regularly mortgaging their futures for short-term gain today. |

## FIRMS OF ENDEARMENT; SUCCESSFUL CAPITALISTS

Are these *Firms of Endearment* (FoEs) successful? Yes. The FoEs make more money on average than any other cohort group among the *Fortune* 500. In Jim Collins' book, *Good to Great,* his "great companies" made an average of 331 percent above the market over a ten-year period. The *Firms of Endearment*, who are focused on Making Meaning, not money, make an average of 1,026 percent above market, with no one company skewing the average to the high side – they all are very profitable.

The belief systems of these businesses are present throughout the organization, and are demonstrated by the Stakeholders in the workplace. Independent researchers looked at Trader Joe's and verified that the culture, beliefs, and values Trader Joe's espouses are actually carried out by the Stakeholders (whom they call "Crew Members") and are also experienced by their customers.[5]

The former CEO of Trader Joe's, John Shields, would talk at the opening of every store and tell the Crew Members that if they weren't still having fun at the end of thirty days, to please resign. What company tells their frontline people that the objective is to have fun and to quit if they're not? A company that understands that Making Meaning also means making more money will be glad to have their Stakeholders focused on such perceived frivolity.

As evidence of a great culture, one researcher said Trader Joe's "customers become part of the culture rather than merely experiencing it."[6] That is a remarkable statement about culture and goes to the core of why Trader Joe's is successful – they know what they believe, they truly believe what they believe, and that is demonstrated by how their culture affects everything they do and everyone who works there.

Why is this so important? Because it is a better business strategy to build a business based on who you ARE, not on what you DO. Industrialist-minded mimics can copy what you do very easily, but if the culture is actually what makes it all *work,* their replication won't work. When companies lift their unique beliefs off the annual report and actually live them out, it puts them in a position where competition is an irrelevant conversation. Anybody can copy what you do, but nobody can copy who you are. Beliefs matter.

Trader Joe's, Whole Foods, Container Store, and a growing number of other well-known brands are also joined together to Make Meaning through a nonprofit founded by John Mackey of Whole Foods, called Conscious Capitalism. They have the nerve to believe – as I do – that Capitalism is a good thing, and that it is one of the best systems we have for doing good in the world around us. Their organization, ConsciousCapitalism.org, is just one more example of companies rejecting twenty-first-

> Anybody can copy what you do, but nobody can copy who you are. Beliefs matter.

century Industrial Age practices, recognizing the difference between Industrialism and Capitalism, and embracing the Participation Age need to Make Meaning, not just money.

## WHAT DO ALL THESE COMPANIES SHARE IN COMMON?

Most of the Participation Age companies we have highlighted have a few things in common.

1. Almost all of them are family or employee owned, and virtually all of them participate in profit-sharing, stock options for all employees, and other forms of ownership.

2. All of them espouse something bigger than just making money; they find a way to Make Meaning in the world around them that also makes a lot of money.

3. None of them are focused on becoming big. All are focused on delivering something special to the world around them, and know that in doing so they might become big, too.

4. None of them talk about their competition or have the *closed market* mindset of the giant twenty-first-century Industrialists. They welcome others into the industry and learn from each other. Some of the leaders and founders of these companies are very close to many other founders in the same industry, and live in a world of abundance, not scarcity.

5. They don't resist progress; they welcome it, and regularly adopt new products and services that replace already successful products. They work together to constantly update and change whole industries for the better.

6. None of them focus on growing by acquisition. Many of them have acquired other companies along the way, but unlike companies like GM, United Services of America, and other twenty-first-century Industrialists, growth by acquisition is not a main strategy or even a core strategy. It wasn't done for the sake of getting bigger, but for getting better.

7. They are highly committed to creating and keeping jobs, not just transferring them via an acquisition. They don't see people as extensions of machines who are as disposable as the machines, but work hard to create cultures and environments in which people will thrive and Make Meaning, not just money.

8. They are not focused on *using* the status quo products or services and squeezing every last dollar out of them, but most are regularly creating, innovating, and looking for the next product.

## THE RESISTANCE FACTORS

If companies like W. L. Gore and Semco can find thousands of Stakeholders, remain highly profitable, and show up on lists of "Best Places to Work" every year, why haven't more companies followed suit? Bill Gore said it all in 1968:

> *"The simplicity and order of an authoritarian organization make it an almost irresistible temptation. Yet it is counter to the principles of individual freedom and smothers the creative growth of man. Freedom requires orderly restraint. The restraints imposed by the need for cooperation are minimized with a lattice organization."* Bill Gore, 1968

The business climate now is very different than in 1968 when Bill Gore said that. As the Participation Age grows around us and the Industrial Age fades in the rear view mirror, more and more companies are seeing the need to transform their business practices. It is becoming clear that an authoritarian organization is not applicable in today's world.[7] The irresistible temptation to create one is no longer justifiable.

For the last hundred years, the majority of Industrial Age companies have been able to trace both their profitability and their demise to other things besides their culture and core business practices. But as leaders begin to see what the Dilbert Society is doing to their bottom line, they will change their own belief systems.

## MANAGERS—THE BANE OF PROGRESS

Which leads us to the second reason why more companies aren't doing this yet. Most companies are full of Industrial Age managers, not leaders. As we said in chapter 5, they are the harbingers of most of the core business diseases of the Industrial Age. That is why the *Dilbert* cartoons pick on managers the most. They have more to protect in maintaining the status quo than anyone else in a company. If they were to promote a transformation into the Participation Age culture, they would be basically firing themselves. So you will not see much initiative from managers to move out of the Industrial Age.

I know many people with the title of manager who are actually leaders. They manage stuff, but lead people, and are more than ready to have their company make the transition to the Participation Age. In a Participation Age company, the majority of managers will need to go back into production, but these few will become the leaders. Any company looking to make the transition should identify those selfless managers who are ready to destroy their own fiefdoms to build a better company. These are the future leaders of every Participation Age company.

## THE COMING WAVE OF
## PARTICIPATION AGE COMPANIES

More and more companies are going to encourage Stakeholders to own, share, participate, create, innovate, be human at work, and share in the profits. Participation Age change will have to come from the CEO. Unless the founder or CEO decides things must change, starting with his chair, nothing will happen. Is it worth it? To date, most Industrial Age companies have said no. But moving forward, they may have no choice, as they begin to get left behind in a new world where everyone demands they be treated like adults.

## NOTES

1. *The Lattice Organization*, William L. Gore, W. L. Gore & Associates, White Paper from Stetson University, http://www2.stetson.edu/~bboozer/Gore_lattice.pdf,1967).

2. *Semco SA--Organization Working on a Participatory Management Model*, Bavi Pate, IRMA, http://www.mbaskool.com/business-articles/human-resource/5327-semco-sa-organization-working-on-participatory-management-model.html.

3. 2010 study by the Canadian Grocery HR Council http://smallbusiness.chron.com/employee-turnover-grocery-15810.html.

4. Rajendra S. Sisodia, David White, and Jagdish Sheth, *Firms of Endearment, How World-Class Companies Profit from Passion and Purpose* (New Jersey: Pearson Prentice Hall), 2007.

5. *Climate versus Culture: Duality in the Consulting Intervention*, Mark Mallinger, Timothy Walter, presented at the Academy of Management, Denver, August 2001.

6. *The Trader Joe's Experience: The Impact of Corporate Culture on Business Strategy*, Mark Mallinger, PhD, and Gerry Rossy, Graziado Business Review 10, Issue 2 (2007).

7. *National Study of Employers,* Kenneth Matos and Ellen Galinsky, Alfred P. Sloan Foundation, 2012.

# From Manager to Leader— Moving Into the Participation Age

Many great books have been written on the subject of leadership and it would be foolish and unnecessary to attempt to write another one here. The purpose of this chapter is to take a quick, practical look at leadership, specifically as it relates to moving a company from the Industrial Age to the Participation Age.

Draft and Steers (and many others) described the traditional Industrial Age management approach in 1986.[1] In 1984, Yankelovich and Immerwahr described Participation Age management (they called it "participatory management") as a system that would open the way for the work ethic to be a powerful resource in the workplace. But they believed "the persistence of the traditional model in American management discouraged workers, even though many wanted to work hard and do good work for its own sake."[2]

On June 1, 2012, I wrote a blog post with the same title as this book, explaining *Why Employees Are Always a Bad Idea.* Stacia Davis was the first one to respond and wrote, "What am I thinking after reading this article?! I am thinking of a way to paper my office with it. To distribute it to the people I work with, the management, my friends, elementary school play dates from twenty-five years ago, and every person I meet on the street. This is an incredibly relevant idea and I thank you for eloquently phrasing it and posting it online. A to the MEN!"

There were a lot of similar comments on my blog and on Twitter. Yankelovich and Immerwhar's comment in 1984 is just as relevant today: "The persistence of the traditional model in American management discourages workers." The Participation Age demands decentralization of management into the hands of those who actually do the work. Frederick Taylor has been proven wrong; they are neither stupid nor lazy, and are, in fact, the best resource for building a great company. The Participation Age companies we profiled in chapter 12 all embrace the disappearance of the manager from the leadership structure of a successful company.

In chapter 5, we described the difference between a manager and a leader, and offered a chart showing the side-by-side differences between the two. It would be good to review that chart as a basis for this chapter, because as a leader, the lens through which you see management and leadership will have more influence on your success in the Participation Age than any three-step process I could offer you. The change starts in the way we view the world around us.

To that end, a manager viewing the world through a life of experience in twenty-first-century Industrialist companies will have a vastly different way of relating to people than someone who has experience working in a Participation Age company. The lens of the Industrial Age manager assumes in some subtle way that people are stupid and lazy, even if only slightly so, and therefore, they need him on a micro level. The Participation Age leader sees the world through the lens of "my coworkers are smart and motivated" and therefore, they are self-motivated and can be self-managed. It is why we have invested so much time and energy in this book to debunk Taylor's fundamental *stupid and lazy* argument.

> Until the leadership of the company is fully on board with moving out of the Industrial Age and into the Participation Age, you might as well attempt to push water up a hill with a garden rake. The odds of being successful are about the same.

## GETTING THE LEADERSHIP ON BOARD

The first thing that has to change is always the mindset of the leadership. It is no different if you want to move your company from Industrial Age management to Participation Age leadership. Henry Ford said, "Whether you believe you can or you believe you can't, you're right." Until the leadership of the company is fully on board with moving out of the Industrial Age and into the Participation Age, you might as well attempt to push water up a hill with a garden rake. The odds of being successful are about the same.

## YOU ARE THE SOLUTION

Please put this book down and walk away if you, as the leader, are not committed to being the first one to change. Go ahead and stick with your twenty-first-century Industrialist model and do it openly. At least then, employees will know to apply, and Stakeholders will know to pass on the "opportunity." Genuinely be an Industrialist, because faking a Participation Age company is not something anyone can pull off.

An alcoholic is not ready for help until he personally embraces being an alcoholic and wants to become something else. It's an old saw, but change happens from the top. If the leaders want passionately to change, then it's "game on." If you're a company leader and you're still reading, I'll assume it's "game on" for you.

> It's an old saw, but change happens from the top.

## I AM A SERVANT

The first thing I would suggest is to get a great grasp on the concept of servant leadership, that you exist to make everyone else more successful than you, and to use your position, resources, and experience to push people out in front of you. If you read Ricardo Semler's book, *Maverick,* which I again highly recommend, you will see a man promoting the development of others over *himself.* "Servant leadership" is an old concept, and really is redundant. If you are leading, you also should be serving. But Industrialist mindsets see leading as a position of power and privilege, and have corrupted and ignored the concept of servant leadership.

If you believe people are self-motivated and can be self-managed, then you will naturally respond to them with a desire to put them in whatever position you can to help them do that.

## GETTING THERE

Effective change is both incremental and yet all at once. Change must come all at once, but only after months of preparation, and even then, to begin with, in as small and controlled an environment as possible. Having a company-wide meeting to announce that tomorrow we will now be a Participation Age company is a bad idea, and will result in nothing but a credibility gap.

In the companies we work with, we begin setting up the change through months of dialogue and demonstration of ownership with those who will be switching from employee to Stakeholder. After months of getting the mindset and the infrastructure set up, we take the first team or department and switch them over all at once.

It's like flipping a light switch – there is a lot of work to be done before you do it. First, you have to wire the room and connect it to the right power source. Then, you have to add light fixtures, bulbs, and switches. Only then can you flip the switch. What you shouldn't try to do is introduce light in small quantities while installing the wiring, connecting to the source, adding a switch, etc. That would not work, and it doesn't work in changing from the Industrial Age to the Participation Age. Change, like installing new lighting, comes all at once after the right preparation is completed. Creating incremental change doesn't work any better than installing incremental lighting.

We "wire" teams (or departments if the company is committed to keeping them) and flip the switch for each team, after making sure the prep work is completed. The big switch is moving from a Time-Based culture to a Results-Based Community culture. That switch gets flipped on a specific day, after months of preparation, and everything then changes at once – how the Stakeholders are measured, who leads, the rewards for good results, and the consequences for not performing. It all changes at once, and by the time it happens, people are usually eagerly looking forward to it.

> Creating incremental change doesn't work any better than installing incremental lighting.

Where the rubber meets the road is in a full-on commitment to replacing employees with Stakeholders and replacing managers with leaders. It shouldn't take years, but it won't happen in a few months, either. Obviously, the more you are already practicing the true Capitalist principals of a Participation Age company, the faster you can get there.

## EMBRACE AND PROMOTE OWNERSHIP

We've said it many times; ownership is the most powerful motivator in creating Stakeholders. The mindset of the leader is to look at everyone in the business as if they owned the business themselves. In a recent meeting with a business owner, he told me he was going to come up with five changes in his business to promote the development of Stakeholders, and then he was going to share them with his staff. I stopped him and asked why he was coming up with those changes. He responded, "Because I'm the owner and it's my responsibility to create the kind of environment that would help them become Stakeholders."

It was the perfect answer because it allowed me to say, "Then let them come up with the changes. If you want them to own those changes, treat them like yourself and ask them to create the list of five changes. They'll likely know better what would actually help them become Stakeholders. Unless they come up with something that is going to materially hurt your business, they are likely to have more ownership in five things they come up with than ones you create." He told me later how surprised he was at the list they created and that it didn't have anything on it he would have done to help them.

In every situation, ask yourself, "If the person I'm trying to help was the owner of this business, what would that owner do?" Then do whatever you can to free them to do that. Create ownership of their tasks, processes, job, team, creativity, and problem solving. Everyone responds to ownership – Stakeholders most of all.

## EVERYONE IS A LEADER

If everyone owns their jobs and their results, everyone can be a leader. In a Participation Age company, people become leaders because others are following them, and for no other reason. Never promote someone to a title on a door. People will only follow them because the title is on the door. Instead, encourage people to lead, find those who are, and give them recognition and more pay than those who chose not to lead.

The Industrial Age model of leadership is completely and utterly broken. Titles like Vice President, Director, Manager, and Supervisor are antithetical to building a great and lasting company. In the typical company, these titles exist in a vacuum. A person is chosen and shoehorned into the title, and now everyone is supposed to magically love, respect, and follow that person's fearless leadership, even if the individual has never before exhibited that fearless leadership. It is much better to anoint people who are already doing it, than to squeeze people into a "position" and hope they grow into it. In a Participation Age company, because everyone leads, you will find you need very few people who are leaders to replace an awful lot of managers.

> Leaders are people whom someone is following. Period.

Leaders are people whom someone is following. Period.

## COMMITTED COMMUNITY MODEL

Adopt the Committed Community organizational structure we talked about in chapter 10 on culture and run with it. Don't be afraid to swish around on the parabola (satellite dish) and end up on the edges sometimes, with others in the middle. Embrace the belief that everyone leads when they have the ball. Semco's turnover is less than 1 percent a year. When everyone gets to lead, they want to stick around.

## LIVING WITH THE DECISION

As a leader, embrace W. L. Gore's great analogy of above-the-waterline and below-the-waterline decision making; any decision that won't sink the business should be made at the level at which it needs to be carried out. If the decision will affect the future of the company or create long-term potential harm, enough people should get involved to ensure it won't. If it's an above-the-waterline decision and it will affect someone else's work a lot more than yours, get out of the way. Ricardo Semler even lets manufacturing Stakeholders decide their own hours and which machine they want to run. And if they want to learn a different machine, they make arrangements to learn how to run that one. For that reason, most of Semco's three thousand Stakeholders are cross-trained at multiple disciplines, something a traditional Industrial Age manufacturing company would say is impossible, impractical, or inefficient. Semco makes a lot more money than most manufacturing companies.

> Any decision that won't sink the business should be made at the level at which it needs to be carried out.

People need to learn, and they will learn best by making mistakes. You have made a lot of them, which is why you want to save everyone else from the experience. But how will you create ownership and free yourself to lead, if you are managing people out of their problems? Let them learn from their experiences. They will make even better decisions without you the next time. You will earn your freedom as a leader by giving them theirs.

## A RESULTS-BASED CULTURE

Moving from a Time-Based culture to a Results-Based culture is not complex, but it does take focused effort. A quick list of things to do (you'll find plenty more as you make the switch):

1. **Vision** – Reframe their world and tell them where we're going, and that we won't get there overnight, but that we are immediately beginning the change. Do it with the whole company, pick one department (the most eager, easiest one), and get on with it.

2. **Freedom Mapping** – Our version of process mapping. Map their positions to find out what people are doing, then get them doing what is the highest and best use of their time. People work much more effectively doing what they are good at. Usually, people can offload work to others that they aren't good at, because the other person is much better at it and loves doing it.

3. **Define the Results Required** – Let the Stakeholders do this. Ask them what result they think they should get in order to get what benefit they want (more time off, more pay, etc.). Again, treat them like owners. If they come up with something that will sink the ship, you can speak to that. But, usually, they will create a results-based system that is more stringent than the one you would have created for them.

4. **Define the Reward** – Encourage them to pick a reward of time. If you can't afford to give more money, then that's a below-the-waterline decision they can't make on their own. And frankly, that would be a good thing. Because they will learn that getting a life will mean more to them in the long run than getting a few extra bucks.

5. **Define the Penalty** – Owners make more money and get more time by upping their own game. What happens if someone decides to start taking time off and performance slides? At Semco, peer groups of ten to fifteen people vote every six months (remember, there are no managers) to decide who gets to stay on the island. As a result, almost no one gets fired for nonperformance.

6. **Review the Process Maps and the System** – Do they have what they need to be successful while switching from a Time-Based culture to a Results-Based culture? Equipment, training, clear results, clear rewards?

7. **Flip the Switch** – Recently, in one company, we took seven months to turn the first department around. Within a month, the entire department was spending seven and a half hours less at work per person. An entire work day came off their week, and productivity did not suffer. An Industrialist reading this would immediately increase the goal so that he could squeeze more productivity out of that "lost" time. He would instead lose his most productive Stakeholders and start on a downward spiral from which he would not recover. Short-term profits would increase, but in the long run, the company would not do well.

8. **Be Quick to Let Employees Go** – Some people will decide very quickly that they like being children and do not want to embrace becoming owners/adults/Stakeholders. They will quit on their own. Others will wait until after you flip the switch and force you to let them go. Make sure people are trained and have what they need to be successful, and if someone is still not performing, be quick to move them along. Nothing grinds the gears of a Stakeholder more than having to do somebody else's work, and nothing communicates to them more that they are valuable than filling the position beside them with another Stakeholder. Most companies are MUCH too slow to let someone go. Ownership has consequences. If you do not hold people to their results, you will not pull your company into the Participation Age. You are not running a day care center – that's for Industrialists.

## STAKEHOLDERS ARE ADULTS AND OWNERS

Remind yourself every day; It will be easy to forget and revert to managing them. When things are going badly, don't revert, require that they step up and help solve the problem or increase their production – whatever the issue is. Your default will be to go back to micromanaging. Instead, ask yourself how to get them involved in leading themselves out of the problem. If you go back to micromanaging, you have just communicated to them that they are not Stakeholders. If it requires removing someone, do it quickly – see step 8 on previous page.

## DECENTRALIZED LEADERSHIP

Bill Gore was never quite sure how many factories he had. He didn't need to know, because he knew that his ten thousand Stakeholders were adults and could make a great decision whether to open another factory without him. He didn't arrive at that trust overnight, but after years of building a decentralized Committed Community, he was able to put highly strategic decisions fully in the hands of others.

Decentralized leadership is scary, but if you ensure that below-the-waterline decisions aren't being made in a vacuum, it's the best way to run an organization.

Use Highest Common Denominator Leadership (HCD) – expect the best out of people and be surprised when it doesn't happen.

You will get a lot more creativity and innovation if you let people make decisions and be full-on adults. Use Highest Common Denominator Leadership (HCD) – expect the best out of people and be surprised when it doesn't happen.

Read at least three books, Ricardo Semler's *Maverick*,[3] Douglas McGregor's *The Human Side of Enterprise*,[4] and *The Starfish and the Spider: The Unstoppable Power of Leaderless Organizations,* by Brafman and Beckstrom.[5] There are many others, like *Rework* by Fried and Hansson, and *Delivering Happiness* by Tony Hsieh. Read a couple, and they will lead you to the others that make sense for you to read.

## TRANSFORMING AN EMPLOYEE INTO A STAKEHOLDER

Anecdotally, I believe at least 20 percent of people are natural Stakeholders, less than 20 percent are hardened employees, and 60 percent or more want to be Stakeholders but have been turned into employees by managers. The best tool I have discovered for transforming employees into Stakeholders is what we call the Decision-Making Scale, which has four levels:

| Identifying Problems | Identifying Solutions |
|---|---|
| Level 1 – Unable to identify problem | Unable to identify solution |
| Level 2 – Able to identify problem | Unable to identify solution |
| Level 3 – Able to identify problem | Able to identify possible solutions and bring them to the boss |
| Level 4 – Able to identify problem | Able to identify and implement solution and send report to the boss |

In a traditional Industrialist company, work identities roughly divide along these decision-making levels:

| Identifying Problems | Identifying Solutions | Identity |
|---|---|---|
| Level 1 – Unable to identify problem | Unable to identify solution | Employee |
| Level 2 – Able to identify problem | Unable to identify solution | Supervisor |
| Level 3 – Able to identify problem | Able to identify possible solutions and bring them to the boss | Manager |
| Level 4 – Able to identify problem | Able to identify and implement solution and send report to the boss | Director or above |

In a Participation Age company, the identities would divide along these lines:

| Identifying Problems | Identifying Solutions | Identity |
|---|---|---|
| Level 1 – Unable to identify problem | Unable to identify solution | Employee |
| Level 2 – Able to identify problem | Unable to identify solution | Employee |
| Level 3 – Able to identify problem | Able to identify possible solutions and bring them to the boss | Employee |
| Level 4 – Able to identify problem | Able to identify and implement solution and send report to the boss | Stakeholder |

If you are an Industrialist, Level 4 Stakeholders are those staff in your business who are annoying because they will not be serfs in your fiefdom and just "go along." You will eventually fire them or they will leave, but neither of you will be happy for the duration. If you are a Capitalist, you might say, "I got really lucky hiring Jenna," and you might feel that way about 20 percent of your workforce. But at least 60 percent of the rest of them can be turned into Jennas if you lead them there. You can play a simple game using this Decision-Making Scale:

1. Whenever you are having a problem-solving conversation with anyone, say this fill-in-the-blank statement to yourself: "This is a Level 'X' (1, 2, 3, or 4) conversation."

2. If it is a Level 1, 2, or 3 conversation, ask yourself, "How do I move this person to the next Level? Don't try to skip levels – there are only four, and you need to make sure that person gets it.

3. If it is a Level 4 conversation, congratulations. You are talking to a Stakeholder.

The process for Step 2 above is simple:

2a. If it is a Level 1 conversation, TRAIN the person to know how to identify the problems. If they aren't spotting problems, it is almost always a training issue – they simply don't know what constitutes a problem in that particular activity. Or, they are a hopeless employee and you need to move them along. Don't be hasty to do that. Make sure it's not a training issue first.

2b. Once they are good at identifying problems and bringing those to you, they are at Level 2. To get them to Level 3, TRAIN them to begin to know how to also identify possible solutions. Have them work with you to do it and watch how you arrive at the solution. Move people out of the organization who will not learn to identify problems and bring them to you.

2c. Once you feel they are beginning to grasp how to develop possible solutions, make the classic leadership statement, "Don't bring me problems anymore, just solutions." Move people out of the organization who continue to bring you problems without possible solutions.

2d. If they are now bringing you possible solutions, they are at Level 3. Once you become comfortable that they are regularly bringing you good solutions, at that point, throw out the classic leadership statement (bring me solutions) and say, "Don't come to me with solutions anymore. You're great at figuring them out yourself. Identify the problem, identify and implement the solution, and just send me a report." Move people out of the organization who continue to need you to bless their solutions before they will take action.

2e. In time, you will be comfortable enough with most people to ask them to stop sending you a report. When you do, you have a leader on your hands. Require that they Make Meaning, not just money. Stretch them, encourage them. Teach them how to lead and show them how to take over. And then get out of the way and go do something productive. Lead by example, not by managing others.

Remember that below-the-waterline decisions require the input of others. Have a process in place for identifying those types of decisions and a process for getting input from the right people. This isn't difficult; Stakeholders have a good sense for what is above and below the waterline. Identify key areas and list them if you have to, and they will take it from there. If you have used the Decision-Making Scale process to train them how to make decisions, it won't be an issue.

## MANAGERS OVERSEE; LEADERS TRAIN AND GET OUT OF THE WAY

The traditional job of the manager is to oversee employees and improve their production with close supervision and improving the process. The role of a Participation Age leader is to also improve Stakeholders' productivity, but by training them to be self-motivated, self-managed adults who are better at improving their own processes than any manager.

## EVERYONE IS A LEADER

In the Participation Age, everyone is a leader. Does that mean we need everyone to be visionary motivators? No, leaders are people who take ownership of their lives, and proactively look for ways to create, innovate, and make an impact in the world around them, and who understand that they can make decisions and are responsible for their own results. Everyone from a boiler tech to a company founder can operate on those principles.

> In the Participation Age, everyone is a leader.

Companies all over the world at every size are demonstrating that people do not need to be managed, and that the company is far better off with self-motivated, self-managed Stakeholders throughout the organization. You can replace a lot of managers with just one leader, and when you do, you will set your workforce free to move your organization forward in ways you couldn't have imagined.

# EMBRACING THE PARTICIPATION AGE

1. What is your mindset? Review the chart in chapter 5 – "Manager vs. Leader." What one thing can you do to become more of a leader and less of a manager in your business? (Pick only one.)

_____

_____

   By When? _____ /_____ / _____ : ____a.m./p.m.

2. Pick one person in your organization to transform from an employee to a Stakeholder. What is the first thing you need to do to get started helping them?

_____

_____

   By When? _____ /_____ / _____ : ____a.m./p.m.

## NOTES

1. Richard L Draft and Richard M. Steers, *Organizations: A Micro-Macro Approach* (New York, NY: Scott Foresman & Co, 1986).

2. D. Yankelovich and J. Immerwahr, *Putting the Work Ethic to Work* (New York, NY: Public Agenda Foundation, Society Press, 1984) 21(2), 58-76.

3. Ricardo Semler, *Maverick* (New York, NY: Warner Books, 1993).

4. Douglas McGregor, *The Human Side of Enterprise* (New York, NY: McGraw-Hill, 2006).

5. Ori Brafman and Rod A. Beckstrom, *The Starfish and the Spider: The Unstoppable Power of Leaderless Organizations* (New York, NY: Penguin Books, 2006).

# How to Hire People You'll Never Have to Manage

*"Nothing we do is more important than hiring and developing people."*
—LARRY BOSSIDY, Chairman, Honeywell International

*"Find the best people you can in the world. And just get out of their way."*
—MATT MULLENWEG, Social Media Entrepreneur

Our original Crankset Group hiring practices were developed to support the Factory System model, and are, not surprisingly, just as outdated as most of the other front-office business practices we inherited from that system. In a Participation Age company, selecting people based on resumes and sitting across the table talking to them is about as effective as wearing flip flops in a snowstorm. But old habits die hard.

In this chapter, we're going to show you what we do now to weed out employees and hire Stakeholders. If your company has the culture right, which comes from the top, this process will help you find Stakeholders and will actually repel employees.

## HOW TO GET EMPLOYEES TO QUIT
## BEFORE YOU HIRE THEM

The objective in our hiring practices is to make sure employees quit before we hire them. It seems like the best time for that to happen. We only want Stakeholders, so our hiring process is built to weed out the employees so they don't get past the first round or so.

Stakeholders and employees have wildly different objectives for getting a job. Industrial Age employees are looking for safety, security, and stability, expressed through a "job" and a regular paycheck. Stakeholders are looking for significance, or to Make Meaning, and they are looking for a place that needs their voice, their creativity, their passion, and their adult desire to make decisions, own their work, and own the results.

Let's be very clear. Employees are not looking for work; they are looking for a job and a paycheck. If the job and corresponding paycheck entails no work, that's even better. Employees don't mind going to work; they just don't want to work when they get there. They don't mind sitting for endless hours without working, as long as the paychecks keep coming. Hire Stakeholders; they love to work.

> The objective in our hiring practices is to make sure employees quit before we hire them.

The traditional hiring process is designed specifically to find employees because it does not require them to do any work to get the job and the paycheck. We fixed that.

Here's our process:

## HIRING PRINCIPLE #1—HIRE FOR CULTURE, THEN TALENT, THEN SKILLS, THEN EXPERIENCE

Hire first for culture. Do they fit in and embrace your beliefs, values, and principles? If you don't know what your beliefs, values, and principles are, read the Appendix section for insight and possible direction. Then make all your hiring decisions (and all your other decisions) based on them.

In principle, you want to hire first for the things that you can't teach. Culture involves someone's deeply held belief system. You don't want to try to teach that – just look for a match with yours.

Hire first for culture, second for talent. Talent is something they are either born with or have developed since they were a kid. It's hard to train someone to be a foot taller, or highly outgoing and friendly, or extremely detailed oriented, or to have a consuming sense of urgency.

Once you find a culture match, and are confident the person has the talent you need, you can move on to

> Employees don't mind going to work; they just don't want to work when they get there. Hire Stakeholders; they love to work.

see what their skills are. In general, talent is innate and skills are learned. Someone may have an innate talent for juggling (eye-hand coordination, dexterity, etc.), but juggling is a learned skill. So are programming, working on a car, and designing a rocket.

Never hire for skills alone. Never. That is nothing short of chasing a shiny object. The skilled person who doesn't fit your culture will be a thorn in your side. It might take a few months or longer, but you will both be miserable. The possible gain of having that highly skilled person on board will be more than offset by the drag they will be on the rest of the company. Don't do it.

If you are presented with two people, one who is a perfect culture match with great innate talent for whatever you want them to do, and a second person who is less of a culture match and maybe not as *talented*, but **Hire first for culture.** who has all the skills and experience you need, always take the first one. Skills can be taught, and experience can be gained, but you won't/can't change their culture fit or their talents.

And almost never hire for experience. Someone's experience at another company may seem to make them the ideal candidate at yours, but context is a very important and elusive variable. What made them great at another company might not work at all in yours.

## HIRING PRINCIPLE #2—RESUMES (OBITUARIES) ARE NEARLY USELESS

You can see why, in a Participation Age company, resumes don't help much at all. You will never get a grasp of someone's belief system and whether they fit in with your company culture from reading that piece of paper. Yet, the culture piece is the single most important factor in hiring. If there isn't a culture match, the hiring process shouldn't even go to the next level. You don't ever need to look at a resume in the first few steps of hiring them.

Resumes also never give you a feel for someone's innate talent. After culture, talent is the most important consideration. You want them to grow with you, and their talent and propensity for going beyond just what they are hired to do will determine whether they have a future with your company. What they know today is almost irrelevant for the future, and if you're hiring only to cover today's production issue, it's a bad hire.

**Obituaries and resumes are both glowing accounts of what people have done in the past, except that resumes are usually more embellished than obituaries.** The traditional role of resumes is to inform you of two things: 1) a candidate's skills, and 2) a candidate's experience. The problem with looking at a piece of paper to determine those is that resumes are like obituaries. People never list the dumb things they've done or their ongoing string of failures. Obituaries and resumes share a common characteristic – they are both glowing accounts of what people have done in the past, except that resumes are usually more embellished than obituaries.

Considering this, when you see a list of software competencies a mile long and you ask, "So, you're competent with all of these?" what answer do you really think you're going to get? And what does *competent* mean?

Likewise, if you ask if those sales listed are ones the candidate actually closed, well, of course they are. In hiring our last salesperson, Kyle Matthews, we asked all of the candidates to give us referrals of three people to which they had actually sold something. Out of fifteen or so semi-finalists, thirteen of them included no past clients, one person gave us one closed referral, and only one candidate, Kyle, gave us three customers as referrals. They all said Kyle was now their friend. We hired Kyle.

Giant corporations have software programs that go through stacks of resumes and pick people based on keywords. If you stop and think about the incredible people they've left on the table and the hacks they hired who simply had a professional resume writer fill in the blanks, it's no wonder Participation Age companies don't have much respect for resumes. We'll use them, but late in the process, and usually not for the traditional purposes.

## HIRING PRINCIPLE #3—TAKE NO DIRECT REFERRALS

This may not work for a few highly seasoned leaders being hired to take over major responsibilities, but for almost all positions we don't take referrals. If a Stakeholder, friend, or neighbor wants to recommend someone, we ask them to send their candidate to the designated website and go through the process blind, like everyone else. We don't want to know their names or anything about them.

I used to hire from referrals, and it was very hit and miss. It took me a while to figure out why. A lot of it has to do with the way our brains work, but in a nutshell, when someone I know, love, and respect refers someone to me and tells me this person hung the moon, I desperately want to believe that. It colors my view of the person from the outset. The person might actually have hung the moon somewhere else, but that doesn't mean he or she will be the right culture fit for us or be able to hang the moon in our context. Referrals have rarely worked out anywhere as glowingly as they were described.

We believe the right candidate will rise to the top of our process, so we simply ask everyone to send their referrals through the established process. This puts them on equal footing with everyone else. The other thing this does for you is it keeps you from having to do *courtesy* interviews for your Aunt Mabel's best friend, or even worse, feel the pressure to hire someone because of relational status. We don't even meet people for the first few rounds of our hiring process, and by then, we've usually got a small group of great cultural fits with the right talent for the position.

Does this really work? We hired Kyle through this blind process. I was one of three people reviewing the responses (not resumes), and it wasn't until after we had narrowed the field to fifteen or so candidates that we finally asked for their resumes. I then saw Kyle's name and realized I knew him very well. His mom and dad are great friends, and they had alerted him to the ad. He came in blind and blew away one of our Stakeholders tasked with checking the applicants and continued to do so through the whole process. He got the job without benefiting from special referral status simply because he was the best candidate.

## HIRING PRINCIPLE #4—DON'T MEET PEOPLE UNTIL VERY LATE IN THE PROCESS

With very few exceptions, there is no good reason to meet people personally until late in the process, even for sales positions. To the contrary, meeting them early on can work out badly. When we meet people, their physical appearance, demeanor, clothing, etc. greatly influences the way we think of them. Some of that matters for sales positions, but a lot of it clouds and distorts our objectivity.

If we have a great personal connection, or we connect (or disconnect) in some superficial way – all of that lodges in our brain and colors the rest of the hiring process. If you're hiring someone to make outbound calls, fix a boiler, program code, or do most other jobs, you want to focus on the culture, talent, and eventually skills that person brings to the job. If you meet people early in the process, you will take some great candidates out of the running and move some others forward who really aren't a fit for the position.

## HIRING PRINCIPLE #5—DESIGN A DIFFERENT HIRING PROCESS FOR EVERY POSITION

Why would you sit across a desk and chat with someone about his or her obituary/resume when you are hiring someone to fix boilers, do sales, program code, or answer phones? It's nuts. You must ask yourself what you really want this person to do well, and then design a process that focuses on those few core competencies. The one-size-fits-all process is lazy and very expensive because of how much retraining it causes. I can't think of a single position in any company that is well-served by sifting through a stack of resumes, blindly picking a few obituaries that look good, and talking over a desk about that obituary.

It takes time and effort, but creating a different process for each position will always bring the best results. Do you want someone who is good on the phone? Design a process that has you talking to them on the phone. Don't meet them in person until you have it down to two to three people. Want a programmer? Give them something to code (again, don't meet them until almost the end – don't be influenced by appearance). You get the idea. Every job is different and every process to fill them should be, too.

## THE HIRING PROCESS

Here's what we do and recommend to other business leaders we work with:

1. Design the ad – our ads are always VERY long. If you don't apply anything else from this process, do this: create a VERY long ad, four to eight written pages. Fill it with your culture – your beliefs, values, principles; your vision, mission, and business objectives. Give your website(s). Tell the candidates why you are the best and what their future looks like with you. Toward the middle or the end, list all the things you think their job will entail. Make it as detailed as possible. Have your friends send all their referrals through this process, without telling you who referred them.

   If you are hiring for a job with any need for attention to detail at all, somewhere in the middle of the ad, bury a sentence like this, "Please do not send your resume to us. Just answer the following questions and email those to xxxx@xxx.com. We will respond to those submissions that resonate with us" – or something similar.

   Give them five to seven questions focused solely on culture – what they value, their beliefs about business in general, the principles they would work from, how they might fit in, what they want out of the experience, etc. Don't ask anything about their skills or experience.

2. Place the ad. Again, we do it largely on free sites, but have used the paid job-hunting sites at times as well.

   Two things will happen.
   First, because the ad is long, you will not be deluged with responses. In fact, you will likely have to put the ad out a couple or more times (even on Craigslist) to get enough responses to move forward. When we first did it for an administrative position, we were told we would get a few hundred responses in a couple hours. We got about one hundred responses, and fifty or so were deleted for sending their resumes.

   The second thing that will happen is that most of the people who do fight their way through the whole ad will be Stakeholders. You will have eliminated almost all of the employees. Why? Remember what I said above, Industrial Age employees have been taught to look for a job, not for work. Even reading this ad will look like work to them, and they're not about to do it. Industrial Age employees are just trolling the ads and slinging resumes, they're not going to stop and take the time to actually read your ad. Most will not even reply, but those who do will not read the ad and will send their resumes even if they read it. Why? Because they can't possibly imagine a job search process starting without one.

3. Read the responses to the culture questions. (Delete any responses that include resumes without opening the emails. Those are employees responding.) Grading is subjective (and looking at a resume isn't?), but you will find yourself gravitating toward people who view business the way you do, and want the right things out of the position (fulfillment, the ability to contribute, be a team player, make an impact, etc.).

We use a Candidate Scoring System on a spreadsheet. The scoring template varies according to the position being filled. We score the responses on the spreadsheet, which begins the process of compiling a number of scores for each candidate into a summary score. At the end, we will still make a subjective decision, but it almost always matches up with the spreadsheet. And the spreadsheet keeps us as objective as possible throughout the process.

4. After weeding out those who don't have the right cultural fit, test for talent. If you're hiring someone as a phone salesperson, talk to them quickly on the phone – two to three minutes. First impressions are key in phone sales. You only want to know if they have the talent to do this.

If you're hiring for an admin position, test for attention to detail, sense of urgency, etc. – whatever you think are the most important talents (not skills). Sometimes, this will include an aptitude test, but in the early stages, you can usually design some other way to find out if they have the talent for the job. Score these on the spreadsheet. Some candidates will obviously not be taken to the next round. And some will drop out because they don't want to do the work to get the job. They have shown themselves to be employees and have done you the favor of quitting before you hired them.

5. Test for skills. Send a potential admin a word doc to format (or fix – find the errors), a presentation to design, a spreadsheet to build or fix – again, whatever skills you are looking for, have them perform these. Have a phone salesperson sell you something. Have a programmer code something. A boiler tech should fix the boiler, or find the problem at least (if it's a liability to have them fix it). A marketing person should design a piece or do copywriting.

For a few of these positions, you will have to meet the person, but for most of them, you can do it blind. As was said before, don't meet people until you absolutely have to.

Score them on the spreadsheet. You will lose some more candidates here because, again, they don't want to do the work and are just looking for a paycheck.

6. Do short phone interviews when appropriate – five to seven minutes, or in the case of a salesperson, maybe seven to ten minutes. This wouldn't make sense for a boiler tech or a lot of technical jobs, but you do want to know if most people can communicate. Again, scoring is subjective, but it all adds up over time to a much more objective opinion than if you were just passing resumes across a table. You will weed out applicants at this point, and a couple more will quit the process, saving you the future headache of letting them go.

7. Request their resumes (and salary requirements if appropriate; never give yours to them first – ask them what would motivate them). By now, you're down to ten to fifteen people, maybe a few more, but not usually. Play detective with the resume. Look for things that aren't there as much as things that are: missing periods of time, too many job changes, erratic job history (no focus, no passion for any one type of work), who they give as references, too much emphasis on education, badly designed or badly formatted resume (lack of attention to detail), cover letter focused on things you aren't interested in, etc.

You can also look at experience and skills, the traditional things people use resumes to share, but remember, skills can be taught, and experience can be fudged. And someone who is very experienced can be inflexible and unable to adjust to your processes. ("We always did it this way at X company.")

Score the resumes on the spreadsheet and weed out any obvious mismatches to your company.

8. Invite the finalists for very short interviews – ten to fifteen minutes max for no more than ten people, fewer if you are confident you have five or so great ones. Just about everyone left at this stage will be Stakeholders and self-motivated, self-managed Stakeholders. They will also have a sense of adventure and a natural curiosity. Nobody else would get through this kind of process.

You don't need more than ten to fifteen minutes to find your two or three finalists. It will be obvious. In many cases, this will be the first time you've met them, but you will have a solid idea of who the final three will be from the rest of the process. The personal meeting is largely for getting an intuitive confirmation that you were right or wrong. Score the short interviews and knock it down to two to three finalists.

9. Thirty to Forty-five Minute Interviews – have them meet first with the people they will work closest with or have the most impact on (have some of these folks in the short interview process as well, or even the phone interview process.) If they don't see the fit, there is no sense taking it any further, even if you love the applicant. If they seem to be a fit, have them meet with as many people as possible throughout the company. (One company I know takes the final two out for happy hour (one candidate one night and the other the next night). The entire company of fifty plus people go along and then vote on which one they would like to hire. It's one of the votes that goes on the spreadsheets.)

10. Call your winner and begin negotiations. Notice, we did not talk much about money before this. It rarely comes up in this process until very near the end. We got their salary requirements when we got their resumes. If they were out of whack, that would be part of the phone interview, to see if there is room to make it work for both of us.

## THINGS TO WATCH FOR

The most important thing to do is to filter everything the candidate says through the culture of your organization and the mindset of a Stakeholder. Employees will ask a lot of questions about benefits, vacation time, work hours, lunch breaks, etc. Stakeholders will ask lots of questions about how they can make an impact, opportunities to grow and learn, and what the culture is like. Interviewing is like having a first date; if something annoys you just a little on the first date, it's likely to drive you crazy a year later. Follow your intuition on these things.

## DO THIS ONE THING

If you do nothing else suggested in this chapter, do this – have everyone (including referrals) respond to a long ad by answering a few culture questions. And request that they not send a resume. That alone will cause most employees to quit before you hire them, and the remaining candidates will, for the most part, be hardcore Stakeholders looking to Make Meaning, not just money.

## DOES THIS SOUND TOO HARD?

I regularly talk to business owners and leaders who are very dissatisfied with their staff. Then they tell me how they hired them and it makes perfect sense. The manager was very busy, the slot needed to be filled, so they shopped for someone highly skilled with a lot of experience, who wouldn't need any training, and stuck that person in the position.

You will get the result of whatever process you run. If you run a quick-hit, resume-scanning hiring process based on chatting across a table, that is the Random Hope strategy of interviewing and you will get pot luck as a result. It's also a very lazy way to approach one of the most important things you will ever do with your business – hire others who can free you up and move the company forward. If you take the time to do it right, you will likely get the right results.

One small company we worked with, who hired people the old-fashioned way for its first three years, (resumes, skills, experience, referrals) have seen all those people either leave or have had to move them along. The people they have hired through this process are all still with them. The founder told me she would be honored to have them with her for decades, and just as honored to help them start their own businesses or find another, better place to Make Meaning.

> If you run a Random Hope strategy of interviewing you will get pot luck as a result.

Hiring isn't a crap shoot. It's what we make it. Take the time to go for Stakeholders. You won't regret it.

---

If you would like to have our Stakeholder's Toolkit, which has copies of a few of our ads and our scoring templates, along with an expanded step-by-step process for hiring, they are available at http://WhyEmployeesAreAlwaysABadIdea.com.
If you bought this book, please email us first at Grow@CranksetGroup. com, and we will give you a code to change the US $157 price to $20.

# EMBRACING THE PARTICIPATION AGE

1. What is your mindset? What one thing can you do to change your hiring process to attract exclusively Stakeholders and to make it unattractive for employees to apply?

_____

_____

By When? _____ /_____ / _____:_____a.m./p.m.

2. Is there anyone in your organization who needs specific assistance with the hiring process, or who can be your champion in this new process? What one thing can you do to move this person forward?

_____

_____

By When? _____ /_____ / _____:_____a.m./p.m.

# PART III

# REFRAMING
Our Business Practices

# Other Business Diseases: Preplanning, Scarcity, Education, Competition, Rugged Individualist, Balance

The seven core business diseases of the Industrial Age are:

1. Big, (for the sake of being big)
2. Industrialist
3. Employees
4. Managers
5. 9 to 5
6. Separation of Work and Play
7. Retirement

But there are other consequences we are experiencing from the Industrial Age.

## IT'S ALL ABOUT BELIEF SYSTEMS

Those seven core business diseases are not the only questionable practices to arise from a system set up to benefit the Bigs at the expense of the Smalls. If a company wants to join the Participation Age or an employee wants to become a Stakeholder, there are a few other prominent business diseases we should understand, all of which flow directly or indirectly from the seven core diseases we discussed in Part I.

> These business diseases are nothing more and nothing less than a belief system.

We have to understand that all of these business diseases are nothing more and nothing less than a belief system on which we have built an entire century of business practices. If you adopt the seven core beliefs above, it naturally guides and affects everything else you touch.

## RUN TOWARD, NOT AWAY

As you build the Participation Age belief system on which you will run your company, notice the connection from the following *sub-diseases* to the seven core business diseases, and then think about how they all play out in our businesses. Build a belief system which guards against falling back into these practices.

Don't try to build your company or career as a negative reaction to Industrialism, but with a strong vision for where you want to end up. People who are running away from something are much less likely to be successful than people running toward something. Don't run away from the Industrial Age. Instead run toward a clear vision for a Participation Age company. Get a good grasp on the core business diseases and those further diseases outlined here, then write down what you believe and run toward that with resolve and unwavering commitment.

> People who are running away from something are much less likely to be successful than people running toward something.

# Preplanning

*"We didn't have any plans when we started. We were just opportunistic. We got into this thing not by design but because it worked out that way."*

—BILL HEWLETT, HP

Building a business is a lot like my trip to Tanzania; you make it up as you go along. I was supposed to meet a Congolese Chief, with whom we planned to do business and also help rebuild the local economy. I got my visa and passport back from the Tanzanian consulate via FedEx only minutes before leaving for Africa. The visa snafu was only a warm-up.

I was supposed to only be there for a quick two-hour meeting, so my return flight out of Tanzania was the same evening, just nine hours after I arrived. I landed and received a text that the Chief would not arrive until the next day. I lost my cheap nonrefundable ticket home and bought an expensive one way for the next night.

I had no knowledge of Dar es Salaam, but managed to find a hotel. Every day for the next few days, the Chief was delayed and was supposed to arrive the next day. I rebooked flights and hotel rooms daily. The fourth day, I took a long walk and took pictures with my phone of some nice trees against a wall on a quiet street, and was quickly confronted by three policemen in fancy uniforms. They let me know it was the president's palace behind the wall, and I had just taken illegal pictures. Then they uttered three words you never want to hear in a developing country from a cop, "Come with us."

I was in the country illegally. My visa was only for three days, and both my visa and passport were back at the hotel and not on me, a big no-no. As I was being walked back to the gate house, I decided to pretend I was in charge. I showed them how I could delete pictures from the phone and made a little small talk in broken Swahili. Then I said, "Nafurahi kukufahamu" (pleased to meet you), shook their hands, turned around and walked away. The role reversal confused them enough for me to turn a corner and melt into a crowd on a busy street. I quickly got lost in the crowd as if I were in an *Indiana Jones* movie.

I finally met the Chief and got to my return flight with only ten minutes to spare, before the gate closed. Had I missed my flight, I wouldn't have had money for a hotel, and all my credit cards were frozen. I got out of the country and returned to the United States with US $10 in my pocket. Thank goodness for lousy airplane food.

## TOO MUCH PREPLANNING IS A DISEASE

Bill Hewlett's statement at the beginning of this section is not unique. I haven't found a single *Fortune* 500 that started with a business plan – not one. I suspect the overwhelming majority of successful businesses have the same history of spontaneous order as he experienced (order coming from perceived chaos). Most of them had early years that sounded more like my trip to Tanzania. They understood that a lot of preplanning was just fortune telling.

Exhaustive preplanning is a disease of the Industrial Age that became popular as companies grew to giant proportions and as educators began imposing their cognitive worldview on an otherwise intuitive business world. When you're propping up a giant factory or trying to take over an entire industry, it lends itself to a lot of preplanning. Business plans became popular in the closing years of the Industrial Age (1950 on), and the rest of us have caught the disease.

## THE PRECAUTIONARY PRINCIPLE

This obsession has evolved into what is called the Precautionary Principle, which generally states that if you can think of something that might go wrong, don't do anything until you have a contingency in place to cover for that possibility. The amazing advances of the Industrial Age have allowed us to focus on levels of safety that would never have been imagined for thousands of years.

Meticulous preplanning before you move forward sounds pretty reasonable, except it is sucking the life out of our willingness and ability to create, innovate, and take the risks to build great things that have been a part of being human since long before the Egyptians imagined the pyramids. The cleaned-up world we inherited from the nineteenth- and twentieth-century Industrialists has nearly sterilized the creativity right out of us. We are becoming so risk-averse that it is a national epidemic. The education system, the government, and big business are all teaching us to live by the Precautionary Principle; don't move until you have it all figured out.

I'm not against planning – we should be doing it at every step along the way as we are moving. I'm not even against a little bit of preplanning. But massive preplanning has near 0 percent effectiveness at doing anything but killing innovation.

Planning never creates movement, but movement can create a good plan. Implement now. Perfect as you go.

Massive preplanning as you see in three-to-five-year business plans is a disease that has its roots in the Factory System. Successful people do it like Bill Hewlett did for HP in the early years. They come up with a very simple idea, get moving, then evaluate and plan as they go. They don't stop to plan, because successful companies understand that planning never creates movement, but movement can create a good plan. Every *Fortune* 500 is a testimonial to this. Stop planning. Get moving.

Massive preplanning is a business disease. The Industrial Age was wrong. Implement now. Perfect as you go.

# Scarcity

*"In the event of a decompression, an oxygen mask will automatically appear in front of you. . . . If you are traveling with a child or someone who requires assistance, secure your mask on first.*

—FLIGHT ATTENDANT, every airline, USA

*"You will get all you want in life if you help enough other people get what they want."*

—ZIG ZIGLAR

## SCARCITY VS. ABUNDANCE

Industrialists live in a world of scarcity. There is only so much to go around, and not enough for everyone, so the game is to get yours before the next guy gets his. And in its worst form, the objective is to get it all and leave none for anyone else, as the early Industrial Age monopolies demonstrated. Industrialists believe there are only so many good ideas or great potential products out there, and after that, it's over. It's a Darwinian world, and the scarcity-minded Industrialist intends to be the last man standing. It has to be that way. If someone else is left standing, their presence might destroy us. It's a zero-sum game.

## TRUE CAPITALISTS LIVE IN A WORLD OF ABUNDANCE

Traditional Capitalists focus on moving the world forward through their creativity and innovation. Capitalists have no fear of destroying the present for the future, and regularly introduce advances that make existing products and services obsolete. In recent years, Apple has been recognized for this, regularly cannibalizing its own products with the next one. Rather than fearing that it might destroy its present market, Apple understood it would create new and even bigger markets. Steve Jobs was willing to destroy his own company's present products for the next great advance, a very Capitalist view of the world.

Google's CEO Eric Schmidt also had it right in the early days, proclaiming that "Google is trying to solve the next problem, not the last problem." But in recent years, Google's early abundance mindset has been challenged regularly. None of us can rest on our laurels. Living in abundance is a focused and ongoing effort.

## THE SCARCE WORLD DOESN'T EXIST

The scarce world the twenty-first-century Industrialists are so afraid of simply doesn't exist. Markets are always expanding, and new products and services are being created at a dizzying pace. Scarcity thinking is just a lousy excuse for being lazy, uncreative, and boorish in a world constantly expanding with new ideas, new markets, and new generations of people. The slow and long-term decline of companies like GM, United Airlines, and other stolidly Industrialist companies is a direct result of this scarcity thinking. It causes them to focus on acquiring the other guy's creativity, eliminating him, then maintaining the status quo so they can milk the existing market.

> Scarcity thinking is just a lousy excuse for being lazy, uncreative, and boorish in a world constantly expanding.

Capitalist companies that live in a world of abundance fundamentally believe that there are plenty of good ideas and expanding markets to go around. They believe they can create more markets and customers out of thin air by being creative, and by building a future, instead of milking the dying throes of the present for one last dollar. Products like fast food, computers, personal printers, cell phones, QR codes, commercial space travel, Angry Birds, Twitter, online education, and a thousand others were unthinkable just a few years ago.

## BE THE BOARD

Some of the most abundant-minded companies live on an entirely different level. The Industrial Age taught us win/lose. Then the modern business world started to get on board with win/win. But in the Participation Age, companies that live in a world of abundance remove themselves altogether from the win/win equation and take it to another level. As Rosamund and Benjamin Zander articulated so well in their book, *The Art of Possibility*, "Great companies simply become the game board on which people play the game of business." They work hard at connecting companies to each other, and figuring out how to make the whole industry successful, believing that what Zig Ziglar said was true – they'll get theirs because they've focused on helping other companies get theirs.

This isn't kum-bah-ya stuff. It is a hard-core Capitalist success habit. It builds a culture of trust, credibility, and service in the world around us. People want to work with those companies, and will go out of their way to find them.

Do you live in a world of abundance or in a world of scarcity? The answer will affect every decision you make in business, and will go directly to the bottom line.

> Do you live in a world of abundance or in a world of scarcity? The answer will affect every decision you make in business, and will go directly to the bottom line.

## NOTES

1. Zander and Zander, *The Art of Possibility* (New York: Penguin Group, 2000).

# Education: The Sacred Cow

*"Most studies show that schools start to do better when they are competing for students."*

—BILL COSBY

Our public education system is the last great monopoly of the Industrial Age. The sacred cow for perpetuating the business practices of the Industrial Age is an education system created by and for the Industrialists, one that is out of sync with the Participation Age.

## EDUCATION WON'T MAKE YOU SUCCESSFUL

Our education system worked to make a few Industrialists rich and powerful. And even though the Industrial Age is over, it's still stuck back there, focused almost exclusively on churning out employees who are taught two things in college: a specific skill, and that they should never challenge the professor's brilliance. The combination of that specific skill and mindless acceptance of the professor's finished view of the world sets them up very well to be cogs in some big corporate machine. What it doesn't do is prepare them to be life-long learners, owners, Stakeholders, or self-managed adults.

## OUR EDUCATION SYSTEM IS
## AN INDUSTRIAL AGE DISEASE

There is one main message I want to convey here. Our education system was designed specifically to feed the Factory System for the benefit of a few Industrialists, to the detriment of the rest of us. It was designed by the Bigs for the benefit of the Bigs. So it is no surprise that the result for the rest of us is not good. Here are some of the less-than-stellar results from depending on a formal education system that is deeply committed to closed markets, the status quo, and keeping out or attempting to discredit all competition:

> Our education system was designed specifically to feed the Factory System for the benefit of a few Industrialists, to the detriment of the rest of us.

1. **Top CEOs**—*Bloomberg Business Week* reported in 2010 that people who never attended or never graduated from college are the number one source of CEOs for S&P 500 companies, not Harvard (it's number three).

2. **Wealth**—Forrester Research reports that 20 percent, or one out of five, of America's millionaires never attended or finished college.

3. **Personal well-being or happiness**—A university degree leads to lower levels of happiness for twenty-three- to twenty-five-year-olds a few years out of college, compared to those twenty-three- to twenty-five-year-olds who instead got an apprenticeship or vocational training.[2]

4. **Learning**—A full third of college graduates gain no measurable skills during their four years in college.[3]

5. **Productivity**—Only 59 percent of high school graduates waste time at work, compared to 66 percent of those with a bachelor's, 65 percent with a master's, and taking the top spot, PhDs at 67 percent.[4]

6. **Annual income**—Millions of nonattendees and nongraduates make significantly more than college graduates. A correlation to annual income is only possible for industries in which the education system has locked out all competition, as is the case for becoming lawyers, doctors, and the like. (Abe Lincoln would never have been allowed to practice law today.)

7. **Lifetime income**—"College graduates make a million dollars more in their lifetime than noncollege graduates." That is an urban myth perpetuated by an Industrial Age education system that needs your money to keep it afloat. It has been debunked many times. In my blog, I used a Georgetown University study to show that high school grads could make as much or even more.[5]

## LIFE-LONG LEARNERS

Our education system, particularly higher education, is still set up to train people in specific skills, but does little to help them learn how to think. It is not set up to produce self-managed, self-motivated Stakeholders who are life-long learners.

## IF NOT HIGHER EDUCATION, THEN WHAT?

We need to stop telling people they need to go to college to be successful, especially when it comes to business. It's not true. It may be necessary in fields where skill sets have been locked down by the education system, but for most of us there are other, better ways to become successful.

> Our education system, is not set up to produce self-managed, self-motivated Stakeholders who are life-long learners.

1. **Be an apprentice.** Business is one of the soft sciences in which formal education is least correlated with success. Let's get back to what worked for centuries before Industrial Age education interrupted us. Apprenticing worked for centuries, and the learning, connections, and experience gained by working with and for someone you want to emulate is worth a great deal more than most bachelor's degrees, and certainly more than any MBA.

2. **Purpose.** As my Irish friend, John Heenan says, "If you don't have a vision for your own life, you'll become part of someone else's vision for theirs." That is the Irish definition of an *employee*. If you don't have a strong purpose for your life, the best you will ever do is make money, but you'll never Make Meaning. (Read my book, *Making Money is Killing Your Business*, and get a Big Why.)

3. **Be a life-long learner.** Adults don't learn unless we're disoriented. Live a disoriented life and wake up every morning knowing how little you know and how much less you have experienced. Life-long learners don't fail or even succeed, they just practice and get better all the time.

4. **Be a doer, not a thinker.** The academics are wrong. *We do not think our way to a new way of acting. We ACT our way to a new way of thinking.*

5. **Chase your dream.** Turn your dream into a vision. Dreamers talk; visionaries walk. Get moving.

6. **Ask Why.** Ask it a lot. And ask it of everyone and everything. It's the most important question you'll ever ask. If you can't ask it where you work, there is a company out there looking for you who can't wait for you to ask it.

7. **Don't be a victim/employee/child and settle for working for an Industrialist.** Start your own business or keep looking until you find a Capitalist who wants Stakeholders who can Make Meaning, not just money.

## ALTERNATIVE EDUCATION MODELS

Today, we have an ever-increasing number of choices for how to become life-long learners, all of which threaten the traditional system of didactic (truth-telling) teaching.

The Sudbury Valley School (SVS) is one emerging model of a *democratic* school. The Sudbury model started in 1968 in Framingham, Massachusetts and has slowly spread across the United States and into other countries around the world. It replaces the traditional K-12 model for those who participate.

Sudbury schools are based on "the twin concepts of trust and responsibility" (students are not stupid or lazy). Like true Stakeholders, the students are treated as members of the school *community*, along with the teachers, and are trusted to manage their time and make their own decisions.

Nobody teaches didactically from a *top down* perspective – there is no sitting in rows listening to the expert. Teachers are more facilitators than teachers. At Sudbury, learning happens in the context of doing, which research regularly shows is one of the best ways to learn.

The percentage of Sudbury students who go on to college is 87 percent, and a staggering 42 percent of them are involved in entrepreneurial pursuits. (Sudbury students come from all economic strata.)[6] They have a Stakeholder's vision for their lives and want to Make Meaning. Peter Gray, who studied the Sudbury model, writes, "The most common complaint that the Sudbury Valley graduates had about college is that their college classmates seemed immature – they acted as if they didn't want to be in college and often behaved irresponsibly."[7]

> The academics are wrong. We do not think our way to a new way of acting. We ACT our way to a new way of thinking.

Sudbury is only one example of Participation Age learning that ranges from charter schools to homeschooling to a myriad of cocreation initiatives, to some pretty creative stuff going on in small pockets inside the formal public education system itself.

## ONLINE EDUCATION:
## "THE THIRD INDUSTRIAL REVOLUTION"

The online world is also helping break the mold. Robert Tracinski, in an article about *The Third Industrial Revolution*, says, "All of the technology we have developed is there waiting to be applied to a revolutionary change in how we learn – and how we work. It reminds me a lot of the Internet in 1995: they're still just figuring out how to take something that has always been done in brick-and-mortar classrooms, and do it online. The obsolescence of the university is only the first step in the revolution."[8]

KhanAcademy.com, an online learning phenomenon, is attracting millions who are rejecting the didactic preaching/teaching model for a *learn-by-doing* model.

ColoradoConnectionsAcademy.com is one of many like it springing up across the nation. It is an online public school for kids, replacing the brick-and-mortar K-12 system.[9] Research shows that kids being educated online are as social or more so than their brick-and-mortar-educated counterparts. Most of them have both online and offline clubs available, and in some cases, more clubs like Chess clubs, Robotics clubs, Academic clubs, Arts clubs, and others.

Coursera.com, started in 2012, is now offering hundreds of free online classes from dozens of elite universities, giving anyone in the world free access to a great education.[10] As these kinds of initiatives grow and expand, the sharing model so central to the Participation Age is going to make it possible to replace the traditional Factory System-based education model and facilitate a return to learning as a way of life.

> The obsolescence of the university is only the first step in the revolution.

Industrialists work hard to maintain the status quo and a closed market, and are focused on destroying the competition instead of getting better. The Participation Age and its hallmark of *sharing* is encouraging the development of new learning models that will replace the education system so committed to its Industrial Age model. It can't happen soon enough.

## NOTES

1. *Top 10 CEO Undergraduate Alma Maters, Bloomberg Business Week:* May 13, 2010, http://buswk.co/YzwQEX.

2. *Employment and Workplace Relations,* Mike Dockery, Curtin Institute of Technology, Australian Department of Education, National Centre for Vocational Education Research (NCVER), , 2010.

3. Richard Arum, Josipa Roksa, *Academically Adrift* (Chicago: University of Chicago Press, 2011).

4. *Wasting Time at Work, 2012, Salary.com,* http://www.salary.com/wasting-time-at-work-2012/slide/7/.

5. *Education: One of the Business Diseases of the Industrial Age,* Chuck Blakeman, ChuckBlakeman.com (blog), July 15, 2013, http://bit.ly/12z7wUQ

6. Peter Gray, *Freedom to Learn: The Roles of Play and Curiosity as Foundations for Learning* (August 13, 2008).

7. Ibid.

8. *The Third Industrial Revolution,* Robert Tracinski, February 20, 2013, http://www.tracinskiletter.com/2013/02/third-industrial-revolution/.

9. K12, *ColoradoConnectionsAcademy.com,* see http://www.k12.com/what-is-k12#.UXp2VIJOMiE.

10. *Online Course Enrollment Climbs for 10th Straight Year,* Kelsey Sheeby, US News & World Report, 2013, http://bit.ly/181o1rA.

# Your Competition, Isn't

*"The problem with competition is that it takes away the requirement to set your own path, to invent your own method, to find a new way."*
—SETH GODIN, best selling author of *The Icarus Deception*

The nineteenth-century Industrialist and the twenty-first-century Industrialist share the same view of competition: it is a threat to be eliminated. Going to work is nothing short of going to war, and the daily objective is to shore up the battlements and take the fight to the enemy. It is the mindset of feudal lords reflected into the business world. But one of the biggest implications of a Participation Age company living in a world of abundance is that you no longer have competition that needs to be eliminated. Hard-core Capitalists just don't see the world that way – only Industrialists do.

I've personally landed millions in contracts from small companies to giant technology and pharmaceutical corporations, and I've never once thought about *competition*. It has never been a factor. I actually don't think I have any, and I don't believe you do, either. If you think you do, you just might be thinking like an Industrialist.

Industrialists teach us to do "SWOT" analyses – Strengths, Weaknesses, Opportunities, and "Threats" – to identify those evil competitors who are going to swoop in and steal our clients away. But the main threats you should be worried about come from within your own company, and inside the heads of your own people.

## WHY NOT STUDY THE COMPETITION?
Competition is a business disease that is very closely related to scarcity disease. In the Participation Age, where the hallmark is *sharing*, there are a lot of reasons why you shouldn't be worried about people entering your market, coming up with great ideas you haven't had, or improving on yours. Following are just a few.

1. *People who focus on trying to figure out what makes their competition successful don't have enough good ideas of their own.*

In a world of Industrial Age scarcity, it's as important, or even more important, to study the *competition* to try to figure out their next great idea, as it is to create your own. General Motors wasn't created as a car company, but as a holding company. For the entire twentieth century, just about all they did was buy other people's creativity. All of the big Industrialists of the 1800s – Vanderbilt, Rockefeller, Carnegie, J.P. Morgan, and others – were famous for focusing more on destroying competitors than on coming up with the next great idea. Today, an Industrialist's objective is to dominate the world by maintaining the status quo, a futile exercise in a rapidly changing world.

In our company, we don't have time to figure out what others are doing. We're too busy breathing life into our own ideas, so we're not worried that the other guys have come up with the last great available idea. When you live in a world of abundance, you know you have another great idea inside you, and your responsibility is to uncover it. We don't watch others in our industry. We focus on being creative and innovative and on getting better all the time. There are plenty of good ideas to go around. What's your next great idea?

2. *Imitation is the sincerest form of flattery, but it's a lousy business strategy.*

Great companies are too busy fleshing out their own ideas to follow others around their industry like mimes at a busker festival. And we're terrible guessers, anyway. I've seen companies dissect the products, services, or marketing of other companies and copy them, only to find out they were mimicking the worst part of what the others were doing.

Mimicking others is born in a world of scarcity, and also speaks of a culture that has little or no creativity of its own. Copycats make cheesy Industrial Age products that never lead them to the next great idea. Explorers and pioneers don't mimic others. A Capitalist would be in it to make an impact or change an industry. The two last words of a company dying from lack of innovation are, "Me, too."

3. *Focus on your clients' needs, not your competitors' products.*

Our company's first focus is on coming up with creative and innovative ideas of our own. Our second focus is on what our clients need. What we are creating and what our clients need aren't always the same thing, and both of them inform the other. Sitting around waiting for your customers to show you what they need isn't a good idea. Henry Ford said, "If I had asked my clients what they wanted, I would have made a faster horse." We should be aware of what our customers need before they know what they need, and then work to get them those products.

If you focus first on coming up with good ideas of your own, and then on meeting the needs of your clients, you won't have time to focus on what others are doing.

### 4. *They Won; Good for Them*

If they "beat" you, they simply have something the customer needs that you don't. Be glad for the customer. If, in turn, you sometimes have things other customers want, you'll attract those relationships and the other guy won't. Don't think in terms of having lost to the other guy; think about continuing to improve what you offer so more people will want and need it. The threat is never external; it's our own laziness or lack of creativity that takes us down.

If you have something meaningful to offer, you will get customers. If you don't, you won't. Simple as that. Blaming "competitors" for "losing" contracts or trying to destroy them so you can win is childish nonsense, not to mention very short-term thinking. And it makes you the hated target by people mistakenly throwing stones at Capitalism, who actually hate Industrialists.

### 5. *Are you a wandering generality or a meaningful specific? (Zig Ziglar)*

The great majority of Industrialist companies are wandering generalities, built on mimicking the success of other companies instead of creating their own. When you try to be all things to all men, you become nothing to anyone. Classic Industrialist companies are selling everything from panty hose to airplane parts, and usually have no passion for any of it. They're just building cash cows.

## SHARING IN THE PARTICIPATION AGE

In the Participation Age, companies don't focus on competition, or even the recently popular term *coopetition*. They focus on getting better, making their industry better, and making the world a better place to live, both through creating more useful products and by their value to society.

> In the Participation Age, companies focus on getting better, making their industry better, and making the world a better place to live.

Get the idea of competition out of your head and focus on being the best at whatever great idea you've birthed. And while you're at it, try to figure out how to make the other guy successful, too. You'll make a lot more money and have a lot more fun. And Stakeholders will come running to work for you.

# The Rugged Individualist

*"The rigorous practice of rugged individualism usually leads to poverty, ostracism, and disgrace. The rugged individualist is too often mistaken for the misfit, the maverick, the spoilsport."*

—LEWIS LAPHAM, *Harper's Magazine*

The first Industrialists created an aura of swashbuckling individualism that was so pervasive that nonsense like "going it alone" almost became a prerequisite for success in the Industrial Age. The rugged individualist has its strongest roots in the Industrialists of the nineteenth and early twentieth centuries, and is a business disease that is ripe for eradication.

I am a recovering John Wayne rugged individualist. It took a number of decades and five business startups for me to realize I didn't have to pretend I had a handle on every aspect of the business, or even a lot of it. As I slowly acquired confidence, I learned everybody is making it up as they go along. A few years back, I remember seeing a survey asking *Fortune* 500 CEOs, "What is your greatest fear?" The biggest response was that they feared someone would find out that they didn't know what they were doing. Join the club.

The need to have it all figured out and never admit you made a mistake is insidious. It's worse in the world of big government (on both sides), but is also a staple of management. In the twenty-first-century Industrialist's view of the world, people who admit mistakes and that they don't have everything figured out are considered weak, and should be easy prey for destruction on the way to world domination. But history says differently. If you look at the great leaders in history, they always surround themselves with people who can call them on the BS in their lives and in their leadership. Those who fail surround themselves with yes-men, and then go it alone.

We are building 3to5 Clubs for business owners all around the world. They meet in groups of twenty-four, twice a month, to work through the fundamentals of how to build a business that makes money when they're not around (see www.3to5Club.com). People love the bi-monthly training, but the most valuable thing 3to5 Clubs have to offer is a place where business owners go to find committed community and to say three magic words: "I don't know."

Where do you go to say, "I don't know?" Harvey McKay, one of the best-known business leaders in the world, made sure he was always in a group of other business leaders who would meet regularly and provide what we call "Outside Eyes" for each other. Benjamin Franklin started his Leather Apron Society with a few apprentices like himself who were trying to figure out how to make it in the world. He credited it for a great deal of his success. A lot of very smart business leaders are deeply committed to great business advisory groups with long-standing records of success, like Entrepreneurs' Organization (www.eonetwork.org), Vistage (www.vistage.com), and others. (You should check one out and join.)

> You can manage the ongoing chaos of a growing business all by yourself, or you can admit "I don't know," get with others who also don't know, and figure it out together.

I've started eight businesses, and while I may have had a good grasp on the *craft* of each one of them, the actual implementation was always a crapshoot. As soon as my idea hit the real world, all bets were off, and we were in a regular evolutionary cycle we call, "Implement now. Perfect as you go." You can manage the ongoing chaos of a growing business all by yourself, or you can admit "I don't know," get with others who also don't know, and figure it out together.

We believe in the Wisdom of Crowds[1], which says that there is almost always a better answer in a diverse group of individuals than any one expert could come up with on his own. I hear regularly from 3to5 Club members, Vistage, and Entrepreneurs' Organization (EO) members around the world who say being in those groups have transformed both their lives and their businesses.

The rugged stance individualist is a blustering, silly, insecure, transparent one to take in the Participation Age. As the Industrial Age fades behind us, great leaders-in-the-making will gladly say "I don't know," and then will doggedly pursue figuring it out in the context of Committed Community with others who don't know.

John Wayne is dead. Let's bury the rugged individualist in his honor.

*"If you want to travel fast, go alone. If you want to travel far, go together."*
                                                    – Chinese Proverb

## NOTES

1. James Surowiecki, *The Wisdom of Crowds*, Reprint edition, (New York: Anchor Books, 2005).

# Balance—How to Lead an Unremarkable Life

*"There's no such thing as work-life balance."*
—JACK WELCH, former CEO, GE

*"I gave up years ago on the concept that you could actually have balance in your life, I think it's a phantom chase."*
—BARBARA CORCORAN, real estate mogul

*"I don't believe in balance, not in the classic way."*
—MARISSA MAYER, CEO, Yahoo

*"Balance is the enemy of art."*
—RICHARD EYRE, international art director

*"I don't like balance."*
—DONATELLA VERSACE, fashion designer

*"Balance is overrated."*
—THOMAS LEONARD, Founder, International Coach Federation

Balance is another lousy Industrial Age artifact. It's a disease, not a cure. Successful people don't live a balanced life. They don't want one, either. Do you want a successful life? Stop seeking balance.

## TEETER-TOTTERS RULE

When a teeter-totter is perfectly balanced, nothing is happening. Both people are sitting there in mid-air, staring blankly at each other, wondering if anything interesting is going to happen, slowly realizing that for what they are experiencing, it was not worth getting on the seesaw.

Does that sound like fun? Welcome to the *Ozzie and Harriet, My Three Sons*, and *Leave It to Beaver* life the Industrial Age wanted us to live. We were taught to seek *balance* so we could live highly predictable, highly balanced, and as an unfortunate result, highly unremarkable lives. Just like the Silent Generation did in the 1950s.

Separation of work and play by the Factory System of the Industrial Age is one of the main reasons we seek such a phony construct as balance. Before the Factory System, work was always fully integrated as part of the rest of our lives. As we started GOING to work, the question, "Which one do I choose, work or play?" became a central theme of the Industrial Age. We became haunted by whether we had worked enough to win the "car in the parking lot longest" contest, and then whether we could balance that with some good family time or down time.

## INTEGRATION, NOT BALANCE

None of the greats lived balanced lives. Jesus, Buddha, Mohammed, and just about any great leader in history you probably revere, didn't seek or live balanced lives. In the Participation Age, successful people don't seek balance – they seek integration.

Work and play are no longer separate things we view as opposing each other or happening in different worlds. As an example, Tony Hsieh moved Zappos' headquarters to Las Vegas specifically to encourage integration of work and play, so Stakeholders wouldn't have to seek balance. In the Participation Age, we bring our whole self to work, and we blur the lines between work and play. We leave at 10:00 a.m. to see our kids in the only fifth-grade play in which they will be the lead raccoon. We take bike rides or go for walks at 3:00 p.m., and we even work in the evenings, or what used to be the "weekends," if it fits the rhythms of our businesses and our lives to do so. I call it living an integrated life. Like we did for thousands of years before the Industrialists made us show up at their factories.

## FULL ENGAGEMENT, NOT BALANCE

Integration is about seeking full engagement with whatever will make us successful.

I've built eight businesses. During the first year of building the Crankset Group, I worked seven days a week. There was no balance at all. I was fully engaged in starting the business. The result of that imbalance is that four years later, I was getting every Friday off, every other Monday off, the last week of every month off, and a month a year. That is around 59 percent of the work year, when most Americans only get 4-8 percent of Mondays through Fridays a year off. My life today is not balanced, either; I get a lot of time off.

My wife and I get to choose what to do with all that time – ride a bike, build businesses in Africa, visit a 3to5 Club in Ireland, go on a vacation. In each instance, we are almost always out of balance, going nuts either in vacation mode, work mode, family mode, etc. People having the most fun on a teeter-totter are fully engaged and always out of balance.

## WORK LESS TIME, BE MORE FULLY ENGAGED

I'm not advocating being a workaholic. Plenty of research shows that workaholics spend twelve hours a day at work but only invest four to eight hours in actually getting something done. What I'm advocating is full engagement in whatever needs the highest and best use of your time right now. Years ago, I passed up a "chance of a lifetime" to lead a company in Napa Valley because I was totally out of balance, focusing on my young kids. I didn't try to balance the two – it would have been nuts. Family was the only priority at the time.

Loehr & Schwartz wrote a book called *The Power of Full Engagement*. They had it right by recommending that we make sure we develop each major area of our life – mental, physical (exercise/diet), emotional, spiritual, and the productive output of work and play. And if we don't, we will atrophy and be much less likely to build successful businesses. That's integration.

> What I'm advocating is full engagement in whatever needs the highest and best use of your time right now.

## GET MORE DONE IN LESS TIME

Too many business owners go into business immediately looking for an *Ozzie and Harriet* "lifestyle business" – assuming that they can step right in working three to four days a week so they can be *balanced*. Success almost never comes that way. Momentum doesn't come from balance; it comes from being very imbalanced and focused on something. You burn a lot of fuel on takeoff. An airplane burns up to 50 percent of its fuel just getting to its cruise altitude. Fred Flintstone did a lot of flailing with his feet before his car ever started moving. Balance, especially in the early stages, doesn't help us build a great life or a great business. It's just another form of playing it safe.

> Balance, especially in the early effort, doesn't help us build a great life or a great business. It's just another form of playing it safe.

## REST WITH FULL ENGAGEMENT

I rarely sit around during that fourth week and seek *balance*. The fourth week of some months I'll be riding my bicycle 50-100 miles a day for six straight days in some great place in the world, completely out of balance. Somebody else might lie on a beach the whole time and sleep – a totally imbalanced approach to vacation. Either way, go off the grid while you do it, which is also imbalanced.

Stop seeking balance. Find something to throw yourself at and do it with everything you have. Then take a break from that and throw yourself at something else just as hard (playing with your kids, another business, writing a book, etc.).

I love my teeter-totter life. If you don't have one, don't expect to be successful, and certainly don't expect to live a life that is built to Make Meaning. The Industrial Age company you work for might want you to live a balanced life and leave your personal stuff at home. It's a trap. Find another company to work for – there are plenty of Participation Age companies out there, and the number is growing fast. You would also do your company a service by leaving. It might just make them face the fact that they need to change to keep up with where the world is going.

## HOW TO LIVE A LIFE THAT MATTERS

Too often the word *balance* is nothing more than code for an aversion to taking risks. Building a life of significance is like climbing a cliff face. Balance is achieved when resting on flat spots and ledges. Balance is a good way to rest on way to something important, but if you make a lifestyle out of it, you are risking an unremarkable life. Either way there is risk. I find great inspiration in the saying of Sydney J. Harris, a great 20th century journalist who wrote, "Regret for the things we did can be tempered by time; it is regret for the things we did not do that is inconsolable."

In the Participation Age, we are called to live a committed, fully engaged, fully integrated, and imbalanced life and to share that life with the world.

You can certainly seek to live a life of balance. But balance, pursued as a lifestyle, is much more apt to leave you with regrets of roads untraveled and dreams not pursued, than with a completed bucket list. In the Participation Age, we are called to live a committed, fully engaged, fully integrated, and imbalanced life and to share that life with the world. As Margaret Thatcher, who lived an imbalanced life, said, "One's life should matter." If you live a balanced one, yours likely won't.

# EMBRACING THE PARTICIPATION AGE

1. What is your mindset? After reviewing these other business diseases of the Industrial Age, what is one action you can take to improve personally and/or as a company in these area?

_____

_____

By When? _____ /_____ / _____ : ____ a.m./p.m.


2. Is there one person in your organization who would benefit from exploring these six business diseases and discussing how those mindsets might be affecting their productivity? How could you facilitate that learning?

_____

_____

By When? _____ /_____ / _____ : ____ a.m./p.m.

# The Solution: Significance

*"A life isn't significant except for its impact on other lives."*

–JACKIE ROBINSON

*"Anyone who thinks they are too small to make a difference has never been to bed with a mosquito."*

–GANDHI

## IT'S HOW YOU RESPOND TO CIRCUMSTANCES THAT COUNTS—THE AFRICAN EGG VENDOR

I sat with the African egg vendor and twenty or so others in a mud-brick building with no doors or windows, just openings. They were from one of the largest and most desperate slums in the world. The average person in the room made between US $30 and $60 per month, which was more than a lot of other people there made.

We were discussing business building principles. I had come from America with notes and handouts, but on the first day, I realized they were worthless and gave them to a small school. They were thrilled to have them because they were blank on one side. They don't see much paper, let alone paper they could still use.

I had rarely felt this helpless. Usually, you can just give me a business topic, wind me up, and I'll interact with a group for as long as the beer or snacks last. Here were a couple dozen business owners waiting to hang on every word and I had nothing.

I turned to the egg vendor and asked her how much she makes each month. She proudly told me US $180.00. But once I had her include the cost of the eggs and her other business expenses, her profit was about US $60.00. And once we added up her personal expenses, including food and rent, she said she usually had about US $2.00 left each month. I helped her see that this was her true net profit, and she was very proud that she actually had a little each month. Many business owners she knew, didn't. I asked her what she did with it, and she said, "I take my children to get a special meal." She was a single mom with three kids.

We then talked about freedom—that wealth is the freedom to choose what to do with your time and money. Net profit represented freedom, the ability to choose. That made her very proud to know she had US $2.00 worth of freedom each month, and the other business owners started to get a little excited about the prospect that they, too, might figure out how to get some net profit. We decided right there to call net profit, "Freedom Money," because it's the only money in business with which you actually get to make a fully free choice. The rest of it is spoken for in one way or the other.

Then I challenged her and the rest of them to stop eating their Freedom Money and reinvest it in their business instead, so they would have even more freedom later. I drew blank stares, so everyone huddled around my laptop with a dying battery, and I built a quick spreadsheet to show what might happen if, for eighteen months, the egg vendor reinvested her US $2.00 of Freedom Money into buying more eggs every month. The next month she would have US $2.50 in Freedom Money. Reinvested in more eggs, the end of the third month she would have US $3.50 in Freedom Money, and so on. By the end of eighteen months, she could stop reinvesting and would have US $60 every month in Freedom Money after that.

I asked her if that would change some things, and she thought it might change her life. I then told her it won't happen that way. She'll break eggs, won't find buyers, will have to hire someone to help, etc. Life is messy and so is business, and her Freedom Money might be US $15 a month, not US $60. But it would no longer be US $2.00. It was a tough thing to challenge a woman not to take her kids for a special meal, but she got on board immediately.

I never saw her again, but I always assume the best, that she built up enough monthly Freedom Money to build a better life for herself and her children. The most powerful thing she got out of the time was that being an owner allowed her to make decisions. She was in charge of her future, not the world around her. I left her with a thought that has been valuable to me over the years, "Circumstances don't make me who I am. How I respond to them, does." She left as a proud business owner, looking forward to creating more Freedom Money with her business. Ownership is a very powerful thing.

## THE THREE S'S OF THE INDUSTRIAL AGE

My mother was born in 1921. She grew up in the Great Depression and entered the workforce in 1943 after nurse's training and taught me to pursue three things in life, the three S's of the Industrial Age:

1. Safety--live in the suburbs, don't live downtown with the icky people.
2. Security--have a big wad of cash in the bank.
3. Stability--every day should look the same, no surprises. Her strongest encouragement--get a job with a giant corporation; they are the best prepared to give you a life of safety, security and stability with no surprises.

> "Circumstances don't make me who I am. How I respond to them, does."

Just about every mother of that generation was teaching their kids the same things. So, it's no surprise that at the height of the Industrial Age after World War II, the suburbs exploded with cookie-cutter Cap Cods, white picket fences, men working for Giant Corporation, Inc., who all left for work in unison with their white shirts, ties, suits, and briefcases at 7:30 a.m. and got home at 6 p.m., and who lived as predictable a life as possible. They came home to a manicured wife and 3.6 freshly scrubbed children. *Ozzie and Harriet* reigned. That may sound great to some, but as we revealed in the introduction to this book, those people were called The Silent Generation and made very little meaning in the world around them with their balanced lives.

Their manic pursuit of safety, security, and stability made them the best extensions of machines in the history of the Industrial Age. It also dehumanized them to the point of silencing their voices, their creativity, and their legacy. (Remember, no presidents and no Supreme Court justices came from this generation; the only generation without a number of them.)

Where are these three S's on Maslow's hierarchy of needs? They are at or nearer the bottom. So, why did my mother teach me to chase these things that were at or near the bottom of what we as humans need to make life meaningful? Because having gone through the Great Depression and World War II, she was looking up at the bottom. It was understandable; she didn't have any of these three fundamental needs, and a life with all three would have seemed like Nirvana to her.

## TODAY'S MILLENNIALS ARE SEARCHING
## FOR THE FOURTH S—SIGNIFICANCE

But Millennials who only grew up in the shadow of the Industrial Age do not understand the language of Safety, Security, and Stability. They are one of the first generations in history, at least in the West, to be born with at least a modicum of all three of those things provided for them at birth. They aren't looking up at the bottom, but are instead reaching up for the fourth S of the Participation Age—Significance. Making money is no longer enough. Being an extension of a machine to do so is not attractive, and the idea that everyday should look the same and that life should be predictable and without surprises is not challenging to them. They want more. They want to Make Meaning.

> Millennials aren't looking up at the bottom, and are instead reaching up for the fourth S of the Participation Age—Significance.

As the cultural influence of the Industrial Age and the Factory System fades behind us, we are all waking up to the need to rehumanize the workplace, reintegrate it back into our lives, and build lives that Make Meaning, not just money. To do so, we must eliminate the arcane business practices that we dragged out of the Industrial Age into the Participation Age—those business practices that turned men and women into machines, and silenced our drive for Significance.

### YOU HAVE A CHOICE

Addressing the business diseases of the Industrial Age is not complex, it's simple. But for those who have built businesses and lives around the inherited constructs of a bygone era, it will be both simple and hard.

I don't envy the task in front of the Bigs who built their companies around the business diseases of the Industrial Age. The legacy culture, legacy systems, and legacy hierarchy that served them so well in dominating their industry in the Industrial Age, will be the very things that make it hard for them to move into the Participation Age. But companies of every size and age are flourishing as Participation Age companies. That should give hope to the Bigs; if others can do it, so can we.

The task in front of the Smalls is no simpler, but it is a little easier. If a Small recognizes that it has inherited some of the business diseases of the Industrial Age, all it needs is the will to change. But it needs to have a strong and determined will, because our past is a strong magnet and will pull us back in if we lack vigilance.

We should be grateful that the Industrial Age provided us with the first three S's— Safety, Security, and Stability—on which to build the fourth

S—Significance. But we must also recognize that the practices that brought us those three will not bring us the fourth.

We have a choice to make. Stay with what we know and slowly atrophy as the world moves on without us, or join the Participation Age and start sharing together in building companies that Make Meaning, not just money.

Which do you choose?

# EMBRACING THE PARTICIPATION AGE

1. What's your mindset? After reviewing this chapter, what practical thing do we need to do differently to promote Significance above the Three S's of the Industrial Age (safety, security and stability)?

_____

_____

By When? \_\_\_\_ /\_\_\_\_/ \_\_\_\_:\_\_a.m./p.m.

2. After reading the book, what am I pretending not to know? Is there anything we need to do on a micro or macro scale that I might be avoiding, that would help us embrace and flourish in the Participation Age?

_____

_____

By When? \_\_\_\_ /\_\_\_\_ / \_\_\_\_:\_\_a.m./p.m.

# Afterword
# How Capitalism Will Solve Poverty

*"No country has ever achieved economic success by depending on aid."*
— DAMBISA MOYO, author of *Dead Aid: Why Aid Is Not Working and How There Is a Better Way for Africa*

The ten poorest countries on earth are all in Sub-Saharan Africa.[1] Over a century of foreign aid and well-meaning non-profit assistance has left Africa worse off economically than it was a hundred years ago. The poverty rate in Sub-Saharan Africa is the same as it was in 1980, except today it includes a few hundred million more people due to population growth.[2] Dambisa Moyo, author of *Dead Aid*, says, "Evidence overwhelmingly demonstrates that aid to Africa has made the poor poorer."[3]

## AND ALL THE KING'S MEN...

We've tried micro-finance and found it wanting, too; up to 90% of loans go to buy televisions and other consumer goods, and most of the rest is disbursed without training on how to build a business.[4] Many former advocates of micro-finance are now saying it is not scalable and cannot solve poverty.[5] Mohammad Yunus, widely credited with starting what is now a US $70 billion microfinance industry said, "I could never believe that the microfinance institutions have become the very same evil money lenders that we attempted to replace."[6]

Others have advocated the formation of a "new kind of capitalism": for-profit companies from which the founders never take a profit, where 100% of the profits are used to solve poverty.[7] But that is simply another form of philanthropy or charity, and has gained little traction over the years. It also doesn't solve the core issue that philanthropy and aid have had a century to solve Africa's poverty and have only made it worse.[8]

Education is necessary, too, but for a century we have educated people from poor nations who migrate to nations with functioning economies where they can get paid for their knowledge.[9] Education is necessary but will never solve poverty.

> We have tried almost every possible solution to break the cycle of poverty in Africa, save one – Capitalism.

Likewise, health improvements are critical and fundamental, and the health of millions of the world's poor has been greatly helped by foreign aid. But improving the health of the poor will never solve poverty.

We have tried almost every possible solution to break the cycle of poverty in Africa, save one – Capitalism. That solution has proved successful for hundreds of millions in China, while Africa, and particularly sub-Saharan Africa, still languishes.

## CHINA THRIVES WHILE AFRICA SUFFERS

In 1981, China had 43% of the world's poorest people. Africa held 11%. Today, China has 13% of the world's poorest, while Africa now holds a devastating 34%.[10] At that time in 1981, China's extreme poverty rate was at least 66% and Africa's was 40%. By 2004, the World Bank reported China's extreme poverty rate at only 8%, while Africa's is to this day still 40%, and in some research, now up to 50%.[11]

| Poverty Rate | China | Sub-Saharan Africa |
|---|---|---|
| 1981 Extreme Poverty Rate | 66% | 40% |
| 2004 Extreme Poverty Rate | 8% | 40% to 50% |

Why the contrast? Very simply, China's people went the route of Capitalism (and the government slowly followed). Africa, on the other hand, became the focus of every major nonprofit and the financial aid of most nations. We can debate whether international aid and nonprofit money is *THE* cause, *A* cause, or not a cause at all, but one thing is sure, it is not a solution. Why?

## OWNERSHIP IS EVERYTHING

We've said throughout this book that ownership is the most powerful motivator in business. The Chinese solution created ownership while the African "solution" created dependency.

In the late 1970s, thousands of local Chinese farmers disobeyed the government and dissolved their collectives with very positive economic results. The government resisted, but finally and reluctantly followed their lead. In

1980-1981 the Household Responsibility System (HRS) was enacted, allowing the rural Chinese to dissolve all the collectives. It allowed them once again to take title to their land and businesses, and take responsibility for their lives – to become Capitalists.

An astonishing 40% of the reduction in Chinese poverty came in the first three years after HRS was enacted, and long before giant corporations swooped in or exports started to roll out. (International trade, it turns out, has had almost no positive effect on the Chinese economy.[12]) It was all small and local capitalism; millions of small and local businesses springing up before the giant corporations ever showed up.

> The Chinese solution created ownership while the African "solution" created dependency.

Restoring ownership took over 600 million people out of poverty in the historical wink of an eye. The Chinese decided *ownership* of the means of production was the most powerful motivator to eliminate poverty.[13] Not a single non-profit or giant corporation can take credit.

## OWNERSHIP WORKS IN AFRICA, TOO

It is happening in Africa, too. Rwanda's largely corrupt government opened their borders to American and UK business people in 2006 and have made it extremely easy to start and own a small and local business. As a result, somewhere between 1-2 million people have come out of poverty in the last few years. In 2013, Rwanda was the ninth fastest growing economy in the world, with sharp poverty reduction, and lessened income inequality.[14]

## WHAT IS THE ANSWER?

The answer isn't government aid. It isn't giant corporations pulling the revenue out and taking it to the west. It isn't much needed education, health improvements or micro-finance. The answer for Africa is the same as it has been for China, the United States, Brazil, Hong Kong, Germany, Rwanda and any other growing economy: millions of small and locally owned businesses. Capitalism on a local level is the only thing that will solve long-term, systemic poverty.

The answer is also in the willingness to build businesses in Africa – real businesses, not micro-financed lifestyles, but businesses with five to fifty employees, that can be bought, sold, inherited and expanded. There is enough socially conscious money flowing into Africa right now to do it, but right now it's going to things that won't solve poverty.

> "Don't send us your money; teach us how to do things for ourselves."

When the money starts flowing into businesses, it *MUST* be accompanied by training. In Africa (and everywhere) training to run a business is even more important than money to build them. As one African named Michale said in a blog post, "As harsh and counter-productive as it might sound, don't send us your money; use it, rather, to pay your doctors, engineers, farmers, businessmen and the like to come to Africa for at least a year at a time to teach us how to do things for ourselves." I believe there is a whole new wave of business owners coming up who will risk investing US $10-$50,000 in building businesses in Africa and, more importantly, invest time there (teleconferencing, etc.) training others to run and eventually own those small and local businesses. I believe with that approach we can do something nonprofits haven't been able to do for over 100 years, solve systemic poverty among the 500-700 million impoverished Africans. And we can do it in less than 20 years.

Visit http://PurposeWithAProfit.com for more on how capitalism will solve poverty.

## NOTES

1. *Top 10 Poorest Countries*, www.mapsoftheworld.com, updated July 26, 2012, http://bit.ly/1abunv6

2. *Are There Lessons for Africa from China's Success against Poverty?*, Martin Ravallion, The World Bank, Development Research Group, 2008, Policy Research Working Paper #4463, http://bit.ly/1cv5SGS

3. *Why Foreign Aid is Hurting Africa*, Dambisa Moyo, The Wall Street Journal, Sunday, March 21, 2009, http://on.wsj.com/1e40mfY

4. Hugh Sinclair, *Confessions of a Microfinance Heretic*, (San-Francisco: Barrett-Koehler Publishers, 2012

5. Hugh Sinclair, *Confessions of a Microfinance Heretic*, (San-Francisco: Barrett-Koehler Publishers, 2012

6. *The Dark Side of Microfinance, An Industry Where the Poor Play Cameo Roles,* Wharton College, Knowledge@Wharton, July 18, 2012, http://bit.ly/1316X6f

7. Mohammad Yunus, *Creating a World Without Poverty*, (New York: PublicAffairs™ Publishing, 2007

8. *Why Foreign Aid is Hurting Africa*, Dambisa Moyo, The Wall Street Journal, Sunday, March 21, 2009, http://on.wsj.com/1e40mfY

9. *Brain Drain and Brain Gain*, Tito Boeri, Herbert Brucker, (Oxford: Oxford University Press, 2012)

10. *Global Poverty Is Falling*, Fareed Zakaria, CNN, Global Public Square Blog, May 1, 2013, http://bit.ly/1dEqGQj

11. *Are There Lessons for Africa from China's Success against Poverty?*, Martin Ravallion, The World Bank, Development Research Group, 2008, Policy Research Working Paper #4463, http://bit.ly/1cv5SGS

12. *Are There Lessons for Africa from China's Success against Poverty?*, Martin Ravallion, The World Bank, Development Research Group, 2008, Policy Research Working Paper #4463, http://bit.ly/1cv5SGS

13. *Are There Lessons for Africa from China's Success against Poverty?*, Martin Ravallion, The World Bank, Development Research Group, 2008, Policy Research Working Paper #4463, http://bit.ly/1cv5SGS

14. *Doing Business in the East African Community 2013*, Author: Doing Business, DoingBusiness.org, International Finance Corporation, May 2, 2013, http://bit.ly/1e4lwdV

15. *How to Really Solve Poverty in Africa*, Fr Alexander Lucie-Smith, The Catholic Herald, CatholicHerald.co.uk, Wednesday, 30 March 2011 http://bit.ly/14Ql5Rf

# Appendix

Throughout *Why Employees Are Always a Bad Idea* (*WEAAABI*), we have highlighted a consistent theme; companies built on a set of deeply and widely held beliefs have a much better chance of success than companies built on other more extrinsic motivations like making money or even building a great product. Beliefs are not things written in an annual report for consumption by investors. The simple proof that a company has deeply and widely held beliefs is that everyone is making decisions based on those beliefs and at every level of the company.

This is not as hard to accomplish as it sounds. When leaders make decisions that way, everyone in the company will either follow suit, leave, or be moved along, creating a company that lives what it believes. That could take a few months to a few years, but any company can do it. Total Renal Care was on its way to bankruptcy when Kent Thiry took over, instilled a set of deeply held beliefs, got everyone either on board or moved out, and turned it into one of the most respected companies in the world.

Following are the deeply and widely held beliefs of the Crankset Group on which we make all our decisions.

## CRANKSET GROUP VISION

Live well by doing good.

## CRANKSET GROUP MISSION

We provide tools for business leaders to make more money in less time, get off the treadmill, and get back to the passion that brought them into business in the first place.

# THE CRANKSET CULTURE

## Live Well by Doing Good

Be the Board

We will lead from our experience, not from our knowledge

Clarity/Hope/Risk

Abundance

## Transformation

## Conation

Lifetime Goals

Community

## Business Maturity Date — Time, Money, Significance

Strategic Plan; Waypoints

## Serve, don't sell

We Implement Now and Perfect as We Go

Outcome-based, Stage 6 or 7

## YPH

## The Priority of the Important

Highest & Best Use of Time

## Trapeze Moments

# CRANKSET GROUP BELIEFS

**We believe in the Worth of the Individual.** All of us are made to do and to be something significant. Work is one way for people to create that significance.

**We believe in Ownership.** It is the most powerful driving force in business. We must all own our tasks, processes, jobs, results, and futures.

**We believe in Transformation, not education.** We lead from our experience, not from our knowledge.

**We believe in Clarity, Hope, and Risk.** We believe in bringing **Clarity**, which creates **Hope**, which allows business leaders to take measured **Risks** to grow.

**We believe in Conation.** Conation is the most important word we train people to use. Conation: committed movement in a purposeful direction.

**We believe the Rugged Individualist is a bad idea.** Business leaders should live in Committed Community. We are all recovering Rugged Individualists.

**We believe Time is the New Money.** Our business should give us time, money, and significance (TMS), not just money.

**We believe in Speed of Execution.** Implement now and perfect as you go. Planning for perfection is a bad idea.

**We believe in Yield Per Hour (YPH).** We expect business leaders to always ask "What is the highest and best use of my time?"

**We believe in Trapeze Moments.** We encourage people to take the risk to grow personally and to build businesses they can enjoy for decades.

**We believe in Advisors,** not in experts or gurus. We advise business leaders to build businesses that produce time, money, and significance (TMS).

# SEVEN TRANSFORMATIONAL TRAINING ASSUMPTIONS

Overarching assumption: We don't care if anyone learns anything. We just want them and their businesses to change for the better.

1. Education doesn't work; learning does. People must be disoriented in order to learn. We are outcome-based, not education-based.

2. Knowledge is NOT power; Experience is power. If knowledge were power, librarians would rule the world. We do not think our way to a new way of acting; we act our way to a new way of thinking. Change comes from doing, not knowing.

3. There is nothing wrong with your business. All businesses are perfect; it is the people who need to change, not the business. The chaos in the business is simply a reflection of the chaos in our heads. When we are transformed, the business will change permanently. Until then, it's all window-dressing. (Consulting doesn't work because it attempts to fix a perfect business and ignore an imperfect leader.)

4. He who makes the rules wins. Most business leaders are reactive to their businesses and let the business (and customers) make all the rules. Take control and USE your business to get you to your Big Why.

5. The most profound things are always simple. We reject complex, fancy solutions because we can hide in them without changing what we do.

6. If you want something to change, you have to change something.

7. These three things change people's lives:
   - Make a decision.
   - Put a date on it.
   - Go public.

Crankset Group Stakeholders will embrace and live out these Training Assumptions, and will use them to help business leaders be successful.

# Acknowledgements

No one actually creates from scratch. In my first book, Making Money Is Killing Your Business, I said, "Everything I know is a summary of what I've learned from other people." The creative process is when we take all that learning from the world around us and wrap it in a fresh narrative for a new time, which is our intention for *Why Employees Are Always A Bad Idea* (*WEAAABI*). Without the ongoing input of those around me, *WEAAABI* would not have been possible.

My wife and fellow explorer in life, Diane Blakeman, who is also our Chief Operations Officer, has her fingerprints all over this book (and Crankset Group), both strategically and tactically. Krista Valentine, our Chief Relationship Officer, took the risk to join us when we were very small and has been deeply involved as we have developed *WEAAABI's* principles and practices into our Committed Community culture. Lauren Kelley, our Chief Results Officer, makes us all look better than we are on a regular basis. And Kyle Matthews, our Chief Connecting Officer is living out *WEAAABI* with us and to our clients.

We have a growing list of Chief Transformation Officers, of which I am one, who facilitate our 3to5 Clubs worldwide. Those who have been most instrumental in helping us develop our *WEAAABI* practices around the world: John Heenan, Eddie Drescher, Julia Gentry, Doug Hawkins, Jon Hokama, John McDonough, Diego Pineda and other CTOs around the U.S., Canada, South America, Africa and China. Some of whom I have never met, but intend to soon.

Those who poured over *WEAAABI's* manuscript include Madalyn Stone, Emily Skaftun, Diane Blakeman, Krista Valentine, Virginia Blakeman Lenz (my wonderful sister), Art McCracken, Bob Spiel, Brenda Abdilla, and my dear friend Kate Warren, who founded Brightlife Consultancy in England in 2006 and is finally expanding to the U.S. Lauren Kelley did the highly detailed work of laying out *WEAAABI*, and Josh Mishell created our great cover.

*THANK YOU* to all of you, and to many more who influenced *WEAAABI* and are not named. I am deeply grateful to have you in my life and to see you reflecting from every page of this book.

# Resources

## ABOUT THE AUTHOR
Chuck Blakeman is a results leader who has built many businesses, two of them with presence on four continents. He now uses his experience to help other business owners and leaders build Participation Age companies. Chuck is available for one2one business advising as well as working with company leadership teams anywhere in the world. Some of Mr. Blakeman's past customers have included Microsoft, Apple, Eli Lilly, TAP Pharmaceuticals, Sun Microsystems, Tyco Healthcare, Johns Manville and many more much smaller businesses.

## KEYNOTES
Based on his books, Chuck regularly delivers the following captivating and transformative keynote presentations and breakout sessions around the world.

## WHY EMPLOYEES ARE ALWAYS A BAD IDEA
For business leaders and managers. The Future of Business is in the new Participation Age. Don't be left behind. Come hear how companies large and small, old and new, are changing their business practices and culture to increase revenue, reduce management expenses, and attract and retain the best talent in the world, by turning their employees into Stakeholders.

## MAKING MONEY IS KILLING YOUR BUSINESS
Based on the "#1 Rated Business Book of the Year"
For business leaders and founders. Get off the treadmill, make more money in less time and get back to the passion that brought you into business in the first place. Use your business to build your Ideal Lifestyle, not just an income.

*"In the 17 years of SCN, he was truly the BEST SPEAKER ever...and SCN prides itself on seeking the best speakers in the business. I had NO IDEA what a profound effect he and his message would have on the attendees."*
—Linda Miles, Founder, Speaking Consulting Network

*"Terrific speaker. Eye opening. One of the highlights of the conference!!"*
—Association of Marketing Service Providers

If you would like to explore how Chuck and his team could serve your company or organization, please connect with us at:
Grow@CranksetGroup.com

# WORKSHOPS

We also conduct workshops and seminars for companies and for business associations. Some examples:

**How to Hire People You'll Never Have to Manage**
- Discuss how and why the traditional employee hurts your business
- Learn our seven-step process to ensure you only hire Stakeholders and never have to manage another employee
- Build a Participation Age company with the right people

**Building a Participation Age Company**
- Learn the Seven Core Business Diseases of the Industrial Age and how to avoid them
- Stop managing & start leading: how to do it
- Three-step process to transform an employee into a Stakeholder
- Practical how-tos for moving someone from manager to leader

**Freedom Mapping—The Key to a Great Business**
- Identify and shift to the highest and best use of your time—stop guessing
- Create Process Maps to deliver consistent customer service
- Create ownership and teamwork for all your Stakeholders—eliminate the *job silos* problem
- Make your company worth exponentially more

**2-Page Strategic Plan Workshop**
- Trade in the ineffective business plan (an Industrial Age concept)
- Clarify or write your vision and mission statements, strategies, and objectives
- Run your business every day from the bottom of Page Two
- Make it easy to measure if each week/month/quarter is accomplishing your objectives
- Develop your Strategic Plan right in the workshop to run your business daily

**No-Nonsense Lifetime Goals for Business People**
- How do you define Success and Significance? Why are you in business? Where is it taking you?
- Have you defined your "Big Why"? What does your Ideal Lifestyle look like? When do you expect to get there? How will your business get you there?
- Get utter clarity on these questions and a new motivation to build your business
- Learn how a business can Make Meaning, not just money

*The Group gained great value from the workshop. It was interesting and stimulating, with considerable take-home value."*
— Brent von Sierakowski, Chairman TEC (Vistage), Auckland, New Zealand

## ONLINE RESOURCES
Learn more about Chuck as a speaker and workshop leader at
http://ChuckBlakemanSpeaker.com

Read Chuck's blog at
http://ChuckBlakeman.com

Learn more about 3to5 Clubs worldwide at
http://3to5Club.com

Buy Chuck's books at
http://MakingMoneyIsKillingYourBusiness.com
http://WhyEmployeesAreAlwaysABadIdea.com

Learn more about Crankset Group at
http://CranksetGroup.com

**THE APEX PROFILE ONLINE:** http://ApexProfile.com
The first profile in the world developed specifically for business owners, founders and leaders.

Apex Profile clarifies why you make decisions the way you do, how you perceive the business world around you, and whom you should hire to complement your strengths.

E-mail our team at grow@cranksetgroup.com and request that a one-time code be sent to you for the Profile. This code will reduce the US $79.00 cost of the profile to only $10.00. You can visit http://apexprofile.com for more information.

**OTHER BOOKS BY THE AUTHOR**
Chuck's book, *Making Money Is Killing Your Business*, was rated the #1 business book of 2010 by the National Federation of Independent Businesses. It is in its second printing. Recent print and online appearances include *Harvard Business Review*, *Entrepreneur Magazine*, CNNMoney.com, NYTimes.com, and many others. He was also quoted in Stephen Covey's final book, *The 3rd Alternative*.

Order today at: www.MakingMoneyIsKillingYourBusiness.com
or on: www.Amazon.com (99% Five-Star Amazon reviews)

**CONNECT WITH US**
If you have any questions or would like to explore a possible engagement, please connect with us at Grow@CranksetGroup.com